Publishing

FINANCE OF INTERNATIONAL TRADE

7th edition

Alastair Watson

This edition updated by
Paul Cowdell & Derek Hyde

institute of financial services

Financial World Publishing
c/o The Chartered Institute of Bankers
Emmanuel House
4-9 Burgate Lane
Canterbury
Kent CT1 2XJ
United Kingdom
e-mail: editorial@cib.org.uk
Telephone: 01227 762600

Financial World Publishing publications are published by The Chartered Institute of Bankers, a non-profit making registered educational charity.

Typeset by Kevin O'Connor
Printed by Communications in Print, Basildon, Essex
© The Chartered Institute of Bankers 2000
ISBN 0-85297-580-5

ICC Uniform Customs and Practice for Documentary Credits – 1993 Revision
ICC Publication N°500 – ISBN 92.842.1155.7 (E)
Published in its official English version by the International Chamber of Commerce
Copyright © 1993 – International Chamber of Commerce (ICC), Paris

ICC Uniform Rules for Collections – 1995 Revision
ICC Publication N°522 – ISBN 92.842.1184.0 (E)
Published in its official English version by the International Chamber of Commerce
Copyright © 1995 – International Chamber of Commerce (ICC), Paris

ICC Uniform Rules for Bank-to-Bank Reimbursements
ICC Publication N°525 – ISBN 92.842.1185.9 (E)
Published in its official English version by the International Chamber of Commerce
Copyright © 1995 – International Chamber of Commerce (ICC), Paris

All available from: *ICC Publishing S.A.,* 38 Cours Albert 1er, 75008 Paris, France and ICC United Kingdom, 14/15 Belgrave Square, London SW1X 8PS, United Kingdom

FINANCIAL
WORLD
Publishing
THE CHARTERED INSTITUTE OF BANKERS

CONTENTS

Contents

Contents

Contents

Acknowledgements

The authors wish to thank Andrew Cantrill of HSBC Sheffield for his helpful comments on this 7th edition. The authors and The Chartered Institute of Bankers would also like to thank Barclays Bank and HSBC for their kind permission to reproduce various documents.

INTRODUCTION

The seventh edition of *Finance of International Trade* has been extensively revised and incorporates all relevant developments up to March 2000.

The book is intended to assist all students and practitioners who seek to acquire the necessary background information to gain an understanding of the finance of international trade, foreign exchange and support services provided for exporters, importers and merchants by London's financial institutions.

It concentrates in particular on the needs of students studying for the following qualifications:

● The *International Trade Finance* option paper of the Associateship/Degree programme of The Chartered Institute of Bankers (CIB) in association with the University of Manchester Institute of Science and Technology (UMIST);

● The Institute of Export: *International Trade and Payments*, and Advanced Certificate in Overseas Trade;

In addition this text is cited as further reading for the Association of Corporate Treasurers Corporate Finance and Funding Unit.

This book is in five parts:

● Part One consists of a single introductory chapter which sets out the rationale for the development and growth of international trade, including balance of payments issues.

● Part Two begins with an examination of the foreign exchange markets. It then analyses the practical applications of hedging techniques, both internal and external, and finally covers foreign exchange and settlement procedures.

● Part Three assesses the role of documents used in international trade and then analyses the way that documents are linked inexorably and logically with the shipping and payment terms agreed between importer and exporter.

● Part Four then examines the implications of the various financial and non-financial services from the point of view of exporters,

● Finally, Part Five analyses documentary credits from the applicant's point of view, and then evaluates the benefits and drawbacks of various specialist forms of documentary credit, such as transferable and back-to-back credits, together with services and facilities for importers.

For easy reference a list of learning objectives appears at the beginning of each unit. In addition, there are appendices covering correspondent banking and electronic data interchange, and copies of various International Chamber of Commerce (ICC) rules covering documentary collections and documentary credits.

The sequence of topics in this book is set from a *teaching* point of view and therefore does not follow the syllabus topic order. the key sections of which for this subject are:

● The Meaning of International Trade Finance/Payment and Risk Management Services

● Financial Services from Banks and Other Sources

● Methods of Trading

The aim of this book is to help readers to acquire a sound understanding of relevant theoretical and practical concepts, coupled with an ability to apply the principles in a given practical situation.

It is anticipated that the student will study this course for one academic year, reading through and studying approximately two units every three weeks. However, it should be noted that because topics vary in size and as knowledge tends not to fall into uniform chunks, some units in this workbook are unavoidably longer than others.

Students are recommended to obtain copies of the examiner's reports from 1997 onwards for the CIB/UMIST *International Trade Finance* papers, because these are a first-class means of updating knowledge and acquiring a practical insight into the subject.

International trade is a rapidly changing subject; hence, careful study of publications such as *The Treasurer*, the *Financial Times*, *Financial World*, *Export Today*, and the various customer leaflets and circulars prepared by banks is essential in order to keep up to date. In addition, both students and practitioners should regularly search the following web sites to keep abreast of new developments.

Foreign exchange markets

Bank of International Settlements Statistics: www.bis.org/pub

Single currency

Bank of England: www.bankofengland.co.uk/euro

Government and government-based export assistance

Trade Partners UK: www.tradepartners.gov.uk

Department of Trade and Industry: www.dti.gov.uk

Other sources of advice for exporters

British Chambers of Commerce: www.britishchambers.org.uk

Confederation of British Industry: www.cbi.org.uk

Federation of Small Businesses: www.fsb.org.uk

Institute of Export: www.export.co.uk

International Chamber of Commerce: www.iccwbo.org

Credit Insurance/Bond Support

Export Credit Guarantee Department: www.ecgd.gov.uk

NCM Group: www.ncmgroup.com

e-commerce

Bolero International Limited: www.bolero.net

European Union Institutions

European Institutions (general): europa.eu.int

World Trade

World Trade Organization: www:wto.org

Suggested further reading

The journals and web sites mentioned above are a first-rate source of information on changes to the subject. However, for readers who want to study the topics in greater depth the following are recommended:

Anon: *Second thoughts about globalization*: *The Economist* June 21 1997 p. 108
A. Buckley: *Multinational Finance* (4th Edition) 2000 Financial Times/Prentice Hall
Anon: *Practical Issues Arising from the Introduction of the Euro* Issues 1, 2, 3 Bank of England
Anon: *Introduction of the Euro, what does it mean for business?* January 1997: Bank of England
Anon: *Panorama of EU Industry 97*: European Commission

International Chamber of Commerce Publications as follows:

Number	Title
590	International Standby Practices ISP98
560	Incoterms 2000
589	Incoterms Questions and Answers
620	Guide to Incoterms 2000

Study Plan

If you are a distance-learning student and have not received your study plan by the beginning of the session, please contact the CIB Tuition Department:

Tel: 01227 818637

Fax: 01227 453547

e-mail: tuition@cib.org.uk

The masculine pronoun 'he' has been used in this workbook to encompass both genders and to avoid the awkwardness of the constant repetition of 'he and/or she'.

PART ONE

Introduction

This first part of this book is intended to provide an overview of international trade. It analyses the rationale for the growth of international trade and examines balance of payment issues.

1

INTERNATIONAL TRADE: INTRODUCTORY OVERVIEW – HOW IT DIFFERS FROM DOMESTIC TRADE AND THE PATTERNS AND REASONS FOR ITS GROWTH, IMPLICATIONS FOR BALANCE OF PAYMENTS

Objectives

On completion of this chapter the student should be able to:

- understand why and how domestic trade and international trade differ;
- understand the concepts of absolute and comparative advantage, and how these concepts, in general, tend to support arguments for increasing the volume of international trade;
- appreciate the role played by GATT, WTO and SMP in promoting the growth of trade;
- understand the concept of the balance of payments and the implications of international trade for the balance of payments.

1   How International Trade Differs from Domestic Trade

Domestic trade has the following characteristics which apply to both parties:

- a common language and culture;

- the same laws;
- absence of customs formalities;
- usually relatively simple documentation;
- a single currency;
- relatively simple formalities to transport goods from buyer to seller.

International trade is much more complex in that, generally speaking, it has the opposite characteristics to those listed above.

Completing a sale of goods overseas can be much more costly than a domestic sale in terms of marketing efforts, coping with customs formalities, dealing with different legal requirements, and organizing relatively complex transport arrangements. Further risk is involved if settlement is in a foreign currency since there is no guarantee of the value in domestic currency terms at the time settlement and conversion are effected. In addition to the risk of buyer default, which can obviously apply in domestic business but which may be more acute with an unknown buyer from overseas, there can be default caused by the overseas government's actions. One government imposed restrictions on payments during the Asian Financial Crisis of 1998.

The immediate reaction to all this is to ask why anyone would wish to trade internationally when domestic trade is so much more simple. The purpose of this book is to explain the theoretical reasons that support the growth of international trade and then to show how organizations such as banks, the International Chamber of Commerce (ICC), and credit insurers can overcome the additional problems posed by overseas trade.

2   Why Do Countries Trade?

This question can best be considered by analysing the relationship between consumption and work. Men or women could possibly produce everything they needed by their own labour, but this would not be appealing to most people because they would find their consumption confined to a narrow range of goods. Thus individuals in modern economies do not try to produce exactly what they consume. Instead individuals work for money, which is then used for consumption purposes.

A person's work may help to produce only a small range of goods, but the wages paid for that work help that person to obtain access to a much wider range of goods and services. The well-known economic concepts of specialization and division of labour, where people specialize in the production of certain items and then obtain other goods through trade, evolved from the above concepts. Trade is therefore necessary if the full benefits of specialization are to be enjoyed.

Even towns and cities are not normally completely self-sufficient. Those cities that might technically be capable of such self-sufficiency would be worse off without trade because the variety and quality of goods would be reduced if trade did not take place.

Because people gain by trading between each other, trade will take place naturally without the need for any encouragement. Trade also takes place naturally between countries, because it would be illogical to expect gains from trade to stop at national boundaries.

In recent times, the increase in the importance of services, the political impetus from the development of free trade areas such as the North America Free Trade Agreement (NAFTA) and the Single European Market Programme (SMP), and pressure from organizations such as the World Trade Organization (the successor to GATT) have resulted in an ever-increasing amount of trade in goods and services between different countries.

3 The Concept of Absolute Advantage and Comparative Advantage in International Trade

a) Absolute Advantage

Absolute advantage is an imperfect explanation for the reasons for international trade, but it paves the way for the more cogent argument of comparative advantage which is covered in (b) below.

Let us take a very simple hypothetical example to illustrate absolute advantage. A country is said to have an absolute advantage in the production of a commodity if it uses fewer resources than another country to produce a given quantity. Thus for a commodity with only one factor of production, say labour, if one country uses less labour than another to make a given amount of the commodity, that country has an absolute advantage. This concept of absolute advantage assumes that one hour of labour in one country has the same characteristics as one hour in another country.

The following table illustrates this by comparing the hypothetical examples of wheat and car production in Canada and the UK. It assumes that the only factor of production is hours of labour and that an hour of labour in one country is identical to an hour of labour in another country. It also assumes that there are only two countries, only two commodities, and that the goods are of the same standard and quality in each country.

Table 1

	WHEAT *Hours to produce one ton*	CARS *Hours to produce one*
United Kingdom	300 hours	150 hours
Canada	200 hours	250 hours

Relying solely on the information above, it is clear that Canada has an absolute advantage in the production of wheat, because it takes fewer hours of labour in Canada to produce a ton of wheat, but the opposite applies to cars where the UK has an absolute advantage. In addition, 450 hours of labour in either the UK or Canada will produce one car and one ton of wheat in each country.

What happens if trade takes place and Canada exchanges one ton of wheat for one car from the UK?

Canada saves 250 hours by obtaining one car from the UK and not having to produce it itself, and it can use those 250 hours to produce 1.25 tons of wheat. Thus 450 hours of labour, after the trade shown above, leave Canada with one car and 1.25 tons of wheat. This is a net benefit to Canada of one quarter of a ton of wheat.

Conversely, the UK will obtain a ton of wheat from Canada and will then use the 300 hours saved to produce two cars, thus obtaining a net benefit of one car.

This phenomenon arises with international trade because each country specializes in producing the commodity in which it has an absolute advantage. In Canada, 450 hours are devoted to wheat, producing 2.25 tons of wheat, one of which is traded for a car. In the UK, 450 hours are devoted to producing three cars, one of which is exchanged for a ton of wheat. Thus specialization and division of labour, whether on the part of individuals, towns or countries, will lead to a greater total output of goods and services.

The prices at which the trade is arranged will determine how the gains from trade are split between the two parties. From the point of view of the UK, the minimum amount of wheat to break even in exchange for one car is 0.5 tons, since 150 hours of labour produce 0.5 tons of wheat or one car in the UK. From the point of view of Canada, the maximum amount of wheat it can give in exchange for one car and still break even is 1.25 tons, since in Canada the 250 hours it takes to produce one car could be used to produce 1.25 tons of wheat. Thus the expected exchange value of one car exported from the UK to Canada would be somewhere between 0.5 and 1.25 tons of wheat. The exchange value between these two parameters that is actually applied will determine the split of the benefits of the trade between the UK and Canada.

b)   Comparative Advantage

While it is clear that, in principle, two countries can gain from trade when one has an absolute advantage in the first commodity and the other has an absolute advantage in the second commodity, this section will show how trade is beneficial in a two-good, two-country economy even when one country has an absolute advantage in both commodities. A country is said to have a comparative advantage in a good if its opportunity cost of producing the good is lower than that of other countries. Likewise, if the opportunity cost of producing the good is higher than that of other countries, a country is said to have a comparative disadvantage in that good. In principle, a country should export goods in which it has a comparative advantage and import goods in which it has a comparative disadvantage.

Let us look at the following simplified example, where Canada is assumed to have an absolute advantage in the production of both wheat and cars:

Table 2

	WHEAT Hours to produce one ton	CARS Hours to produce one
United Kingdom	400 hours	375 hours
Canada	200 hours	300 Hours

Here Canada has an absolute advantage in both goods because it requires fewer hours of labour to produce both cars and wheat in Canada. The opportunity cost of producing these goods can be shown as follows:

Table 3

	Wheat One Ton	Cars One Car
United Kingdom	1.07 cars	0.94 tons of wheat
Canada	0.67 cars	1.50 tons of wheat

Explanation: If the UK uses 400 hours to produce cars instead of wheat, it will produce 400/375 of a car, i.e. 1.07 cars.

From the above, we can conclude that Canada has a comparative advantage in wheat production, having a lower opportunity cost than the UK, but the UK has a comparative advantage in the production of cars due to the lower opportunity cost of car production in the UK.

Similar principles to those shown in (a) above will apply in the determination of the exchange value of one car. However, if we assume for the moment that one car can be traded for one ton of wheat, what will happen if Canada exchanges one ton of wheat for one car from the UK?

Canada will utilise 500 hours of labour to produce 2.5 tons of wheat, and after exchanging one ton for one car, will have a total of 1.5 tons of wheat and one car. Thus Canada benefits by 0.5 tons of wheat.

What about the United Kingdom under this transaction? The UK will utilise 775 hours in producing 2.07 cars. One car will then be exchanged for one ton of wheat resulting in a net gain for the UK of 0.07 cars.

c)   Comparative Advantage with Money Inputs

Let us retain the two commodities, two countries, one factor of production model already used, but let us assume that the hourly rate of pay for labour is Can$ 40 in Canada and £20 in the UK. On this basis, and excluding any profit element, the price of the goods from our comparative advantage example would be:

Table 4

	Wheat (per ton)	Per car
United Kingdom	£8,000	£7,500
Canada	Can $8,000	Can $12,000

If the rate of exchange between the Canadian $ and the £ is Can $1.5 = £1, the cost in sterling terms of wheat produced in Canada is £5,333.33 per ton (i.e. £2666.67 cheaper than UK-produced wheat), and the cost of a car produced in the UK in terms of Canadian $ is Can $11,250 (i.e. Can $750 below the cost of a car produced in Canada).

Much, of course, depends on the rate of exchange between the two currencies, and on the hourly wage rates in the two countries. However, it can be seen that the Canadian $ equivalent of the UK hourly wage is Can $30 at the current rate of exchange, whereas the actual hourly rate in Canada is Can $40. The explanation for this could lie in the fact that the Canadian worker was, in this hypothetical example, more efficient than the UK worker and thus earned a greater hourly rate. In practice this efficiency could be an illusion because the Canadian worker could be better supported by capital equipment.

Whatever the reasons, traders will wish to buy wheat in Canada to sell in the UK and to buy cars in the UK to sell to Canada, ignoring transaction costs of the deal.

d) Further Comments on the Implications of Comparative Advantage for International Trade

The purpose of the preceding sections was to demonstrate, in general terms, that there is a gain from trade when countries export goods in which they have a comparative advantage and import goods in which they have a comparative disadvantage. If these 'rules' are followed, there is a total gain from international trade, because the total quantity of goods available expands as a result of more efficient resource allocation.

However, there are practical difficulties that can arise from the implementation of a policy of trade based on the principle of comparative advantage. When imports are suddenly allowed, there are immediate practical problems for the importing country:

● home-based producers could go into liquidation, with resultant unemployment;

● alternatively, home-based producers will reduce wages to compete;

● other sectors of the home economy which relied upon the defunct firms for their income will also suffer.

Logically, the unemployment and loss of trade caused by allowing imports will not last forever, because labour and resources will be moved into other industries with a comparative advantage, but there is considerable argument as to the size and duration of the immediate losses caused when imports are allowed. In general, countries which have liberalized trade have seen economic growth (the 'tiger economies' of the Far East, for example), but there are massive short-term problems when home industry is first exposed to external competition, as can be seen from recent events in Eastern Europe. The analysis of absolute advantage and comparative advantage ignores these issues, as well as ignoring the more obvious difficulties of whether goods produced in different countries are identical, the effects of transaction costs of trade and the implications of exchange rate movements.

This book is not the place for a full in-depth analysis of the various facets of the theory of comparative advantage as a driver of international trade; the purpose here is simply to demonstrate that international trade should normally result in economic growth due to more efficient resource allocation.

4 The General Agreement on Tariffs and Trade (GATT), The World Trade Organization (WTO) and the Single European Market Programme (SMP)

a) Introduction

Now that we have studied the theoretical concept of comparative advantage as the basis of international trade, we shall look at how GATT, the WTO and the SMP have begun to overcome the obstacles to trade that exist in practice.

GATT was set up in 1948 and since that time it has initiated various sets of negotiations (known as 'Rounds') to try to reduce or, ideally, eliminate import tariffs and technical standard requirements with a view to encouraging economic growth through world trade. The final GATT Round, known as the Uruguay Round, began in 1986 and was successfully completed in 1995, at which time the WTO came into existence.

b) The Uruguay Round of GATT

The negotiators' initial target was to reduce tariff barriers by at least a third within five years, but the world's major trading countries finally agreed to more substantial cuts. As a result, the final level of tariffs for industrialized countries fell from an average of 5% to 3.5%. The EU reduced customs duties from 6.8% to 4.1% and the United States from 6.6% to 3.4%. Before the first GATT negotiations in 1947, average tariffs stood at a far higher 40%.

As far as the EU is concerned, the concessions will affect exports valued at around £8.5b and EU imports valued at around £5.5b. More than 40% of EU imports are now duty-free.

The Uruguay Round also simplified non-tariff barriers by examining various rules and procedures that can lead to delays, extra costs and frustration in international trade. These cover such technical questions as customs valuation, pre-shipment inspection and procedures for securing import licences. The changes are aimed at making information on the various requirements more readily available, at keeping paperwork to a minimum and ensuring documents are processed speedily.

In addition, the negotiations examined health and safety regulations and quality standards to ensure these are not covert forms of protectionism. These must be better publicized and notified to the WTO where a more efficient procedure has been set up for handling complaints from aggrieved exporters.

Before the Uruguay Round, services such as banking, consulting and pop music were subject to very different national rules. Now, governments must in effect apply the same conditions to both domestic and foreign suppliers. As a result, a wide range of banking, securities and insurance activities will be answerable to multilateral rules for the first time. Services have been estimated to make up 20% of world trade.

Finally, the Uruguay Round made an attempt to clamp down on intellectual piracy, the copying of the rights of owners of ideas.

c)   The WTO

The WTO came into existence in January 1995. It enjoys equal status with the International Monetary Fund (IMF) and the World Bank and has a potential membership larger than the countries signed up to GATT. It also has a wider remit. GATT supervised just trade in merchandise goods, but WTO covers that and more, with responsibility over trade in goods, services and ideas, or in intellectual property.

One of the WTO's key roles will be to administer the new procedures for settling disputes between its members. Now strict deadlines are set for each stage of the process; non-confidential evidence is made public for the first time; interested parties like consumer groups can give evidence; and no single member can block the decision of the new Disputes Settlement Board.

The creation of the WTO has not entirely eliminated GATT. Countries that were members of GATT prior to the Uruguay Round but did not enter into the final Uruguay Round agreement, will continue to be members of GATT. However, they will be unable to make use of the WTO disputes mechanism if they feel that their exports are suffering discrimination under the Uruguay Round provisions.

At the time of writing, 131 countries are members of the WTO, while another 20 countries (including Russia, China, Taiwan and Saudi Arabia) are currently involved in accession negotiations.

One area where negotiations are currently stalled is in that of services. Although most industrial countries have opened their financial services markets to international competition under the General Agreement in Trade and Services (GATS), market access remains blocked in many emerging economies. There is a continuing debate as to whether the liberalization of financial services markets would be beneficial or not to emerging economies.

This matter, among others, was to have been discussed at the third WTO Ministerial Conference that took place in Seattle, USA, from 30 November 1999 to 3 December 1999. The meeting was suspended without achieving formal agreement. However, despite this setback, the objectives of the WTO remain unchanged. These objectives are set out in the WTO Press Release Press/160 dated 7 December 1999 as:

● To continue to negotiate the progressive liberalization of international trade.

● To put trade to work more effectively for economic development and poverty alleviation.

● To confirm the central role that the rules-based trading system plays for our member governments in managing their economic affairs cooperatively.

● To organize the WTO on lines that more truly represent the needs of all members.

d)   The SMP

Up to the mid-1980s, cross-border trade in the EU was subject to the same obstacles as cross-border trade outside the EU.

Examples of such obstacles were:

● all goods were stopped and checked at frontiers;

● most products had to comply with different laws in different member states;

● services, such as banking, transport and telecommunications, were largely insulated from competition from other EU states.

The SMP began with an agreement by member states, signed in February 1986, containing around 270 measures to create a single market. The measures currently adopted relate in the main to:

● the liberalization of public procurement, which involved making the rules on works and supplies contracts more transparent, stepping up checks and extending the rules to important new areas such as transport, energy and telecommunications;

● the harmonization of taxation, which meant aligning national provisions on indirect taxes, VAT and excise markets and financial services;

● recognition of the 'equivalence of national standards' harmonization of safety and environmental standards;

● the removal of technical barriers;

● the creation of an environment that encourage business cooperation by harmonizing company law and approximating legislation on intellectual and industrial property;

● the removal of the automatic need for customs clearance when goods cross EU boundaries, although customs authorities have a right to check goods if there are any suspicious circumstances.

e)   Future Action on the SMP

The liberalization of inter-community trade in the EU is by no means complete. In an article in the *Financial Times Exporter* July 1997 (p. 2), Margaret Beckett, the UK Trade and Industry Secretary, called for the following improvements:

● better and more even enforcement of the harmonization rules;

● more liberal energy markets;

● a better single market in financial services and public procurement;

● further progress in telecommunications.

The political will to implement the full provisions of the Single Market would appear to be as great as ever. In November 1999 Romano Prodi, currently President of the European Commission, was quoted as saying 'I want the potential of the Internal Market to be unlocked for consumers. The Commission must lead the drive for an Internal Market that delivers for the consumer: in terms of choice, quality and value for money, above all in the areas of services such as financial services.'

Perhaps a more down-to-earth comment was made at the same time by Frits Bolkestein, the EU Commissioner responsible for financial services, who was quoted as saying 'The opportunities the Single Market provides for all, citizens, consumers, and businesses alike are enormous. What we must do now is to make it work in practice.'

5 The Balance of Payments (BoP)

a) Introduction

The remainder of this chapter will focus on the concept of balance of payments, taking the UK position to illustrate what are widely applicable concepts.

We shall examine the concept of the balance of payments as a record of international economic transactions. This provides the base for a discussion of the composition of the balance of payments accounts, and the crucial difference between the accounting balance (which must always occur) and economic equilibrium in the BoP. The concept of the terms of trade will then be considered, together with its relationship to the balance of trade. Finally, the problems involved in interpreting BoP statistics will be examined.

b) The Concept of the Balance of Payments

The BoP may be defined as a systematic record, over a given period of time, of all transactions between domestic residents (including government agencies and military forces located abroad) and residents of foreign nations. For the UK, all transactions are recorded in sterling. When invoiced in foreign currency, the conversion is at the appropriate exchange rate at the time.

By convention, all credit items (i.e. those that increase net money claims on non- residents) enter the accounts with a positive sign (e.g. exports of goods and services, foreign investment in the UK); all debit items (i.e. those that decrease net money claims on foreigners) enter the accounts with a negative sign (e.g. imports of goods and services, UK investment abroad).

c)   The Structure of the Balance of Payments Accounts

The accounts may be divided into three parts:

i)   The current account comprises visible trade (exports and imports of raw materials, foods, manufactured goods, etc.) and invisibles (credits and debits for services such as insurance, banking, shipping, tourism, government expenditure on armed forces overseas and embassies; interest, profits and dividends; and current transfers including payments to/from the EU budget, foreign aid, immigrants' remittances, etc.).

The net balances on the visible trade and invisibles elements are added together to give the current account balance.

ii)   Transactions in UK external assets and liabilities (the capital account) includes items such as direct and portfolio investment by foreigners in the UK and by UK residents overseas; sterling and foreign currency borrowing (+) and lending (-) abroad by UK banks; net values for other private-sector external financial transactions; changes in UK official reserves and official borrowing from and repayments to the IMF, Bank for International Settlements and overseas central banks.

iii)   The balancing item arises because of errors and omissions in the recording of payments, and it is simply the difference between the total value of recorded transactions and the recorded flows of currency. If the item is positive, this means that, in net terms, more foreign currency has come into the country than the total of recorded transactions shows. The value can be extremely volatile.

d)   Official Financing

Prior to 1987, the UK BoP accounts were divided into four parts. The additional part arose from the sub-division of 'transactions in UK external assets and liabilities' into government capital flows and 'official financing' (which included net transactions with overseas monetary authorities, foreign currency borrowing on international financial markets, and the usage of official gold and foreign currency reserves). Today, there remains a separate category for changes in UK official reserves, but it is somewhat more difficult to identify the other elements of official financing in the general capital account. Nevertheless, it should still be recognized that if the overall value of official financing is positive, then there is said to be a BoP deficit (i.e. all other items in the BoP, which are largely private sector items, but including certain amounts of non-financial government sector items, have a negative value in aggregate); conversely, a negative value for official financing means that the BoP is in surplus.

e)   Accounting Equality and Economic Equilibrium

There can never be BoP accounts that do not balance in accounting terms, i.e. all negative items taken together exactly balance the sum of the positive items. The reason for this is that the accounts are constructed on the principle of double-entry book-keeping. Effectively, each item is entered twice into the accounts: first to show the original transaction, and secondly to indicate how it has been financed.

There is an economic equilibrium only when official financing is zero. When a BoP surplus or deficit occurs, a disequilibrium position (an economic imbalance) exists. A persistent deficit or surplus on the BoP is referred to as a fundamental disequilibrium, and this concept is of importance in determining whether or not policy actions are required. However, in recent years there has been an increasing tendency for commentators to focus attention upon the current account of the BoP, in the light of its crucial importance in respect of the country's ability to pay its way internationally. Hence, both private and government sector capital items tend to be grouped together to give a broad measure of the level of net borrowing by the country as a whole.

f)   The Terms of Trade and Price Elasticity of Demand

An important concept that affects the current account is the 'terms of trade'. This is defined as the ratio of an index of export prices to an index of import prices (for the UK, prices are expressed in sterling). If the index of export prices falls relative to the index of import prices, the terms of trade are said to 'deteriorate'. An 'improvement' in the terms of trade occurs when export prices rise relative to import prices. In effect, movements in the terms of trade show changes in the real purchasing power of a given quantity of exports in terms of imports. However, whether an improvement in the terms of trade is good for the country (or a deterioration is bad) will depend upon the reason for the change.

If UK export prices rise because of increased domestic costs, then while this will cause the UK's terms of trade to improve (other things being equal), the effects on the balance of trade (and UK output and jobs) will depend upon the elasticity of demand for traded goods.

For most items traded, if the price falls, other things being equal, the quantity demanded will rise. In order to ascertain how trade values are affected by price changes, it is necessary to consider the price elasticity of demand for imported goods, and foreigners' price elasticity of demand for domestic exports. Price elasticity of demand may be defined as

$$e = \frac{\% \text{ change in quantity demanded}}{\% \text{ change in price of goods}}$$

The following sums up the implications of price elasticity of demand for the sterling values of UK imports and exports:

Table 4

Price elasticity of demand	Whether prices reduced/ increased	Effect on total revenue
e < 1	reduced prices	reduced revenue
e < 1	increased prices	increased revenue
e > 1	reduced prices	increased revenue
e > 1	increased prices	reduced revenue

Thus, if UK export prices can be reduced, then the price elasticity of demand for UK exports must be greater than 1 if the total sterling value of exports is to rise. To reduce the total sterling value of imports, following a rise in the sterling price of imports, the UK price elasticity of demand for imports must also be greater than 1.

The variables usually listed as being important to export/import flows are prices, income, the exchange rate, and the non-price attributes of goods and services (i.e. quality, after-sales service, delivery dates, etc.). The non-price attributes of goods and services are difficult to quantify.

To sum up, a higher price for UK exports may lead to a proportionately greater reduction in demand, thus having adverse effects on the balance of trade. Indeed, as imports become relatively cheaper, these may also increase in volume, thus making matters even worse. However, by contrast, if UK export prices rise in response to an increase in demand for UK goods overseas, this is much more likely to have positive effects on the balance of trade, and on the UK economy as a whole.

PART TWO

Introduction

This part of the book commences with an overview of the foreign exchange market. It then analyses the techniques, both internal and external, that could be used by corporates to manage foreign exchange risk, and then assesses the arguments for and against the management of such risks. Finally this part examines the mechanics of money transfer across national boundaries.

2

THE FOREIGN EXCHANGE MARKET: SPOT MARKETS, FORWARD MARKETS, DIFFERENT EXCHAGNE RATE REGIMES, THE EURO

Objectives

On completion of this chapter the student should be able to:

Understand the basic operations of the foreign exchange market and its participants;

Appreciate the factors that influence the forward rates in foreign exchange;

Appreciate the benefits and drawbacks of the various exchange rate regimes;

Understand the factors that affect foreign exchange rate movements in the spot market;

Appreciate the nature of the ECU;

Understand the broad significance of the developments concerning the single European currency, the euro.

Note:

1. The authors wish to acknowledge their indebtedness to May 1996 Bank of England Fact Sheet on The Foreign Exchange Market for parts of the section on foreign currency exchange markets in this chapter. Extracts from the statistics in the Bank of England's 1998 triennial survey of turnover in the UK foreign exchange and over-the-counter (OTC) derivatives markets are also quoted in this chapter.

2. The single European currency, which commenced in January 1999, is called the 'euro'. Readers should take care not to confuse the word 'euro' in the context of a single currency with the word 'euro' in the context of 'euro dollar' or 'euro sterling' etc. The

euro dollar market can be looked upon as the wholesale market for depositing and lending dollars, and the euro sterling market can likewise be looked upon as the wholesale market for the deposit and lending of sterling.

When the 'euro' in the sense of a single currency comes into being, and when the transitional period is over (see later in this chapter) then the 'euro markets' for currencies of participating countries will cease to exist. However, the 'euro dollar' market, for instance, will continue because the dollar will not be a participating currency. Similar considerations will apply to 'euro yen' and to 'euro sterling' unless the pound joins the single currency.

1   Foreign Currency Exchange Markets

Market Size

The Bank of England conducted its 1998 triennial survey of turnover in the UK foreign exchange and over-the-counter (OTC) derivatives markets as part of the latest worldwide survey organized by the Bank for International Settlements (BIS). All comparisons are with the previous survey in 1995 and are explained in US$bn, unless otherwise stated. The main findings of the UK survey were:

● Average daily spot and forward foreign exchange turnover was $637bn, 37% higher than the $464bn per day recorded three years before (an annualized growth rate of 11%).

● The forward foreign exchange market continued to grow more rapidly than the spot market, which now represents only 35% of total foreign exchange turnover.

● The top twenty organizations' share of foreign exchange turnover increased from 68% to 69%.

For details of a worldwide comparison of forward exchange markets, readers may wish to consult the Bank for International Settlements' web site at www.bis.org/publ

Operation of Market

These markets have no physical form, in the sense of there being an actual market place where dealers in currencies meet. Rather the markets exist through a sophisticated network of communications, involving telephone, telex and computer links. London is the world's largest foreign exchange market, largely due to the business generated from other financial activities relating to products such as insurance and eurobonds and to shipping, commodities and banking. In addition, London benefits from its geographical location and time zone which enables trade to take place with Europe throughout the day, with Japan, Hong Kong and Singapore in the morning and with the USA after 1pm.

The markets in different countries are closely associated, and exchange market activity is today a truly international occupation. Further, it is often suggested that the foreign exchanges constitute almost perfect markets, with the prices of currencies (exchange rates) responding immediately to the finest changes in demand and supply conditions.

Broadly speaking, participants in the foreign exchange markets can be classified into four categories: customers, banks, brokers and official monetary authorities.

- Customers are companies that use the market because they require foreign currency in connection with their cross-border business.

- Some banks act as market makers who undertake at all times to quote buy and sell rates for foreign exchange transactions. Market makers profit from the spread between their buy and sell rates (bid/offer rates) but they must be ready to adjust prices very quickly to avoid being short of a rapidly appreciating currency or being over-stocked with a rapidly depreciating one.

- Brokers act as intermediaries and make their profit from commissions. Brokers have dedicated communication links with banks (telephones, telex, and computer-based links) and they should be aware at any given time of the trends in the market makers' prices and which market makers currently offer the best deal for their clients' needs.

- In many countries, the official monetary authorities are important participants in the markets, buying and selling currencies with the objective of either stabilizing or altering currency exchange rates for economic policy purposes.

Dealings in the market may be 'spot' (where transactions take place at current market prices with settlement being within two business days of the deal being contracted) or 'forward' (where a price is agreed for currency to be delivered at a future date, with settlement being more than two business days after dealing). The Bank of England Fact Sheet (May 1996) gives the following example of how a deal might be carried out.

To execute a *spot* deal a broker could contact a market maker and ask for the rate, for example 'dollar-mark' (i.e. deutschemarks to the US dollar). The market maker normally quotes a two-way price – that is he stands ready to bid for or offer up to some standard amount. The *spread* is the difference between these two prices and favours the market maker against the price taker to whom the quote has been made. During interbank trading where participants know the 'big figures' (i.e. dollars and cents, deutschemarks and pfennigs) the dealer might quote only the *points* (the last two figures of the price). For example, if the rate for dollars against the deutschemark was US\$ 1 = DM 1.5050 -1.5060 then the market maker would quote 'fifty-sixty': he bids for dollars at DM 1.5050 and offers them at DM 1.5060. If the caller wishes to deal he will *hit*, that is accept, one side of the price. Confirmation of this oral contract will be exchanged and instructions concerning payment given, and passed on to the settlements staff who ensure that the respective currency amounts are transferred into the designated accounts on the value date.

As an aside it might be mentioned that as a precaution against internal fraud, the functions of dealing, confirmation and settlement are segregated to try to avoid problems such as occurred for Barings Bank when Nick Leeson was allowed to fulfil more than one of these roles for the same transaction.

2   The Forward Exchange Market

(a) Introductory example

Example One

A forward deal is an agreement between two parties (usually a market maker and a customer) to set a rate at the outset for a deal (covering a set amount of foreign currency) which is to be settled at a future date (or between two set future dates).

Let us first of all take a highly simplified example to illustrate the principles that lie behind the relationship of the forward rate to the spot rate. Suppose a UK exporter, who expects to receive US\$ 1m in one year's time, asks a UK bank for a forward rate. The following process could take place, given the following information:

Spot Rate £1 = US\$ 1.5

Eurodollar one-year fixed interest rates 6%

Eurosterling one-year fixed interest rates 10%

The eurocurrency interest rates for convenience can be considered as the wholesale rates of interest.

Action taken by the bank

1.   At the outset, the bank will agree a forward rate of 1.4455 (after calculating the consequences of the actions shown below). This rate will ensure that the bank is not at risk from any subsequent exchange rate movements, provided the delivery of the US\$ takes place to restore the bank's position to the status quo.

2.   Today the bank will borrow US \$ 943,396.23 and convert it to sterling £628,930.82 at the spot rate of 1.5.

3.   The bank will pay debit interest of 6% on the US \$ funds, but will receive credit interest of 10% on its new sterling balances.

4.   In one year's time the sterling balances will total £691,823.90 (with interest).

5.   In one year's time the US \$ debit balance will amount to US\$1,000,000.00 (with interest).

6.   At the end of the year, the exporter will deliver US\$ 1m and the bank will pay him £691,823.90.

7.   The bank will then use the customer's US\$ 1m to repay its own dollar advance.

8.   Thus the forward rate will have been calculated at the outset as

$$\frac{1,000,000.00}{691,823.90} = 1.4455$$

The purpose of the above example is to illustrate the general principle that the forward rate is derived from the spot rate and relative interest rate differentials. It does, however, make several simplifying assumptions that do not apply in practice:

- It ignores the spread between the bank's bid and offer rates for foreign exchange transactions. In practice these spreads apply to both spot and forward rates.

- It ignores the difference between deposit and lending rates of interest.

- It ignores transaction costs.

- It assumes that the above is the only transaction by the bank in the forward dollar market. In practice there is endless scope for the bank to match its positions by other deals and by transactions in other markets such as futures.

- It assumes that there are no government restrictions or tax distortions on such funds transfers

Note on use of a swap to cover the bank's position

In practice, the bank would almost certainly have covered its potential liability under the forward contract by a swap, rather than by borrowing US$. Thus the bank would have 'swapped' (i.e. paid over to the another, possibly US, bank) £666,667 in exchange for US$1m. At the end of the year the principals would have been swapped back (i.e. the transaction would have been reversed) with the UK bank's exporter customer funding the US$ 1m and the US bank providing sterling which would be used to fund the purchase of the dollars from the customer. The two banks would have agreed at the outset an interest payment to cover the fact that the US bank was gaining interest from its increased sterling balances. The interest payment calculation would be based on the differential between the interest rates on dollar and sterling.

A summary of the swap now follows:

1. Today, as soon as the forward contract has been agreed, UK bank and US bank swap. UK bank pays £ 666,667 to the US bank and receives US$ 1m in exchange.

2. The two banks agree to reverse the transaction in one year, with the US bank to make an additional payment to the UK bank to compensate the UK bank for losing out on the higher sterling interest rates.

3. In one year's time the following transactions take place:

    - The UK bank receives US $ 1m from its exporter customer and pays them over to the US bank.

    - The US bank pays the UK bank £ 666,667, plus interest as follows:

$$\frac{666,667 \times 0.04}{1.06} = £25,157$$

thus the total sterling paid is £ 691,824

- Thus the forward rate would be agreed as

    $$\frac{1,000000}{691,824} = 1.4455,$$ the same result as for currency borrowing.

- For banks this method is more convenient than currency borrowing. In practice, the interest rate differential on the swap might be finer than for straight conventional currency borrowing.

(b) Simplified explanation of why arbitrage will support the forward rate shown in the above

Example Two

4. If the one-year forward rate had been agreed at a different figure, say 1.60, and assuming that a large UK corporate could borrow and deposit at the rates shown in the above example, there would have been scope for a risk-free profit as follows:

5. The UK customer could have borrowed, say, US $ 1m for one year, and agreed a forward contract for the bank to sell US $ 1, 060,000 (the balance plus interest) at 1.60 one year forward.

6. The US$ would have been converted to sterling immediately at 1.5, giving a sterling equivalent of £666,666.67, which would have been deposited at 10 %.

7. The US $ advance to be repaid after one year's interest would be 1,060,000.

8. At the end of the year, the sterling balances would have amounted to £733,333.34 and only £662,500 would have been used to acquire the US$ 1,060,000 at the agreed forward rate of 1.60.

9. Thus there would have been a risk-free profit of £70,833 for the customer.

10. Obviously if a forward rate of 1.60 was on general offer in such circumstances, there would be an immediate demand by customers for US$ borrowing which would tend to raise the US$ interest rate and there would be a demand for spot sterling which would tend to make spot sterling appreciate. Thus by a process known as arbitrage, market forces would tend to remove this anomaly, thus moving the forward rate back to its logical interest rate parity figure.

11. Likewise if the forward rate had been set at 1.40, a profit could be made by customers from borrowing £ 1m sterling, converting it to dollars, covering forward at 1.40, investing the dollars at 6% and then converting dollar principal in one year of $1,590,000 back to sterling . The resultant sterling sum of £1,135,714 would have exceeded the sterling advance of £1,100,000 (including interest).

(c) The determination of forward rates, by way of premium, or discount.

When a forward currency is more valuable than spot currency, the forward rate is said to be at a premium. In the example above the forward dollar rate would have been at a premium to spot rate because it required fewer dollars (1.4455 at the one-year forward rate) in exchange for one pound than the US $ 1.50 required in exchange for one pound in spot deals.

We shall see in Chapter 3 that the forward premium is deducted from the spot rate when calculating the forward rate.

The following acronym can be used to determine when a forward currency is likely to be at a premium to spot:

> LIP (The forward currency with the **L**ower **I**nterest rates will be at a **P**remium to its spot value)

If we look at the above hypothetical example of the US$ spot being at 1.50 and the one-year forwards being at 1.4455, we can see that the reason behind this is that the US$ interest rates are lower than sterling. Thus, in the course of the operation to cover (or hedge) its position under the forward contract, the bank 'gains' by borrowing at 6% in dollars, but investing the sterling proceeds at 10%. Hence, ignoring bid/offer spreads, the bank can afford to pay out more sterling against one-year forward dollars than against spot dollars. If there is more forward sterling than spot sterling against a given amount of dollars, then forward sterling is weaker and conversely the forward dollar is stronger. Hence the forward dollar is said to be at a premium to spot.

Conversely when the forward currency is weaker than the spot, it is said to be at a discount to spot. Had the forward rate been at 1.60 at the time the spot rate was 1.50, then it would have required more one-year forward dollars than spot dollars in exchange for one pound. Thus the forward dollar would have been at a discount to spot in £: $ deals.

We shall see in Chapter 3 that a discount is added to spot rates in calculations of forward rates.

The following acronym can be used to decide when a forward rate is at a discount to spot:

> HID (The forward currency with the **H**igher **I**nterest rates will be at a **D**iscount to its spot value)

If eurodollar interest rates had been higher than eurosterling (say 10% and 6% respectively) in the above example, the bank would have had to pay 10% interest on its dollar borrowing and would have received only 6 % on the sterling deposit. Thus the bank would have wished to pay out less sterling to its customer under the forward contract than it would have paid out at spot rates. If there is less forward sterling than spot sterling against a given amount of dollars, then the forward pound is stronger than the spot pound and the forward dollar is weaker than the spot dollar in £: $ deals.

(c) Example of the use of premiums and discounts to calculate a forward rate

For convenience, forward rates are not quoted outright (1.4455 in the example one above). What is quoted is the differential between the spot and the outright forward (the premium or discount). Premiums and discounts are subject to much less fluctuation than spot rates, so quoting differentials requires far fewer changes to any published forward rates. Most writers show the forward premium or discount to be determined by means of the following general formula.

$$\frac{\text{spot rate x interest differential x time in days}}{360 \times 100}$$

When the forward period is for less than a year, the number of days can complicate the calculation because some countries calculate interest on the basis of a 360-day year, whereas for sterling the number of days is taken as 365. In any event, to be strictly accurate the effects of compounding should be taken into account for periods of less than one year. In addition, this formula requires adjustment to take account of whether the bank's bid or offer rate is used.

Let us for convenience repeat the details in the original hypothetical example:

Spot rate	US$ 1.50 - £1
One-year fixed eurodollar interest rate	6%
One-year fixed eurosterling interest rate	10%
One-year forward rate	US$ 1.4455 = £1

As the forward dollar is at a premium to spot because of the nature of the interest differential, the above formula could be used, without concerning ourselves about the number of days because the period is one whole year, to calculate a premium of

$$\frac{1.50 \times 4}{100} = 0.06$$

The premium will then be deducted from the spot to show an outright forward rate of 1.44.

To be strictly accurate the formula could be re- written to calculate the premium as:

$$\frac{\text{spot rate x interest differential time in days}}{(1+i) \times 360 \times 100}$$

Thus the premium to be deducted from the spot (ignoring the complexities of periods under one year) to show an outright forward rate is calculated as:

$$\frac{1.50 \times 0.04}{1.10} = 0.0545$$

The outright forward rate would then be	1.5000
Less one year forward premium	0.0545
	1.4455

When the forward rate is at a discount, the lower interest rate should be applied to the denominator of the above formula, and the resultant discount would be added to the spot rate to calculate the outright forward.

Let us use the formula to demonstrate the position where the interest rate position is the opposite way round:

Spot rate US$ 1.50 = £1
One-year fixed eurodollar interest rates: 10%
One-year fixed eurosterling interest rates: 6%
The forward discount would be:

$$\frac{1.5 \times 0.04}{1.06} = 0.0566 \text{ discount}$$

So the one-year forward rate would be 1.50 + 0.0566 = 1.5566

If the rate of exchange has a direct quote, that is a number of home currency units is equal to one unit of foreign currency, then the formula will have to be adjusted to take account of this change in quote.

(d) The premium/discount as a percentage of spot

By simply rearranging the above formula, the premium or discount as a percentage of spot can be calculated. This percentage should equate to the interest rate differentials in the two centres, subject to the caveats expressed concerning the above calculations.

3 The Relationship between Spot, Forward, Relative Interest Rates and Relative Inflation Rates

(a) Interest Rates and inflation

There are many theories that explore the factors which determine the level of interest rates. However, for the purposes of this book we are concerned solely with the link between inflation, real rates of interest and nominal rates.

The nominal rate is the rate actually quoted in a transaction, and the real rate is the nominal rate adjusted to take account of inflation. For new transactions, the nominal rate will incorporate the real rate, plus an allowance for anticipated inflation over the relevant period of the transaction, so as to provide the lender with an anticipated real rate of return. This effect is often called the Fisher effect, after Irvine Fisher, one of the pioneers of the theory of interest rate determination.

(b) Interest rate parity

We have demonstrated in the examples in 2.2 above that there is a link between the spot rate and relative interest rate differentials, and the forward rate for a given future period. If we then assume that real rates of interest are the same internationally, the difference in the rates of interest on deposits of different currencies with equally creditworthy banks would arise solely from different inflationary expectations.

(c) The link between interest rates, inflation, forward and spot rates

When Fisher's link between inflationary expectations and interest rates holds, when real rates of interest are equalized between countries, and when interest rate parity holds, spot and forward rates are linked to interest rates and anticipated levels of inflation in the two countries concerned.

There are many obvious limiting assumptions to this general principle, among which are:

●   the effects of transaction costs

●   the possibility of government restrictions on funds transfer

●   the possibility of government intervention in the markets

●   differential taxation treatment of the transactions in different countries

(d) The forward rate as an unbiased predictor of the future spot rate

The forward rate is generally found to be an unbiased predictor of the future spot rate for the relevant period. 'Unbiased predictor' means that if the forward rate is used to predict the future spot rate at the end of the equivalent period of time, then in the long run the sum of the gains will equal the sum of the losses. However, empirical evidence has shown that in the short term the forward rate has consistently undervalued the future spot rate when the spot rate has been rising strongly, and conversely the forward rate has consistently overvalued the future spot rate when the spot rate has been falling rapidly.

4   Different Types of Exchange Rate Regimes

This chapter so far has largely ignored the potential effects of government intervention in the exchange markets. The remainder of the chapter will analyse the effects of the different degrees of intervention by governments in the markets.

In theory, there are many different forms of exchange rate regimes that may be operated. At one extreme there is the rigidly fixed exchange rate regime, where currencies are given fixed parities by a administrative edict. (In this case the normal exchange market mechanism is bypassed entirely.) At the other extreme, exchange rates may be left to float cleanly, with no deliberate official interference, so that the market forces determine the exchange rates. Between the two extremes there are many variants of the basic forms, each involving differing degrees of official exchange market intervention.

(a) Clean floating exchange rates

The advocates of clean floating exchange rates, where market forces alone determine the spot rates, argue that a country's monetary and fiscal policies should not be constrained by the need to defend a fixed exchange rate. They believe that exchange rates should be determined by the supply of and the demand for currencies in the free market.

The main disadvantages of clean floating are:

It can cause uncertainty in relation to business transactions.

Time lags in adjustment may make the BoP situation worse in the short run (i.e. when home currency has depreciated, relative export and import prices alter before relative quantities traded; this results in the J-curve effect where the balance of payments current account initially deteriorates and only subsequently moves into surplus).

Domestic inflationary pressures may be generated as import prices rise from a depreciation of home currency.

Official financial discipline may be undermined because there will be no requirement to curb inflationary expectations to protect the exchange value of home currency.

The main advantages of a freely floating currency are that:

It provides an automatic adjustment mechanism for dealing with balance of payments problems. Thus in theory a surplus on the balance of payments should result in an appreciating exchange rate which will then cause a rise in relative export prices, resulting in the surplus being eroded. However, leaving aside the problems of elasticity of demand and the J-curve effect, it must be remembered that there are many factors other than the balance of payments position that cause exchange rate movements.

There should be no need for restrictive measures by the authorities to interfere with trade because of the need to defend a fixed rate.

At least in theory, international currency reserves are no longer required (except for occasional stabilization of the exchange rate) because the government no longer has to choose the exchange rate that it believes to be 'correct'.

(b) The factors that influence exchange rate movements in a clean floating regime

In the short term the most important factor affecting exchange rates is usually the relative levels of interest rates, or rather the anticipated short-term changes therein.

The following quote from an anonymous writer in the *Daily Telegraph Business News* of 5 July 1997 illustrates this phenomenon:

> *The pound soared yesterday as investors poured money into the currency in anticipation of an early rise in interest rates...Against the mark, the pound was up 1.5 pfennigs to*

2.96, a six-year high, and against the dollar it rose 0.25 cents to 1.6875.

Obviously, at times such as when sterling was taken out of the ERM in September 1992, speculative pressures rather than factors such as relative interest rates (and expectations of changes therein) can affect the short-term value of a currency. However, under 'normal' economic circumstances short-term interest rates play a major role in short-term currency movements.

To the extent that exchange rates are allowed to float freely, then any factor that affects the component parts of the current account and/or capital account of the balance of payments, and hence which affects the supply and demand conditions on the currency markets, may potentially influence the pattern of currency exchange rates. The major factors affecting international trade and capital flows include:

i) Real economic variables, e.g. consumer tastes, real income levels, and technological innovation.

ii) Relative inflation rates.

iii) Relative interest rates, which must be viewed in real terms with expectations of inflation rates taken into account.

iv) Non-economic factors, e.g. the social and political environment.

v) Government policies, which may often affect the balance of payments indirectly.

(c) The theory of purchasing power parity

This offers an explanation of movements in currency exchange rates in the long run. The theory states that the equilibrium exchange rate between any two currencies is that rate which equalizes the domestic purchasing powers of the two currencies. E.g. if a bundle of goods has a price of £5 in the UK and $10 in the USA, then according to the theory the equilibrium exchange rate is £1 = $2. Trade flows will bring about this value by altering the supplies of and demands for currencies.

There are major problems with the theory:

- the theory ignores the existence of international capital flows, as well as the transport and transactions costs associated with trade.

- it fails to recognize the fact that many goods/services are not traded internationally.

- the role of news is not considered. In the real world major unpredicted events often occur and these unexpected events are often referred to as news. Exchange rates respond very quickly to new information, so news can often have an immediate impact on spot rates. However, prices of goods normally change much less quickly as a result of news, so the relevant price indices do not adjust as quickly as the spot rates.

A study by R. MacDonald (1988) Floating Exchange Rates Theories and Evidence, Unwin

Hyman reviewed fourteen empirical studies of the purchasing power parity theory. Ten rejected the PPP as a long-run predictor of exchange rates, while four showed the PPP as being valid in the long term. The general consensus is that there are substantial deviations from the PPP in the short run, but the case is less clear in the long term.

On the other hand, the *Economist* uses the McDonalds hamburger as its benchmark for assessing the validity of the PPP on the basis that this is a standard product which is sold in over 100 countries. In April 1997 the *Economist* reported that the average American price of a Big Mac was US $ 2.42, whereas the dollar equivalent of the Swiss franc price at the current rate of exchange was $ 4.02, and the Chinese equivalent was only $ 1.16. Those who believe that the PPP holds and who are satisfied that the Big Mac represents an adequate basket of goods will conclude that the Swiss franc is overvalued and the Chinese yuan is undervalued. The paper then reported that research by Robert Cumby of Georgetown University showed that the past year's Big Mac survey had correctly forecast the direction of the movement of 6 out of 7 currencies whose value had changed by 10% or more.

The 1998 Bank of England survey of the foreign exchange markets showed that the forward foreign exchange market continued to grow more rapidly than the spot market, which now represents only 35% of total foreign exchange turnover.

Thus factors other than the balance of payments and purchasing power parity theory must influence spot rate changes.

It is therefore suggested that the main relevance of the PPP is when trading partners' inflation rates differ. In such cases it is likely that the exchange rate of the currency issued by the high-inflation country will depreciate in the long run.

(d) Adjustable peg system (Bretton Woods system)

From the end of World War II until the early 1970s most countries were on the 'adjustable peg' system (often referred to as the Bretton Woods system). The basic notion was that a fixed parity exchange rate system would provide a stable basis for international economic activity, but that allowance must be made for the occurrence of fundamental changes in the underlying real economic positions of countries participating in the scheme. Thus, although countries agreed to intervene in the foreign exchange market and to implement appropriate economic policies in order to hold the value of their currencies to within a narrow band around fixed dollar par values, in the event of a 'fundamental disequilibrium' on the balance of payments they were allowed to adjust their exchange rates.

The problem of the adjustable peg system comes from:

- the difficulty in defining what is meant by fundamental disequilibrium.

- deciding when and by how much to adjust the exchange rate.

- the risk of retaliation (including competitive devaluation when one currency has been adjusted downwards in value to try to improve the balance of payments position).

● speculative pressure can also make the problem worse, as was seen when sterling left the European Monetary system in 1992.

The benefits of the adjustable peg, which were certainly apparent in the less volatile economic conditions prior to the 1970s, are that this type of 'fixed' rate system may encourage international trade (through the reduction of exchange rate risks), and longer-term business planning is made easier. Governments are also encouraged to pursue sound economic and financial policies (especially in respect of inflation) in order to support the existing exchange rate.

(e) Managed floating

Since 1972, with the exception of the period October 1990 to September 1992, the UK has followed a regime of 'managed floating'. The Bretton Woods system had proved to be too inflexible, particularly when confidence was lost in its base, the US $. Initially, it was hoped that floating would be only temporary, until an alternative basis for a worldwide fixed rate system could be found. However, managed floating has worked reasonably well, and is widely used throughout the world.

A serious practical problem with clean floating is that exchange rates may become unstable, and financial uncertainty may be created. With managed floating, the authorities intervene to iron out short-term fluctuations, leaving market forces to determine long-term trends; the problem here is in deciding when a movement is short term. Furthermore, there are limits to the extent to which the authorities are able to intervene because their stock of foreign currency reserves is finite.

5 Monetary Arrangements within the EU

For many years, there has been much debate on the view that the EU should move towards full economic and monetary union (EMU). With the introduction of a single EU currency, with monetary controls being implemented by a European Central Bank, and with a much greater power over economic policy being vested with EU institutions, it could be argued that the EMU project was moving towards completion at least so far as the participating countries are concerned.

(a) The EMS (The European Monetary System)

The objectives of the EMS related primarily to the stabilization of EU currency exchange rates (i.e. the creation of a zone of currency stability in Europe), and mutual financial support for member states. Nevertheless, the successful operation of the EMS was generally seen as being an important first step on the road towards EMU, and the requirements for its operation were considered to be a necessary precondition for the successful implementation of the single European currency.

The EMS operated through the Exchange Rate Mechanism as follows:

i) Limitation of EU members' currency exchange rate fluctuations. The Exchange Rate Mechanism (ERM) operated on the basis of two criteria:

  (i) A 'parity grid' arrangement sets upper and lower intervention rates for each pair of currencies – initially the grid allowed a maximum +/- 2¼% relative movement (with 6% for a small number of currencies). However, following extreme turbulence on the currency exchange markets in July 1993, the band was widened to +/- 15% for most currencies (officially as a temporary expedient). Once any two currencies reach their relative value limits the central bank of the country with the weak currency was required to sell the other country's (strong) currency on the foreign exchange markets, while the central bank of the country with the strong currency was required to buy the weaker currency. These purchases and sales, with supporting currency 'swaps' among central banks if required, should continue until pressure was taken off the currencies' values and they were pushed away from their parity limits.

  (ii) The European Currency Unit Divergence Indicator – the ECU (see below) – was used as the basis for calculating a central rate for each member's currency. Each currency is allocated divergence limits against its ECU central rate. In the event of a currency's value moving beyond 75% of the maximum deviation permitted, it was expected that the relevant government would take some form of remedial action. For a country with a weak currency this may involve the raising of domestic interest rates or perhaps a tightening of fiscal policy. For a strong currency country, some form of expansionary policy might be expected. Thus, the ECU indicator related to the broad position of a currency relative to all other EU currencies taken as a group.

  In addition, the values of individual currencies could be realigned within the parity grid and in terms of the ECU central rate if the fundamental economic relationships underlying the exchange rates alter. However, the EMS rules were intended to impose a certain amount of financial discipline on member states, and hence it has been argued that realignments should take place only as the very last resort.

(b) How the EMS operated

Between its establishment in March 1979 and September 1992, the EMS would appear to have operated reasonably successfully, although it was necessary to realign currency exchange values on a number of occasions. The benefits of the system could be summarized as:

- despite these realignments, the exchange rates of ERM participants were more stable than those of the other main Western currencies, and to the extent that this helps to support business confidence this is clearly a positive outcome.

- because the EU now accounts for over a half of all the UK's overseas trade, a more stable relationship between sterling and other EU currencies should help both exporters and importers in their business planning and pricing decisions.

- if UK producers were no longer able to rely upon a depreciating value for sterling in order to maintain their international competitiveness, they would be under greater pressure to hold down wage and price rises, in the face of generally modest inflation rates within the rest of the EU (failure to hold down UK inflation rates relative to other ERM members could have dire consequences for UK output and jobs, assuming that devaluation of sterling was not seen as an acceptable option).

However, some critics of the ERM have argued that:

● its operation has tended to undermine economic growth within the participating countries. Immediately prior to September 1992, there was a strong body of opinion within the UK supporting a reduction in interest rates to stimulate economic growth to offset the effects of the recession. However, in order to keep sterling at its agreed central parity (commonly known by the DM rate of 2.95), UK interest rates had to be kept relatively high.

● in order to achieve exchange rate stability in the longer term, it is necessary that the economic performances of the countries involved should be broadly similar. In practice the UK, for example, seems usually to be at a different stage of the business cycle from its EU partners,

● the successful operation of the EMS may require the subordination of domestic policies within individual countries for the purpose harmonizing economic performance. That coordination of policies would be directed towards bringing inflation rates in member states to similar low levels, reducing interest rate differentials between the respective countries, and limiting the extent of balance of payments imbalances in the medium term. While these objectives command substantial support, convergence of economic conditions is not easy to achieve in practice.

● when sterling was put into the mechanism, in October 1990, there was much controversy over the parity chosen. Indeed the fears that because of sterling's importance in international trade and investment, its entry into the ERM might generate instability within the mechanism (especially relative to the DEM), and thus require excessive exchange market intervention, proved to be well-founded.

● excessive speculation against sterling caused it to be withdrawn from the ERM in September 1992. This had a damaging effect on the economic credibility of the UK government at the time.

6   The ECU

The ECU was a 'basket' of EU currencies, and was regarded as a form of international money, performing all the functions that are normally associated with money assets. Thus, for example, the ECU was used as a means of payment between EU central banks; it was used as the unit of account for both the intervention and credit elements of the EMS.

Since its introduction, in March 1979, the ECU developed along two distinct routes. The official ECU was used to settle intra-government fund transfers and was quite separate from the private ECU which was created by private institutions out of the ECU's component currencies. The private ECU could be bought and sold on the foreign exchange market. Both individuals and companies could hold ECU assets (such as bank deposits and marketable securities) and could incur ECU liabilities (such as bank loans and securitized debts). The major advantage in using the ECU was that its international purchasing power value was likely to be more stable than the corresponding values of the individual component currencies.

The value of the ECU was calculated as a weighted average of all EU members' currencies. The weights were set to reflect each member's relative economic size in terms of gross national product and the importance of its trade within the EU.

The ECU has now been superseded by the euro.

7 The Single European Currency (the Euro)

(a) Background

The Maastricht Treaty envisaged that there could be irrevocable fixing of exchange rates within the EU, as the precursor to the introduction of a single EU currency. This move was to be subject to a qualified majority of EU states being in favour (meaning that no one member state could veto the move) and at least seven member states meeting the economic convergence criteria. Among the convergence criteria were:

● annual inflation to be not more than 1.5 % higher than the average inflation rate of the three lowest inflation EU countries.

● annual budget deficit must not exceed 3% of gross domestic product, unless the ratio 'has declined substantially and continuously and comes close to 3%, or alternatively the excess is only exceptional and the ratio remains close to 3%'. It is unclear exactly what is meant by these additional clarifications to the 3% rule.

● total government debt must not to exceed 60% of GDP, unless the ratio is sufficiently diminishing at a satisfactory pace (again it is not too clear what the precise meaning is).

● the exchange rate must have been within the normal bands of the ERM for at least two years.

Prior to the introduction of the single European currency in 1999, there were some interesting financial manoeuvres as certain EU governments tried to meet the fiscal criteria above, the most spectacular being the proposal in May 1997 by the German Finance Ministry to revalue its gold reserves and pass the paper gain off as public sector income. However, to the amazement of some, it was announced 1 May 1998 that all eleven countries due to join in 1999 had met the criteria.

An important aspect of the Maastricht Treaty is the proposal that a European Central Bank (ECB) will be established, and will take up its full powers when a single EU currency is introduced. It is intended that the ECB will be politically independent, and will have as its main objective the maintenance of price stability within the EU.

A member state's own central bank will be maintained as part of the European System of Central Banks, and will be expected to support the ECB in the implementation of agreed policy. Each individual central bank will also be required to be politically independent of its own country's government. The responsibilities of the ECB will include the conduct of EU monetary policy, foreign exchange market operations, the holding and management of member states' foreign exchange reserves, and the promotion of the smooth operation of EU payments systems.

Some have questioned the wisdom of having a single interest rate covering countries at different stages of economic development. A single interest rate could be set too low for countries where demand needs to be adjusted downwards to offset inflationary pressures (as with the UK's current situation), whereas in other parts of the EU the single rate of interest might be too high because lower rates are needed to stimulate economic activity.

(b) Proposed timetable for full implementation of the single currency

- From 1 January 1999 the first phase of EMU began.

- From January 1999 to December 2001, there will be a three-year transition period during which national currencies and the euro could run in tandem. It would be up to individuals and companies to decide whether to adopt the euro or to use national currencies, or to use a mixture of the two. Notes and coins of national currencies will continue to be legal tender.

- During the period Jan-July 2002, notes and coins in national currencies will be exchanged for the euro. From July 2002, national coins and notes of participating countries will cease to be legal tender.

(c) Which countries participated in the first wave in January 1999?

The acronym BAFFLINGSPI could be used to name the participating countries in the first wave in January 1999:

Belgium

Austria

France

Finland

Luxembourg

Ireland

Netherlands

Germany

Spain

Portugal

Italy

Greece is a member of the EU, but did not join the single currency in the first wave in January 1999. However, Greece is expected to join during 2000. EU countries that have exercised the right to opt out are Sweden, UK and Denmark.

(d) Are the advantages and disadvantages of a country joining a fixed rate exchange system, such as the Exchange Rate Mechanism, equivalent to those of joining a single currency system such as the euro?

The benefits and drawbacks of joining a fixed exchange rate system are not the same as those of joining a single currency such as the euro.

- With a fixed rate system the country retains the right to manage its domestic interest rates and money supply. Leaving the system is always a possibility if circumstances dictate this. This is what happened to sterling when it left the ERM in 1992.

- None of the above is possible with a single currency. There is one interest rate and one policy on money supply (set by the European Central Bank) which may not suit countries at different stages of the economic cycle. Although it is possible to leave a single currency, the political and economic ramifications would be much greater than those involved in leaving a fixed rate regime.

- In a single currency, there will be the same exchange rate for every participating member against non-participating members. This is not the case with a fixed rate regime, although arbitrage will ensure that the rates are not too far apart except at times of strong speculative pressure.

- If the devaluation option is removed, then there will be pressure from euro participating countries with relatively high domestic inflation to be helped to lower their export prices by way EU subsidies.

- There is pressure for a single government in a single currency area, because domestic policies need to be harmonized to make the single currency succeed. This does not apply to the same extent with a fixed rate regime.

(e) · at are the implications of the euro for Europe's foreign e markets?

  ɔ will replace the DEM as a reserve currency for central banks.

  l ECU has been exchanged for euros on a 1:1 basis. The ECU no longer

- Foreign exchange markets between participating currencies will ultimate exist. This will mean that the participating banks and brokers will lose a source of income from the spreads on forward and spot rates, and from their trad options and futures in the participating currencies.

- Research commissioned by the Geneva-based international trade union body FIET has predicted that large numbers of banking jobs could be lost throughout Europe if the single currency if fully adopted.

- The euro may become the unit of pricing for some commodities now denominated in US$, paper/pulp being possible examples because they are produced in Europe but currently priced in US$.

- The government bonds of participating countries, both those in existence as at 1 January 1999 and those subsequently issued, will be denominated euros. There will be a common basis for interest, that of the euro, but the different credit quality of the various governments will ensure that there is some difference in bond yields of participating governments.

- Steps will be taken to harmonize market practices among the participating countries. For example, the basis on which short-term interest yields on bonds are calculated can vary in different countries. Some bond yields are calculated on the basis that a year consists of 360 days whereas others assume a 365-day year as the basis of interest calculations.

(f) Issues for consideration by non–bank businesses post 1999

- Large companies from participating countries involved in cross-border EU trade may switch their accounting systems to the euro as soon as possible because most of their settlements will be by way of bank accounts denominated in euros.

- However, retail and medium-sized companies will still use national (also known as legacy) currency during the transitional period of 1999- 2002 and will only switch to the euro at the last minute. This is because retail customers will have to use national currencies because there will not be any notes and coin denominated in euros until 2002.

- Businesses that have dealings with companies located in countries which are in the 'first wave' of EMU should ask these trading partners whether there will be a need to offer dual pricing for the transitional period from 1999 - 2001. Such businesses should check whether their cash management systems could cope with the transition. For instance euros could be received for credit to a DEM account or vice versa.

- Pricing should be transparent within countries tha have adopted the euro. Thus differential pricing of the same goods in different participating EU countries will ultimately be as difficult as it would be in two different US states.

- Differential pricing in participating countries will probably survive only for goods and

ilt to move across national boundaries. Examples are perishable
i as French television, which runs on a different standard from

cy, accompanied by the existing Single European Market
easier for efficient and flexible companies in one participating
:ss efficient companies that have traditionally concentrated on
.... i his assumes that there will be no EU directive restricting such
actions.

- Price transparency will make non-price factors (for instance quality, reliability, image) more important than ever in the competitive marketplace.

- Businesses may wish to set individual modifications for their products in different EU countries. This could help justify different pricing within the euro zone and could overcome some of the difficulties caused by price transparency of the single currency.

- Transaction costs will be lower with a single currency. Indeed the European Commission has estimated that there will be savings of 0.4% of European gross domestic product.

- The European Commission has estimated that transaction cost savings for one year will cover the cost of adapting IT systems to cope with the euro, but it is hard to see how these IT costs can be reliably estimated.

- Companies may need to adjust their IT systems to take account of the euro.

(g) Implications of the euro for UK financial services

Much depended on whether the euro became a strong and stable currency after its launch in January 1999. If that was indeed the case, London could be have been perceived as an 'off shore' centre which was cut off from the financial hub of Frankfurt where the European Central bank was situated.

However, given the fact that the UK should be able to join the single currency quite easily (since it is one of the few countries that actually meets the economic convergence criteria) there should be no great problem.

In any case, the UK already has the largest US$ foreign exchange dealings of all the EU countries, so there is ample expertise within London to cope with foreign exchange transactions in yet another foreign currency, albeit a major one.

On the other hand, if the euro is seen as a weak currency, the UK may be seen as a safe haven in which to do business. Thus the euro on its own would not seem to be a major source of competitive disadvantage for the UK financial services industry. Other factors, such as the relative cost savings and efficiencies of the various IT systems, may prove to be more significant in the determination of the relative competitive position of London and Frankfurt.

Since its launch in January 1999 at a spot rate of euro 1.40 = £1, (or euro 1 = £0.71p), the euro has depreciated steadily in value. At the time of writing, April 2000, the spot rates are quoted at around:

£1 = Euro 1.65 or Euro 1 = £ 0.60p

This shows a depreciation in value of about 17% over sixteen months. A similar depreciation of the euro has applied to other currencies, notably to the US$.

Economic forecasters seem to differ on whether the initial changes in the value of the euro are just a passing phase or whether there is some deeper fundamental reason for the depreciation.

Position of the euro during the transitional phase

- Many businesses from the participating countries are still invoicing in their national currency (these are known as the legacy currencies) during the transition.

- Rates of exchange continue to be quoted for the legacy currencies, along with the rate for the euro. It must be remembered that the rates of the legacy currencies are in effect fixed against the euro during the transitional period.

- There seems to be some confusion as to whether the sterling euro rate is to be quoted by the direct or indirect method. Hence the use of both quotes in the section above.

(h) Will the UK join the single currency?

It would seem that the UK will only join if approval is given in a referendum. Such a referendum seems unlikely to be held until after the next election, which could be as late as April/May 2002.

Various economic criteria have been set by the present UK government and until the government is satisfied that they have been met the referendum will not be called.

3

SPOT RATES AND FORWARD RATES

Objectives

On completion of this chapter the student should be able to:

- define a rate of exchange and appreciate how rates are quoted;
- differentiate between the bank's buy and sell rates;
- understand the difference between fixed forward exchange contracts and option forward exchange contracts;
- calculate fixed forward rates and option forward rates using the spot as a base and adjusting for the premium or discount.

1   Rates of Exchange and How They are Quoted

A rate of exchange is the price of one currency in terms of another. In the UK, rates of exchange are normally quoted as the number of foreign currency units, that are equivalent to one pound sterling. This method of quotation is termed the indirect quote. By contrast, most EU currencies are quoted as the number of units of home currency that are equivalent to one unit of overseas currency. This is termed the direct quote. In this book we concentrate on the indirect quote method.

Bank dealers normally quote two rates of exchange, one the buying rate and the other the selling rate. Since the bank wishes to make a profit on the 'turn' (i.e. the difference between the two rates), it will use the higher rate for buying and the lower one for selling. Thus, if the rate quoted for the US $ is 1.8525-1.8535, the bank will buy at 1.8535 and sell at 1.8525. The reason for this is quite logical. The bank wants to receive as many dollars for each pound as possible when it buys them and the bank wants to give out as few dollars as possible in exchange for every pound when it sells them.

When dealing with exchange rates, **always work from the point of view of the bank.** Hence the rule is:

BUY HIGH: SELL LOW

---

2 Spot Rates of Exchange and the Exchange Risk

A spot rate of exchange is a rate of exchange for a foreign currency transaction which is to be settled within two working days of agreeing the rate.

As you will know from your economics studies, spot rates of exchange can fluctuate violently from day to day or week to week. Hence, for example, UK traders who have receipts or payments denominated in foreign currency which are to be settled in the future, cannot be sure of the ultimate sterling amounts if the currency is simply converted at the spot rate ruling on the date of receipt or payment. This uncertainty as to the exact ultimate sterling receipt or payment is called the exchange risk. The exchange risk runs from the moment a commercial contract is entered into which involves receipt or payment of foreign currency, and it lasts until the currency receipt/payment has been converted into sterling. The management of exchange rate exposure in its widest sense is analysed in Chapters 7 and 8.

3 Forward Exchange Rates and Forward Contracts

A forward rate is a rate of exchange that is fixed now for a deal which will take place at a fixed date, or between two dates, in the future. Forward contracts can be arranged to cover periods for as long as 10 years ahead in some of the major currencies, but periods of between one and 12 months are the most common.

When a forward currency is more valuable than the spot currency, the forward is said to be 'at a premium'. Likewise when the forward currency is less valuable than the spot, it is said to be 'at a discount'. The term 'par', in connection with forward exchange, means that the spot and forward currencies are of equal value; hence, the spot rate and the forward rates are identical.

A forward exchange contract is a binding contract between a bank and its customer for a purchase or sale of a specified amount of a particular foreign currency at an agreed future date, at a rate of exchange fixed at the time the contract is made.

When the contract is a 'fixed' forward exchange contract, the future date at which the transaction will take place is a fixed date, whereas when the contract is an 'option' contract, the time at which the transaction will take place is any time within a specified future period. The customer has the 'option' to choose which day within the specified future period he will complete the transaction, but apart from this particular aspect the 'option' contract is just as binding as a fixed contract.

While the advantages of forward contracts will be considered later on in more detail, it should be briefly mentioned that the main purpose of a forward contract is to enable exporters to know what the home currency value will be for an amount of foreign currency that will be received at a future date, and likewise to enable UK importerss, say, to calculate the sterling cost of a foreign currency payment that is to be made in the future. When the exact timing of the receipt or payment is uncertain, option forward contracts could apply.

When traders do not take out forward exchange contracts or use some other method to cover known receipts or payments of foreign currency in the future, they are gambling. Nobody can predict with any accuracy what the spot rate will be on any future date, so that the amount of home currency received or paid will be an unknown quantity. The trader may, of course, benefit if the spot rate has moved in his favour when the transaction actually takes place, but he could equally well lose if the rate has moved against him.

4 How to Calculate Forward Rates for Fixed Forward Contracts

The forward rate is calculated by using the spot rate on the day of calculation and adjusting for the appropriate premium or discount. Let us consider two examples, bearing in mind that this book always works on the UK system of indirect quotes for exchange rates.

Example 1
On 1 January a UK bank quotes the following rates for the US $:

Spot	One month forward
1.9425-1.9435	0.53c-0.43c pm

The bank's one-month forward rates, quoted on 1 January for deals that will take place on 1 February, will be calculated as follows:

Buying rate	
Spot (buy high)	1.9435
Deduct: Premium	0.0043
One-month forward fixed buying rate	1.9392

Note

a) A premium is always deducted from the spot rate because if a currency is more expensive in terms of the pound, fewer units of it will be needed to be equivalent to a pound.

b) The bank must deduct when it quotes currency at a premium, but it can deduct either 0.53 cents or 0.43 cents. The bank will always use the premium that is most favourable to it. Because the bank will wish to obtain as much currency as possible for every pound, given that it must deduct either 0.43 cents or 0.53 cents from the spot rate, the bank will deduct 0.43.

Selling rate	
Spot (sell low)	1.9425
Deduct: Premium	0.0053
One-month forward fixed selling rate	1.9372

Note

The premium is always deducted from the spot rate. The bank has a choice between deducting 0.43 cents or 0.53 cents. Because the bank wishes to give as little currency as possible in exchange for a pound, it deducts the greater amount, 0.53 cents.

Example 2

On 1 January a UK bank quotes the following rates for the French franc:

Spot	*One month forward*
9.43-9.44	3c-4c discount

On 1 January the bank will quote its one-month forward fixed rate for French Francs as:

Buying rate	
Spot (buy high)	9.44
Add: Discount	0.04
One-month forward buying rate	9.48

The bank must add the discount to the spot rate. It has a choice of adding 4 cents (or centimes) or 3 cents. Because the bank always acts in its own best interests, it will add 4 cents to the spot rate, thus buying as high as possible.

Selling rate	
Spot (sell low)	9.43
Add: Discount	0.03
One-month forward selling rate	9.46

The bank must add the discount to the spot rate. It has a choice of adding 4 cents or 3 cents. Because the bank always acts in its own best interests, it will add 3 cents, thus selling as low as possible.

Note

The basic rules can now be seen. Spot: buy high sell low. Adjustment for premium or discount: deduct premium, add discount. Use the premium or discount that favours the bank.

5 The Importance of the Decimal Point

In the first US$ example above, the relevant forward premium was expressed as 0.43 cents. One dollar equals one hundred cents; hence, one cent is 0.01 of one dollar. Since 0.43 cents must be less than one cent, the expression of this amount in dollar terms must be 0.0043.

In the first French franc example, the relevant forward discount was expressed as 4 cents (or centimes). One cent is 0.01 of a franc, hence 4 cents must be expressed as 0.04 of a franc.

The following table should prove useful:

Table 1

Country	Name of currency (with standard abbreviations†)	Unit quoted for premium or discount	Relationship of currency unit to unit quoted for premium or discount
United States	Dollar ($) (USD)	Cent (c)	100c = 1USD or 1c = 0.01USD
Canada	Dollar ($) (CAD)	Cent (c)	100c = 1CAD or 1c = 0.01CAD
Netherlands‡	Guilder (NLG)	Cent (c)	100c = 1 NLG or 1c = 0.01NLG
Belgium‡	Franc (BEF)	Centime (c)	100c = 1BEF or 1c = 0.01BEF
Ireland‡	Punt (IEP)	Pence (p)	100p = 1 IEP or 1p = 0.01 IEP
Germany‡	Deutschmark (DEM)	Pfennig (pf)	100pf = 1 DEM or 1 pf = 0.01 DEM
Portugal‡	Escudo (PTE)	Cent (c)	100c = 1PTE or 1c = 0.01PTE
Spain‡	Peseta (ESB)	Cent (c)	100c = 1 ESB or 1c = 0.01 ESB
Italy*‡	Lira (ITL)	Lira (ITL)	1ITL = 1ITL = 1Lira
Norway	Kroner (NOK)	Ore (ore)	100ore = 1NOK or 1 ore = 0.01NOK
Denmark	Kroner (DKK)	Ore (ore)	100ore = 1DKK or 1 ore = 0.01DKK
Sweden	Kroner (SEK)	Ore (ore)	100ore = 1 SEK or 1 ore = 0.01 SEK
Japan*	Yen (JPY)	Yen (JPY)	1JPY = 1JPY = 1 Yen
Austria‡	Schilling (ATS)	Groschen (gro)	100gro = 1ATS or 1gro = 0.01ATS
Switzerland	Franc (CHF)	Centime (c)	100c = 1CHF or 1c = 0.01CHF
France‡	Franc (FRF)	Centime (c)	100c = 1FRF or 1c = 0.01FRF
EU	Euro (EUR)		100c = 1 EUR or 1c = 0.01 EUR

* For the Italian lira and the Japanese yen, the unit of currency is also used for quotation of the premium and discount. For all other currencies, premiums and discounts are quoted in smaller units.

† These standard abbreviations (e.g. USD) are used on international money transfers and in dealing transactions to show the name of the currency. These abbreviations are acceptable worldwide. The standard abbreviation for the £ is GBP.

‡ The legacy currencies of the euro can continue to be used during the transitional period and are still quoted in the press and in other media.

6 How to Calculate Rates for Option Forward Contracts

An option forward contract means that the customer can select on which day he will complete the transaction, provided the choice falls within the option period.

The bank will calculate the forward rates that it would offer for fixed contracts maturing on the first and last days of the option contract and would then choose the rate that was more favourable to itself.

Example 1

On 1 January an importer enters into a contract to buy goods costing a total of US $100,000. Payment has to be made when the goods are shipped and shipment is to be some time during March.

The rates ruling on 1 January are:

Spot	2 months forward	3 months forward
1.9425-1.9525	0.90c-0.80c pm	1.40c-1.20c pm

If the importer enters into a forward exchange contract to cover the exchange risk, he will require an option forward contract, with the option period of between two and three months. The bank will calculate the rates as follows:

Spot (sell low)	1.9425	Spot	1.9425
Less: Two-months premium	0.0090	Less: Three-months premium	0.0140
Two-months forward rate	1.9335	Three-months forward rate	1.9285

The bank will choose 1.9285 because this is the most favourable selling rate for the option period. Remember that a bank sells currency to importers, and buys currency from exporters.

Example 2

Using the rates quoted in Example 1, the bank would calculate its option buying rate for the proceeds of exports invoiced in dollars to be received in March as:

Spot (buy high)	1.9525	Spot	1.9525
Less: Two-months premium	0.0080	Less: Three-months premium	0.0120
Two-months forward buy	1.9445	Three-months forward buy	1.9405

The bank will therefore quote 1.9445 as its option buying rate because this is the higher rate and hence the one more favourable to the bank.

Note

In practice, bank dealers are involved in a very competitive market. For major customers, the bank may not quote the better of the two rates from its own point of view, but it may compromise by setting the rate somewhere between the two extremes. However, for exam purposes, you must complete the calculations as shown above.

4

CLOSE-OUTS AND EXTENSIONS OF FORWARD CONTRACTS

Objectives

On completion of this chapter the student should be able to:

● understand the contractual position between a bank and a customer as regards forward contracts;

● appreciate the close-out procedure that a bank must take if a customer fails to fulfil his contractual obligations under forward contracts;

● understand why the forward contract involves a contingent liability on the part of the customer, and why a bank 'marks a limit' on the customer's account when it grants a forward contract;

● deal with extensions to forward contracts, as opposed to straight close-outs.

1 The Contractual Position

A forward exchange contract is a binding contract and the customer must ensure that he fulfils his obligations thereunder.

It can happen that a customer, through no fault of his own, cannot complete the agreed transaction. In this case the bank will have to 'close out' the deal.

If on the due date an exporter cannot provide the currency that the bank has agreed to buy from him, the bank will calculate the cost of the sale of the relevant amount of foreign currency at the spot rate ruling on the date of default. The bank will also calculate the amount it would have credited to the customer had the forward contract been fulfilled. The bank will then pass the net debit or credit to the customer's account.

Likewise, where an importer is concerned, the bank will calculate the amount that would have been debited had the forward contract been completed; it will then calculate the value of the currency at the bank's spot buying rate ruling on the date of default. The net debit or credit will again be passed to the customer's account.

2   Examples of Close-out Procedures

Example 1

The bank agreed to enter into a forward contract to buy US $100,000 from an exporter. The contract was a fixed forward contract for a transaction due to take place in three months' time.

Unfortunately, the proceeds were not received by the exporter and he had to default. What action would the bank take? The rates on the date the forward contract was agreed were:

Spot	Three months forward
1.8525-1.8535	0.94c pm 0.89c pm

The spot rates three months later were 1.92-1.93.

Answer

The agreed forward buying rate would be:

Spot	1.8535
Less: Premium	0.0089
Three months forward	1.8446

On the due date the bank would calculate as follows:

(Dr) Cost of sale of $100,000 at 1.92	£52,083.33
(Cr) Proceeds of purchase of $100,000 at 1.8446	£54,212.30
Net credit passed to customer's account	£2,128.97

Example 2

Using the rates in Example 1, calculate the amount to be passed through the account of an importer where a forward exchange contract was made for the bank to sell US $100,000 for completion in three months and a close-out has to be effected.

Answer

The agreed forward rate would be:

Spot	1.8525
Less: Premium	0.0094
Three months forward	1.8431

On the due date the bank would calculate as follows:

(Cr) Proceeds of repurchase of $100,000 at spot rate 1.93	£51,813.48
(Dr) Amount which would have been debited had forward contract been completed ($100,000 at 1.8431)	£54,256.42
Net debit to customer's account	£2,442.94

Example 3 (covers partial close-outs)

An importer had arranged a fixed forward contract for the bank to sell US$50,000 at 1.55. On the maturity date the importer informed the bank that he required only US$ 40,000.

The spot rates ruling on the date of the maturity of the forward contract were:

    Spot   US$ 1.50- 1.51

Answer

The bank will sell the US$ 50,000 at the agreed forward rate, but will buy back any unwanted currency at the spot rate.

(Dr) US$ 50.000 at 1.55	£ 32,258.06
(Cr) US$ 10,000 at 1.51	£ 6,622.52
Net debit	£ 25,635.54

Example 4 (covers early close-outs)

If a customer realizes that he will be unable to fulfil his obligations well before the expiry date, he can effectively fix the loss or gain under the close-out at maturity by arranging a matching forward contract with the same expiry date.

For example, an exporter may have entered into a three-month fixed forward contract for the bank to buy US$ 100,000. One month after the commencement of the contract, the underlying commercial deal may fall through. In this instance, the exporter could arrange a two-month fixed forward contract for the bank to sell him US $100,000.

Two months later, at maturity of the two forward contracts, the bank will notionally debit the customer with the sterling equivalent of the two-month forward contract, and will notionally credit him with the sterling equivalent of the original three-month forward contract. The net difference between these two amounts will be debited or credited to the account.

The net effect of such a transaction is to fix the loss/gain on the close-out from the time of the creation of the matching forward contract.

Note

Banks are developing new variations of the forward contract and, in practice, the customer should check out what the bank's procedures and advice would be for his particular circumstances, should this situation arise.

3   Why is it Necessary for the Bank to Close Out?

Many customers believe that the bank is somehow punishing them when they are debited on a close-out. (Their thoughts if they are credited on a close-out are no doubt different.)

However, there is no element of punishment.

If the bank enters into a forward contract with a customer, the bank will take action to offset any exchange risk to itself. The action could take the form of a temporary 'swap', as described in Chapter 2, or some other way of covering the exchange risk could be undertaken. However, the point is that once a bank agrees a forward contract with a customer, the bank itself enters into a contractual obligation with a third party so as to match or offset its own risk. The bank's customer must fulfil his obligations under the forward contract so that the bank can honour its 'matching' commitments to third parties.

If the customer cannot, or will not, fulfil his obligation under the forward contract, the bank must take action to enable it to honour its matching obligation to the third party.

The procedure adopted is the close-out procedure shown in the examples above.

In effect, the bank makes the customer fulfil his obligations under the forward contract by using the spot market. The resultant gain or loss is then credited or debited to the customer's account, as shown in the examples.

4 Why the Bank 'Marks a Limit' on the Customer's Account When it Agrees a Forward Contract

If the customer fulfils his obligation to deliver, or to take delivery of the appropriate amount of currency, the bank is not in any danger. However, if the customer fails to fulfil those obligations, the bank is at risk, because there is a possible loss on the close-out. If the customer has insufficient funds to meet the loss on the close-out, the bank will have incurred a bad debt.

Thus, banks usually mark up a limit when they agree a forward contract. The amount of that limit is the bank's estimate of the maximum possible loss on any close-out. This amount will depend on the length of time to the contract's maturity and on the volatility of the currency concerned. The limit marked is usually between 10% and 20% of the sterling value of the forward contract.

The risk involved in a forward contract is called a 'contingent liability', in that it is a liability that may or may not occur. The contingent liability must, however, be borne in mind by the bank, and that is why a limit is marked on the customer's account. Such a limit will reduce the scope for borrowing in other ways, say, by overdraft. Indeed, the bank's criteria for deciding whether to agree to a forward contract are very similar to those for granting an overdraft.

5 Close-out/Extension of Forward Contracts

When a customer cannot fulfil the transaction where a forward contract has been entered into, the bank will 'close out', as has already been described.

If the customer exports, the bank will buy the currency at the agreed forward rate and sell it to the customer at the spot selling rate ruling on the day the contract should have been completed.

The resultant profit or loss will be the customer's.

Likewise, if the customer imports, the bank will sell at the agreed forward rate and buy it back at the current spot rate.

It sometimes arises that the underlying commercial transaction is merely delayed instead of being totally frustrated. In such a case, the customer would be able to fulfil the contract in due course but after the date(s) specified in the forward contract.

In these cases, where the completion of the forward contract will merely be delayed, the bank will extend it. What happens is that the bank 'closes out' in the normal way but then arranges a new forward contract for completion at the time the customer expects to have the necessary currency.

In an extension the new forward rate is always based on the spot rate used in the close-out. Discount or premium is applied to the spot close-out rate in the normal way to calculate the new forward rate.

Example

The bank arranged a forward contract with its exporter customer to buy US$ 40,725 at US$ 1.40 = £1.00. The receipt of proceeds was delayed and the exporter asked for an extension of one month fixed. Show the transactions on the customer's account, if the rates ruling on the maturity date of the forward contract were:

Spot	1.45-1.46
One month forward	2 c-l c premium
(ignore commission)	

Solution

(a) On the date of maturity of the original forward contract, the bank will close out in the usual way:

(Cr) The bank will buy US$ 40,725 at the agreed rate of 1.40 = £29,089.29
(Dr) The bank will sell US$ 40,725 at the spot rate of 1.45 = £28,086.21
Net amount credited to customer's account £1,003.08

(b) On the same date as in (a), the bank will agree a new forward contract, one month forward fixed:

Spot close-out rate	1.45
Deduct: Premium	0.01
	1.44

(c) One month later, provided the exporter delivers the currency, he will be credited:

40,725 at 1.44 = £28,281.25

Notes

a) Those of you who have previously studied for this subject may have learned the 'diagonal rule' as a means of calculating forward rates. If you know this rule, and can apply it correctly to calculate the forward rate on an extension, then continue to use it. However, many students are totally confused when applying this rule to extensions. As a result, the diagonal rule is not used in this book.

b) The reason the bank applies the spot close-out rate to extension is that it has already made its 'turn' from the difference between buying and selling rates on the original contract.

5

FOREIGN CURRENCY OPTIONS/ PURE OPTIONS

Objectives

On completion of this chapter the student should be able to:

  appreciate the reasons for the development of currency options;

  understand the terminology that applies to currency options;

  appreciate how a currency option differs from a forward contract;

  evaluate the customer benefits of currency options;

  be aware of the competition that exchange traded options provide;

  understand the customer benefits of currency options provided by banks, as opposed to the customer benefits of exchange traded options;

  appreciate the implications of hybrid products, such as cylinder options, for both banks and customers.

1   The Reasons for the Development of Foreign Currency Options

Foreign currency options give customers far more flexibility than is provided by the conventional, traditional forward contract.

Before defining these options, let us examine the main causes of customer dissatisfaction with the traditional forward exchange contract.

Customers' complaints when currency options were not widely available were as follows:

a)   The customer could have lost money if he failed to comply with the forward contract and the bank had to close out. Customers conveniently chose to forget that, if rates had moved in their favour, they could be credited with the net profit on a close-out;

b) Customers did not appreciate that the term 'option' in an option forward exchange contract related solely to the period during which the agreed transaction could be carried out. Many customers wrongly thought 'option' in a forward contract meant that the customer could choose whether or not he wished to complete the transaction; in other words, the customer thought the word 'option' gave him the right to walk away from the forward exchange commitment if he so wished;

c) The following situation was a particularly strong cause of customer dissatisfaction:

   i) An option forward exchange contract was arranged;

   ii) The customer could not fulfil it because of a breakdown in the terms of the underlying commercial contract;

   iii) The bank had to debit the customer on close-out because the spot rates had moved against the customer;

d) Customers felt aggrieved when they took out forward contracts and were then unable to take advantage if spot rates on the date of execution had moved in their favour.

These complaints led to the development of the foreign currency option, which, at a price, overcomes all the real or perceived customer complaints regarding traditional forward contracts.

The development of the foreign currency option as a widely available foreign exchange risk management tool can indeed be said to be 'market-driven'.

2   What is a Foreign Currency Option?

It is an agreement whereby a customer can pay a premium to the bank for the right but not the obligation to buy from or sell to the bank a specified amount of a foreign currency at an agreed rate of exchange. Generally speaking, the option can be exercised, at the customer's discretion, at any time up to a specified expiry date, or it can be allowed to lapse by the customer at the expiry date.

As an alternative to exercising the option or allowing it to lapse, it may be possible to sell the option back to the bank. (This situation is covered later.)

Watch your terminology, and that of the exam question, when dealing with currency options (the common abbreviation of foreign currency options). In forward contracts the rates are always quoted from the bank's point of view so that the fixed forward buying rate relates to the rate at which a bank would buy, and the fixed forward selling rate relates to the rate at which a bank would sell to a customer. In currency options, however, it is the customer who purchases the right to buy from or sell to the bank the specified amount of foreign currency at the agreed rate of exchange.

3 Glossary of Terms Relating to Foreign Currency Options

Writer or Grantor

This is the bank (or any other organization) which, in exchange for a fee, known as the 'option premium', grants the right but not the obligation for a purchaser to buy or sell the currency at the agreed rate during a specified period.

Purchaser

This is the person, usually a customer, who pays an option premium to bank for the right but not the obligation to deal under the terms of the option.

Holder

This can be the original purchaser of the option, or someone to whom the original purchaser has assigned the rights under the option.

Call Option and Put Option

A call option gives the purchaser the right to buy the currency from the writer and a put option gives him the right to sell to the writer. Exporters will normally require put options. Importers will normally require call options. You are reminded that the terminology differs from that of forward contracts.

Base/Counter/Underlying Currencies

The base currency (sometimes called the counter currency) is usually US dollars or sterling. The underlying currency is foreign currency, e.g. Deutschmarks, which the customer will wish to buy (call option) or sell (put option) to the writer. For example a sterling-based UK exporter who invoices in Deutschmarks would take out a put option in which the base currency would be sterling and the underlying currency would be Deutschmarks. The put option would give the customer the right but not the obligation to sell a certain amount of Deutschmarks to the bank during a specified period at a pre-set rate of exchange.

Strike Price

This is the rate of exchange that will be applied if the currency option is exercised.

Option Premium

This is the 'up-front' payment made by the purchaser to the writer and it is usually paid at the time the option contract is granted. Once paid, the premium cannot be recovered, irrespective of whether the holder subsequently exercises the option or not.

The option premium is usually denominated in the base currency, i.e. US dollars or sterling, and is expressed as a percentage of the principal amount. The option premium is determined by the following main factors: the strike price and its relationship to the relevant spot and forward rates; the period of the option; the volatility of the exchange rates of the underlying currencies; and the relevant rates of interest.

Boston Option

Occasionally for approved customers the 'up-front' condition concerning the premium can be waived so that the premium, plus interest, is paid at maturity. If the option is exercised, the premium and interest are added to the cost (call option), or deducted from the proceeds (put option). If the option is abandoned, the premium plus interest is claimed from the purchaser at maturity.

Obviously, only highly creditworthy customers can be granted Boston-type options and such options are not common.

Intrinsic Value at Maturity

An alternative to exercising the option is to sell it back to the bank at its intrinsic value (if any). The intrinsic value at maturity is the difference between the strike price and the current spot rate of the underlying currency.

For example, a call option may have the following characteristics on the expiry date:

Strike price	3.40
Base currency	Sterling
Underlying currency	Deutschmarks
Current spot rate	3.10
Amount of base currency	£12,500
Type of option	Call option

The intrinsic value on the expiry day would be:

a)   Deutschmarks, which can be bought by the customer under the terms of the option:

   (12,500 x 3.40) = DEM 42,500 at a cost of £12,500;

b)   Sterling equivalent of DEM 42,500 which the customer could sell back at the current spot rate:

   DEM 42,500 @ 3.10 = £13,710;

c)   Intrinsic value:

   £13,710 - £12,500 = £1,210.

Thus, on the expiry date, the bank would be prepared to pay £1,210 (ignoring dealing costs) if the holder decided that he wished to sell the option back to the bank, rather than exercise it.

Therefore, if the underlying commercial deal had fallen through, the importer could sell the option back to the bank for its intrinsic value.

Intrinsic Value and Time Value Prior to Maturity

Prior to maturity, the amount of the premium consists of two elements: the intrinsic value and the time value. For a European option prior to maturity, the intrinsic value (if any) in terms of base currency is calculated from the difference between the value of the underlying currency converted at the strike rate (the 'option value') and the value of the underlying currency converted at the forward rate for the unexpired period of the option (the forward value). The principles are similar to those shown in the intrinsic value calculation immediately above, except that for intrinsic values on the expiry dates, the spot rate, as opposed to the forward rate, is the one applied.

For a call option, when the option value is below the forward value, the option is said to be 'in the money', because it has intrinsic value. When the option value of the underlying currency at the strike price is more than the value at the appropriate forward rate, the call option is said to be 'out of the money'. However, out-of-the-money options (whether puts or calls) can never have a negative intrinsic value, because the holder is not obliged to exercise them.

Put options work on the same principles, but they are in the money when the option value is above the forward value and they are out of the money when the option value is below the forward value. When the option value and the forward value are the same, the option is said to be 'at the money'.

The other element of the premium is time value. The greater the time to maturity, and the greater the volatility of the exchange rate for the currency pairs, the greater the time value.

When an option is first arranged, the writer will use a computer program to calculate the 'fair value' of an option, but then the premium that is actually quoted is adjusted in the light of the writer's own position in the market and market demand.

Notification Date, Exercise Date, Expiry Date

These terms are synonymous. Once the expiry date has passed, the option will automatically lapse unless the holder has notified the writer that he intends to exercise his rights.

Settlement Date

Once the holder has notified the writer that he intends to exercise the option, he has up to two working days to settle the deal. For example, if a call option, with sterling as the base currency, expires on a Monday, the holder must notify the writer by that day of his intention to exercise the option. If notification takes place on the Monday, the holder has until close of business on Wednesday to provide the necessary sterling to purchase the underlying currency from the bank.

Note

It is too late to notify the writer on Tuesday of the intention to exercise, because the option will have lapsed at close of business on Monday.

American Options and European Options

With an American option, the holder can notify the writer of his intention to exercise the option on any business day between the granting of the option and the expiry date. Notification can be for all or for part of the amount of currency covered by the option. The final settlement date for an American option is two working days after the expiry date. Note that some banks may limit the number of drawdowns by placing a minimum drawing amount.

With European options, there is a single expiry date and a single settlement date. The holder can notify the bank of his intention to exercise only on the one expiry date, and he must then complete the underlying deal within two working days.

The option premium is higher for American options because of the greater flexibility for the customer and the greater risk to the writer of the option, who must manage the overall options book.

American options are readily available in the UK.

Over-the-counter Options (OTC Options)

These are foreign currency options negotiated as separate, individual contracts between the purchaser customer and the writer bank. Thus the OTC option can be tailor-made to meet a customer's specific needs. Each bank has a minimum amount below which it will not grant currency options.

Exchange Traded Options

These are currency options that are dealt with on organized exchanges. At one time such options were available via London International Financial Futures Exchange (LIFFE), but LIFFE no longer offers this type of option. However, exchanges in the USA and other parts of the world offer currency options.

Exchange traded options are standardized and cannot be tailor-made to meet specific customer needs. Quite often banks themselves take out exchange traded options to cover their own obligations on OTC options that they have written.

4 Comparison of Forward Exchange Contracts and Foreign Currency Options

Table 1

Forward Contracts	Foreign Currency Options
a) These are firm and binding contracts between the customer and his bank, whereby the customer has an obligation to deliver or take delivery of the foreign currency in accordance with the terms of the contract.	a) This is the right, but not the obligation, for the customer to deliver or take delivery of foreign currency in accordance with the terms of the agreement.
b) If a customer fails to fulfil the terms of the forward contract, the bank will 'close out'. In this case the customer will have to stand the loss, or he will receive the gain, depending on the spot rate of exchange on the day of close-out.	b) The currency option gives the holder the right but not the obligation to deal on the terms set out. There is no question of a close-out taking place. The holder has three choices on the expiry date of a currency option: i) exercise it ii) abandon it iii) sell it if the currency option has an intrinsic value.
c) If a bank grants a forward contract, the bank usually marks up a contingent liability facility of between 10% and 20%, of the full contract value. This facility is marked to cover the fact that, if the customer defaults, the bank may need to debit the customer with a loss on the close-out. Thus the granting of a forward contract will reduce the available credit facilities for the customer.	c) A currency option is not classed as a contingent liability, because the customer is under no obligation to deal on the terms set out. Thus, the currency option does not affect the available credit facilities for the customer.
d) From a customer's point of view, the forward contract eliminates the exchange risk, but he cannot gain the benefit if spot rates move in his favour. However, if the underlying commercial deal falls through, the customer will make a gain or loss on the close-out. Thus, forward contracts that are not matched by an underlying currency deal create an exposure.	d) Under the currency option, the holder can take full advantage if spot rates move in his favour. If the holder has the underlying currency, he can deal spot and abandon the option.

Table 1 (Continued)	
Forward Contracts	**Foreign Currency Options**
e) A forward contract is inflexible and affects the credit facilities of the customer. However, the cost of arranging forward contracts is relatively low compared to the cost of a currency option (usually just the bid offer spread).	e) The currency option gives a holder much greater flexibility. Hence the cost (the option premium) is much more than for a forward contract
f) A forward contract is a contract between a customer and his bank. A customer cannot normally sell his rights to a third party.	f) It may be possible for a holder to sell his rights under a currency option, depending on whether it has an intrinsic value. The right to sell is an alternative to the other two rights: the right to exercise the option or the right to abandon it.

5 The Customer Benefits of Currency Traded Options

The benefits to the customer can be summarized as follows:

a) The purchaser can choose the strike price. (One of the factors that influences the option premium is how far the strike price differs from the relevant forward rate.)

b) The currency option provides far more flexibility than forward contracts or other methods of covering exchange risks. The option period can be chosen by the purchaser.

c) There is no question of marking a limit on the customer's account with currency options, because there is no obligation whatsoever for the customer to deal in accordance with the terms of the option. Hence, currency options do not affect the available borrowing facilities, because they are not a contingent liability. However, settlement risk must be considered upon exercise of the option. The bank must be sure that the customer will deliver or take delivery of the relevant currency prior to the end of the settlement period.

d) The purchaser can take advantage if spot rates move in his favour, by simply abandoning the option.

e) If the underlying commercial deal falls through, the purchaser will be able to sell the option back to the bank, provided the option has an intrinsic value.

f) The purchaser's costs are known at the outset, and are limited to the amount of the option premium.

g)   The documentation required to set up the option is simple and straightforward.

6   Customer Benefits of OTC Options as Opposed to Exchange Traded Options

As we saw in the definitions at 5.3, OTC options are provided by banks whereas exchange traded options are obtained on organized exchanges, such as the Philadelphia Exchange in the United States.

The main customer benefits of OTC options as opposed to exchange traded options are:

a)   OTC options are tailor-made whereas exchange traded options are standardized and may not match the customer's requirements.

b)   OTC options involve less administration on the part of the purchaser. With exchange traded options it is necessary to deal via authorized brokers. In addition, purchasers of such options are required to deposit cash margins, and there may be extra cash margins required during the life of the option. None of this is required with bank OTC options, which have simple documentation and no cash margin requirements.

7   Cylinder Options

A cylinder option is a combination of an option and a forward contract. In exchange for a reduced premium, the holder acquires some, but not all, of the benefits of an option. Let us first of all look at a particular situation when cylinder options could be used.

Example

i)   *Today*

X plc expects to have to pay out US $100,000 in 3 months.

X plc buys a call option from its bank, strike price US $1.45.

X plc writes a put option in favour of its bank, strike price US $1.55=£1.

Both options cover an underlying principal of US $ 100,000.

Both options have an expiry date in three months and are European.

The premiums net out exactly. (This is not always the case, it depends on the terms of each option. Sometimes the bank's premium as writer will exceed that for the customer as writer, but the opposite could equally apply.)

Table 2

	Outcome i	Outcome ii	Outcome iii
Spot Rate	US $1.30 = £1	US $1.50 = £1	US $1.60 = £1
Sterling value at spot	£76,923	£66,667	£62,500
Sterling value of call	£68,966	£68,966	£68,966
Sterling value of put	£64,516	£64,516	£64,516
Action by call holder	exercise	abandon	abandon
Action by put holder	abandon	abandon	exercise
Result	X plc obtain the US $ at a cost of £68,966 using call rate of 1.45. If the US $ are not required, the call will be sold for its intrinsic value.	Both options are abandoned. X plc acquires the US $ at spot rate, cost £66,667, if the dollars are needed.	The bank sells US $100,000 at 1.55. The cost is £64,516.

ii)   At maturity in three months the outcome depends on the spot rate

From the above example, we can see the features and benefits of the cylinder option from this customer's point of view are:

● the premium will be lower than for a conventional option, because the customer can offset the premium on the option written by him against the premium on the option written by the bank. In this case the net premium is nil.

● if the spot rate at maturity is in between the two strike prices (i.e. within the 'cylinder'), both options will be abandoned, and the US $ payment, if made, will be settled at spot. If the US $ are not required, no action is required on the part of the customer.

● if the rate is outside the cylinder (i.e. above or below the two strike prices), the call will be exercised if the underlying currency has strengthened, and the put will be exercised if the underlying currency has weakened. Likewise, the put will be abandoned if the underlying currency has strengthened and the call will be abandoned if the underlying currency has weakened.

● provided the customer still has the underlying currency position at maturity (e.g. to make a payment of US $100,000), the deal will be transacted as follows:

- at call strike rate if the currency has strengthened at maturity;

- at spot rate if this falls within the cylinder;

- at put strike rate if the underlying currency has weakened at maturity.

- banks look upon a cylinder option as a credit facility, for the same reason that the forward contract is deemed to carry default risk in the case of a close-out. In this instance, if the underlying currency had weakened at maturity, the bank would need to be sure that X plc would honour its obligations under the put.

- cylinder options are useful where:

  - the underlying currency position in the cash market at maturity is 'certain';

  - the customer wishes to take advantage (to a limited extent) of the upside potential if the spot rates do move in his favour, but will not pay the full option premium;

  - the customer wishes to cover himself by setting the 'worst rate' that can be applied if rates have moved adversely at maturity.

- thus in exchange for a reduced premium, the customer gains a limited maximum upward potential, coupled with the danger of exposure to risk should the underlying currency receipt/payment not come to fruition.

Conclusion on Cylinder Options

There are infinite variations on the way in which banks can use 'financial engineering' skills to offer a hybrid product that combines the features of options and forwards. The net effect is that in exchange for a lower premium the customer forgoes some of the benefits of an option.

6

ALTERNATIVES TO FORWARD CONTRACTS AND CURRENCY OPTIONS, AND BENEFITS OF FOREIGN CURRENCY INVOICING FOR EXPORTERS

Objectives

On completion of this chapter the student should be able to:

● understand the benefits of forward contracts;

● appreciate the alternative techniques for covering the exchange risk;

● understand the benefits and drawbacks of foreign currency invoicing for exporters.

1 The Benefits of Forward Contracts for Sterling-based Importers and Alternative Methods of Covering the Exchange Risk

a) The sterling cost of the imports is fixed; thus, the importer can set his prices and profit margins more accurately.

b) In theory, there is no limit to the amount of sterling the importer could require on the due date, if he has not covered the exchange risk, because the £ floats freely. The forward contract eliminates this exchange risk.

c) Failure to take any action to cover the exchange risk amounts to gambling. The importer will be legally liable to acquire the necessary foreign currency from the date he signs a commercial contract.

Some major corporate customers deliberately allow themselves to be exposed to the exchange risk in certain currencies, because they expect spot rates to move in their favour. However, such companies are quick to cover the exchange risk if the outlook for the currency in question changes adversely.

Normally, smaller companies should cover the exchange risk, because they probably could not survive a catastrophic change in spot rates.

Alternative forms of hedging are:

i)   Currency call options, which are more expensive than forward contracts and may not be available for the currency and amount required. However, the currency option enables the importer to deal at the spot rate on the due date, without penalty, if the rates move in his favour. (Full details of currency options are given in Chapter 5.)

ii)   The bank could sell the importer the necessary currency immediately at the current spot rate. The currency could then be kept on deposit until required. Much depends on the post-tax value of the deposit in the two countries as to whether this method is worthwhile.

iii) Open a foreign currency account but only if there are receipts and payments in the currency. The importer can then take out a forward contract to cover the anticipated balance, or he can delay conversion of the balance until rates move in his favour, or he can buy a currency option to cover the anticipated balance. It is possible to have a cheque book for a currency account.

iv)   When a trader has receipts in one foreign currency and payments in another, he can convert the receipts directly into the currency of the payment, using cross rates. Forward contracts may well be available for cross rates.

2   Exporters: Means of Protection against Exchange Risk

The following methods of protection may be adopted:

a)   Forward contracts.

b)   Borrow foreign currency now, let the bank then convert it at the current spot rate to sterling and then credit the current account with the proceeds at once. The currency loan is subsequently repaid from the currency proceeds of the exports. The interest rate is based on the interest rates ruling in the overseas centre.

c)   Foreign currency account but only if there are receipts and payments in the currency.

d)   Currency put options.

Note
A more detailed analysis of the wider issues regarding exchange rate risks can be found in Chapters 7 and 8.

3 Advantages of Foreign Currency Invoicing for Exporters

The basic benefit is that currency invoicing gives a product a competitive advantage. The product is more attractive to the buyer because:

i) The buyer does not run any exchange risk;

ii) The buyer can easily understand the price implications if quoted in local currency;

iii) It is easier for the buyer to compare the price quoted by local competitors.

Note

a) Where the exporter has both receipts and payments in currency, it will be more efficient to open a foreign currency account. Forward contracts could be arranged to cover the anticipated net balance.

b) Where applicable, a currency option can cover the exchange risk while allowing the customer to 'walk away' if the spot rates move in his favour. Alternatively, a less flexible method, such as the forward contract, could be used.

4 Disadvantages of Foreign Currency Invoicing

The following four disadvantages should be borne in mind:

a) The exporter runs the exchange risk, which runs from the moment the commercial contract is signed until conversion of the currency;

b) Although the exchange risk can be covered, there is a cost involved (for example, the management time and/or the cost of the premiums for options);

c) Currency invoicing creates problems for the accounts staff, unless specialist help such as export factoring is employed (covered in Part Four of this book);

d) Published price lists may need frequent revision.

7

OVERVIEW OF MANAGEMENT OF FOREIGN CURRENCY EXPOSURE

Objectives

On completion of this chapter the student should be able to:

- differentiate between the three basic classifications of foreign currency exposure;

- understand the differences between the three main corporate hedging philosophies;

- appreciate the link between hedging philosophy and business and operating risk;

- differentiate between internal and external techniques;

- understand the wider practical and theoretical issues relating to whether, and if so how, companies should manage foreign exchange exposures;

- appreciate the relevance of the budget rate of exchange in the formulation of projections.

1   The Three Main Classifications of Foreign Currency Exposure

In the preceding chapters, we have simply looked at techniques that can be employed to manage exchange rate risk. Now is the time to formally define what is meant by exchange rate risk and to differentiate between the three main categories.

Foreign currency exposure can be defined as the vulnerability of a company to changes in its profit and loss and balance sheet position arising from exchange rate movements. 'Foreign currency' is any currency other than the company's reporting currency in which the company's published accounts are denominated,

Foreign exchange exposure is usually classified under three main categories; transaction, translation and economic. In this chapter, we shall concern ourselves with transaction exposure and its various subdivisions.

2 Transaction Exposure

This can arise out of normal overseas trading activities. For exporters who invoice in foreign currency, the transaction exposure exists between the date of the commercial contract and the date of conversion of the receivables into home currency. For importers who are invoiced in foreign currency, the transaction exposure exists between the date of the commercial contract and the date of conversion of home currency into the requisite sum of foreign currency. Transaction exposure also arises in respect of any cash transfer between domestic currency and overseas currency, thus cash expenditure or capital receipts, such as dividends denominated in foreign currency, will give rise to transaction exposures.

The above is the traditional definition of foreign exchange transaction exposure. However, another view is that, over and above the traditional exposure, there is an 'extended transaction exposure', which applies whenever a company is committed to selling to certain countries or to buying from certain countries. This exposure will last for the period of time required before the corporate could switch to other countries. (Some authorities would classify extended transaction exposure as 'economic' exposure).

A third category of transaction exposure, 'pre-transaction' exposure, occurs when a company is committed to receiving payment in a foreign currency if buyers decide to purchase. The two major manifestations of pre-transaction exposure are:

i) When a company has submitted a tender for a contract which is to be settled in foreign currency. If the contract is awarded, the company will incur a foreign currency transaction exposure and the spot rate of exchange may well be different from the one ruling on the day of tender. However, taking out a forward contract at the time of the tender could be unwise, because, if the tender proves unsuccessful, the forward contract will have created an exposure.

Readers will no doubt recall from Chapter 4 that the close-out procedure will mean that a corporate that is a party to a forward contract has created an exposure when there is no underlying transaction to facilitate the fulfilment of obligations.

ii) A similar exposure applies when a company issues price lists denominated in foreign currency. There is no guarantee of the amount of sales that will actually be made, but the company is committed to fulfilling any sales that may arise at the price set out in the published list.

3 Corporate Hedging Philosophies

a) Introduction

A hedge is some action taken by a company to cover itself against risk. The techniques of hedging can usually be categorized as either internal or external. For the moment let us consider only external techniques. These are usually instruments known as 'derivatives', which are available from external providers, such as banks and organized futures exchanges.

A derivative is simply a financial instrument whose value depends on (or is derived from) another financial instrument or commodity. When a company wishes to hedge an underlying transaction exposure, it can take a position in the derivatives market that is equal and opposite to the underlying transaction exposure. Examples of the use of derivatives such as currency options have already been seen in Chapters 3, 4 and 5.

However, it is difficult to hedge transaction risks for long periods ahead. For example, a UK-based car maker may incur most of its costs in sterling and about half of its sales revenue in US $. Obviously, the company will suffer if the US$ falls against the £. In theory, the company could have sold its anticipated dollar receipts forward for five years, but the problem then arises of how the company can accurately predict its dollar sales over such a long period. If forward contracts were arranged, the company would incur an exposure on a close-out if it could not fulfil the contracts.

b)   Hedging Philosophies

The three main philosophies are:

i)   hedge nothing;

ii)   hedge everything;

iii)   hedge selectively.

i)   Hedge nothing

Small companies that are new to overseas trade often hedge nothing because they are unaware of the risks of exchange rate exposure and because they do not know about the techniques of hedging. This situation is clearly dangerous because a small firm is unlikely to have the capacity to absorb any significant exchange rate losses.

In theory, there is a case for larger companies to hedge nothing, because academic economic studies indicate that in the long term a 'no-hedge' policy should produce the same results as a fully hedged policy. The arguments for and against corporate hedging will be discussed at the end of this chapter.

If a company is a 'price maker' in the overseas market, or if demand for its products is inelastic, it may decide not to hedge extended transaction exposure. Such a company can simply raise the price of its goods in foreign currency to cover currency depreciation.

ii)   Hedge everything

Such a policy can eliminate transaction exposures, but it cannot eliminate economic exposures, and it gives rise to an 'opportunity cost'.

For example, if the spot rates were to move in favour of the company between the date of the invoice and the conversion of the currency, the company will have 'lost out' or incurred an opportunity cost if it has hedged the exchange exposure. A hedge-everything philosophy is common in heavy engineering companies when currency transactions are large and 'one-off' and where profit margins are tight.

In practice, many corporations with a hedge-everything philosophy use forward contracts to cover 'certain' cash flows in foreign currency and use options to cover cash flows that may arise but cannot be considered as 'certain'.

iii) Hedge selectively

Selective hedging involves taking a view on the future movements of exchange rates, the object being to hedge only those exposures where the anticipated risk of loss exceeds the opportunity for gain.

One system of selective hedging is to set a maximum permissible exposure, which will be based on the company's capital base, cash flow and profitability, and also the degree of the company's risk aversion. Any exposure above the maximum would have to be hedged. Any exposure below the stated maximum would either be left uncovered or it would be hedged, depending on the treasurer's perception of exchange rate movements.

In practice, limits on the size of an individual exposure and on the size of exposure to a particular currency will be set, so that the company does not 'use up' its exposure 'allowance' in just one uncovered position.

An open currency position should be monitored on a daily basis and a level set at which cover will be taken. One mechanism for doing this is the use of a stop loss order. For example, if a UK company is due to receive FRF10m from its overseas customer in three months' time, it may set the stop loss so as to sell the FRF in the forward market if the exchange rate is 5% above the original rate. The stop will be moved downwards but never upwards. If the exchange rate starts to move up from a low, the stop will be triggered close to although not at the lowest rate. (If the rate 'moves up', it means that the French franc is depreciating, because there are more francs than previously required to equal £1.)

A policy of selective hedging makes heavy demands on executive time and professional expertise. It requires a treasury system that is integrated into the budgetary control system so that future exchange exposures can be identified in a systematic way.

Many small and medium-sized companies lack the expertise to hedge selectively, and in practice such companies hedge everything. On the other hand, some multinational companies will hedge selectively, unless they are mainly in heavy engineering or similar industries with large, one-off transactions and tight margins.

c) The Link between Hedging Philosophy and Business and Operational Risk

Companies that have a high business risk (e.g. contractors) or high operating risks (where there are high fixed costs which cannot be easily reduced in an economic downturn) should tend towards a 'hedge-everything' policy. The riskier a business, the greater its cost of capital.

These companies with a high business and operating risk cannot usually afford a high financial risk from foreign currency exposure. (Similar principles apply to gearing and interest rate exposure.)

Whatever hedging philosophy is adopted, there must be clear internal documentation setting out the general philosophy and detailing the techniques that can be used.

4 Internal Techniques for Hedging Transaction Exposures

a) Matching

This involves the use of foreign currency bank accounts when a company has both receipts and payments in overseas currency. When payments are due before receipts, the company can arrange overdraft facilities, subject to creditworthiness, and when there are receipts due before payments, interest can be negotiated for the credit balances. Interest rates will be based on those ruling in the overseas centre.

Companies can arrange to hedge the anticipated balances at periodic intervals.

The major benefit of foreign currency accounts is that the company can avoid consistently buying and selling the same currency. In other words, the company avoids the bank's spread between its buying and selling rates.

b) Multilateral Netting

This system is useful for large groups of companies with a centralized treasury function. Each operating subsidiary must report the following details to the centre:

a) anticipated receipts and payments in every currency other than its own domestic currency;

b) an estimate of the subsidiary's exposed position in every currency other than its own domestic currency.

The central treasury will then act as a clearing house and will hedge the group's net exposure in any particular currency. This system is only really applicable in large multinational companies that have an efficient centralized treasury function. The requirements for successful implementation are:

a) the budget periods for all operating subsidiaries must be synchronized, otherwise the reported net exposures of the group could be distorted;

b) the savings from netting must be sufficient to cover the costs of the information system between the group and its subsidiaries;

c) the system must not contravene any local exchange-control or tax regulations.

c) Leads and Lags

This technique applies when a company has not purchased a bank product such as a forward exchange contract to hedge a transaction exposure in foreign currency. In other words, this is not really a hedging technique at all, but simply an attempt to forecast exchange rates and then to take action based on the forecasts.

If the company has to make a payment in, say, three months in a foreign currency that is expected to appreciate in value, it will 'lead', i.e. it will attempt to pay early so as to reduce the home currency cost of the payment. Naturally, the company will attempt to negotiate a discount to compensate for the early payment.

Obviously, the converse would apply if the foreign currency were expected to be about to fall in value. In that case, the company would attempt to 'lag', i.e. delay payment for as long as possible, subject to contractual obligations.

A similar process applies with exporters who try to lead, i.e. speed up, receipts if the foreign currency is expected to fall and who try to lag when the currency is expected to rise in value.

When the underlying commercial transactions are between different operating subsidiaries of the same group, there could be tax complications in leading and lagging. Expert tax advice is required; in addition, care must be taken to ensure that any overseas exchange control regulations are not contravened.

In order to decide whether leading or lagging is a viable proposition, the treasurer needs to know:

i)   the amount of discount to be paid or received in the leading or lagging;

ii)   the forward rates that are currently available;

iii)   interest rates;

iv)   tax and exchange control implications.

The treasurer can then compare the benefits of leading or lagging with the benefits of using other hedging techniques.

d)   Other Internal Techniques

i)   Local suppliers may be prepared to invoice in a different currency from their home currency, e.g. UK-based subsidiaries of US multinationals may be happy to invoice in US $ to UK purchasers.

ii)   The company may, as a long-term strategy, switch its manufacture to other locations, to change the currency of its cost base.

5   Theoretical Arguments Concerning Foreign Exchange Exposure Management by Corporates

Introduction

There has been considerable academic debate as to whether foreign currency exposures should be managed by corporates. If foreign exchange exposure should be managed by corporates, which principles apply and what techniques could be used ?

a)   Summary of Arguments against Foreign Currency Hedging

i)   *Purchasing power parity theory*

Movements in foreign exchange rates will be offset by changes in relative price levels. (This is a simplistic summary of the PPP theory. A more detailed explanation has already been given in Chapter 2.)

If the above version of the PPP theory applied in practice, without any time lags, there would be no such thing as foreign exchange exposure, because any loss due to foreign exchange rate movements would be compensated for by a gain in price, and vice versa.

ii)   *Capital asset pricing model (CAPM)*

Unsystematic risks are risks that apply to particular individual companies.

If exchange rate risk (and interest rate risk, for that matter) can be considered as unsystematic risks, then investors can eliminate such risks by holding a diversified portfolio of shares. Gains on some shares due to exchange rate movements would be offset by losses on other shares which would be adversely affected by the same exchange rate fluctuations.

If, however, foreign exchange risk is considered as a systematic risk, which is one that is embodied in the market as a whole, then hedging instruments will be priced in a rational way to take account of the volatility of the relevant currencies. Hence, there will be no added value from hedging, and indeed the cost of hedging, as represented by option premiums, management time and bid/offer spreads, will destroy shareholder value. When hedging instruments are priced in a rational way, the market can be said to be 'efficient'.

iii)   *Modigliani and Miller (M & M) propositions 1958*

M & M argued, in connection with corporate gearing, that shareholders could obtain 'home-made leverage' by borrowing on their own account instead of leaving the borrowing to be carried out by the companies in which they owned shares. Taking this proposition a step further, it could be argued that investors should obtain 'home-made hedging' by hedging on their own account. Individual shareholders could each make their own personal arrangements to hedge currency exposures from their own portfolio of shares. Hedging by individual corporate entities from the investors' portfolio would be counterproductive, because this corporate hedging would counteract the hedging of the individual investor.

iv)   *Market efficiency*

Currency markets do not provide bargains; rather they provide fair gambles based on fair prices. In the long run, gains and losses on unhedged foreign exchange exposures tend to average out. Readers will recall from Chapter 2 that the forward rate, over time, is an unbiased predictor of the spot rate.

Thus, in the long run, there will be no benefit from hedging. The argument concludes that corporates could 'self-insure' by simply allowing gains and losses to cancel out in the long run.

Hedging, so the argument says, will reduce the value of the firm because the premium paid will exceed the potential loss after taking into account the probability of that loss actually occurring.

b)   Summary of Arguments that Contradict the Above

i)   *Purchasing power parity*

Major deviations have occurred in the PPP (see Chapter 2). If relative inflation and relative exchange rates do not immediately offset each other, corporates are exposed to exchange rate risk. Even if the relative levels in the countries concerned did immediately offset each other, the input and output prices of a particular company may not adjust in line with the general change in price levels in the countries concerned.

ii)   *CAPM and market efficiency*

Even if the CAPM is considered valid with regard to foreign exchange exposures, and even if it can be accepted that foreign exchange markets are efficient, there could still be adverse consequences from failure to manage a corporate's currency exposure. If large adverse changes in exchange rates coincided with the receipt or payment of a large sum of foreign currency, the exchange rate movement could give rise to serious liquidity problems.

Although, in the long run, all such gains and losses should cancel out, that would be of little consolation to shareholders, managers and creditors if the liquidity crisis had forced the corporate to go into liquidation.

iii)   *M & M*

Individual investors are unlikely to be able to diversify exchange risk as efficiently as corporates. There are minimum amounts for hedging instruments such as forward exchange contracts, options and futures, so it may not be possible for an individual investor to tailor a hedge to meet his own requirements. Major corporates also might have access to techniques such as accelerating or delaying inter-company payments in accordance with foreign exchange market conditions. In addition, the managers have access to information on their companies' foreign exchange exposures that is just not available to the private investor, and the cost of hedging may be far lower for corporates than it is for individual shareholders.

It may be that the above arguments are less cogent in the case of institutional investors such as pension funds, which should have the same 'bulk power' as major corporates. In addition, the managers of institutions may be capable of hedging the foreign exchange risk from their portfolio of investments in a more cost-effective manner than relying on the managers of the various companies to hedge the risk of each corporate entity independently.

However, the majority of listed shares in the UK are owned by institutions, such as pension funds. These organizations need stability of earnings in sterling terms, because their own liabilities (pensions) are denominated in sterling.

c)   Other Arguments Supporting Management of Currency Exposures by Corporates

i)   Corporate hedging reduces the volatility of earnings and the volatility of future cash flows. This in turn reduces the risk of incurring the costs of financial distress (a technical term describing the costs incurred in a liquidation from legal fees and other transaction costs).

ii)   Lower risk should result in a lower cost of capital. The cost of capital (after some adjustments) is the basis of the discount rate applied to future cash flows when valuing the business; thus, the lower the discount rate the higher the value of the firm.

iii)   Lower risk of financial distress may increase debt capacity for a hedged company.

iv)   Managers and employees cannot hold a diversified portfolio of jobs. Good managers should be attracted to firms that manage foreign currency exposures, because such firms are likely to be affected to a lesser extent by the costs of financial distress.

v)   In some tax regimes, fortuitous foreign currency gains may be liable to taxation, whereas foreign currency losses may not be tax-deductible.

vi)   Suppliers and customers prefer to deal with less risky firms.

6   The Use of a 'Budget' Rate of Exchange in Projections

a)   How Budget Rates are Used

Nowadays even the smallest businesses must plan, and one essential basic planning tool is the projected profit-and-loss account (known as an operating budget) and a projected cash budget. For a business with anticipated receipts or purchases denominated in foreign currency, there is an added complication: the projected spot rates at which the receipts or payments will be converted.

A typical planning exercise would take place in October, and would cover the twelve months starting in the following January.

Most businesses decide upon a 'budget rate of exchange' and this rate is used to convert all anticipated currency receipts or payments into home currency for the purposes of the operating and cash budgets. The company can select any rate it wishes for this exercise but, in practice, the three-month or six-month or twelve-month forward rate is usually chosen. The forward rate does not claim to predict what the spot will be at the end of the relevant period, it simply reflects the current spot rate today and the current interest rate differentials in the two countries. However, the forward rate is usually selected, simply because it is the one that is available at the time the budget is prepared.

If all other parts of the budget are totally accurate (which is most unlikely in practice!), any actual conversions made at more favourable rates will result in extra profit and more cash than that projected in the budgets, and the converse will apply if the actual rates used for conversion are less favourable. By making regular comparisons between the actual rates of exchange used for conversions and the budget rate, companies should be able to assess the likely effect of exchange rate movements on the company's year-end profits and cash position, and should be able to evaluate the success of any hedging action taken.

b) How Internal Communication Can Help Contain Transaction Exposure

Transaction exposure arises from decisions taken by purchasing and sales personnel who cannot be expected to have a detailed knowledge of the treasury function.

However, it is essential that sales and purchasing personnel are broadly aware of the impact of their decisions on the company's exposure position, and to this end they require a broad understanding of:

● hedging techniques and forward rates;

● how to use forward rates in comparison to leading and lagging.

Likewise the treasurer must be made aware of the likely long-term sales volumes in different currencies and how sensitive such sales are to price changes. This information will be particularly important in monitoring 'extended transaction exposure'.

Treasurers should also liaise on a regular basis with sales and purchasing staff to ensure that these people know the current rates (spot or forward) and can therefore quickly calculate whether a particular deal will be profitable in home currency terms.

Note
A new accountancy standard (FAS 133) is currently coming into force. This requires companies to follow strict formalities as regards the monitoring and reporting of derivatives exposures. These formalities will add to the cost of derivatives.

8

FOREIGN CURRENCY TRANSLATION EXPOSURE AND FOREIGN CURRENCY ECONOMIC EXPOSURE

Objectives

On completion of this chapter the student should be able to:

● understand the nature and implications of translation exposure;

● differentiate between profit-and-loss and balance sheet translation exposure;

● understand how currency borrowing and swaps can be used to manage translation exposure;

● evaluate the benefits and drawbacks of managing translation exposure;

● understand the nature of foreign currency economic exposure;

● appreciate the difficulties in the management of foreign currency economic exposure.

1   Translation Exposure

a)   The Nature of Translation Exposure

This exposure arises from the changes in the value in home currency of overseas assets and liabilities from one balance sheet date to the next. It also relates to the consolidations of the year's profits and the effect on earnings per share when some of the profits relate to an overseas subsidiary.

This chapter does not seek to provide a detailed understanding of the accountancy treatment of translation gain or loss, but merely seeks to explain the broad principles.

b)   Translation Exposures and Balance Sheets

The largest translation effect for most international groups is the result of translating the net worth of overseas subsidiaries into the company's reporting currency for the purpose of producing consolidated accounts. The value in the reporting currency of the group is calculated by using the rate of exchange that applied at the balance sheet date. Hence, even if the net worth of the subsidiary remained unchanged between balance sheet dates when denominated in the currency of that subsidiary, there would be a translation gain or loss in the reporting currency of the consolidated accounts, depending on the movement of exchange rates between the two balance sheet dates.

c)   Translation Exposure and its Effect on the Profit and Loss Account

This is easily explained by an example. A UK-based company may have a subsidiary located in the USA. Naturally the year's profits, denominated in US $, will have to be included in sterling terms in the consolidated accounts. This consolidation will occur even though the profits may be retained in the subsidiary. (Under SSAP 20, UK companies can use year-end exchange rates or average exchange rates for the year. The American equivalent, FASB52, in practice allows a weighted average exchange rate to be applied to the profit-and-loss statement.)

The sterling figure produced in the consolidated profit-and-loss account will affect the group's annual reported earnings and the reported earnings per share.

2   Specific Examples of Translation Exposure on Profit-and-loss Accounts

In this example we shall look at a UK company with a French subsidiary, which uses the year-end rate to translate its overseas profits for the published accounts.

The profit forecasts by City analysts for the current financial year are £95m, based on forecast UK profits of £45m and forecast profits of the French subsidiary of FRF 500m at a forecast exchange rate of FRF10=£1.

The following table shows the various outcomes at different year-end exchange rates, assuming that the UK profits are actually $45m and the French profits are actually FRF 500m.

Year-end Rate/£	FRF8=£1	FRF10=£1	FRF12=£1
UK profits £m	45	45	45
French profits FF500m	62.5	50	41.7
Group total	107.5	95	86.7

There are various possible solutions to overcome this potential translation exposure.

i) Arrange a forward contract for the bank to buy FRF 500m at the year end. This contract will not be fulfilled, but will be closed out on maturity at the year end.

   If the FRF has weakened at the year end, the paper loss on consolidated earnings will be matched by a cash gain on the close-out of the forward contract. However, if the FRF has gained in value at the year end, there will be a paper gain on consolidated earnings matched by a cash loss on close-out.

ii) Arrange a currency put option for FRF 500m. If the FRF has weakened, the currency option can be sold for its intrinsic value to offset the paper loss on consolidated earnings. If the FRF has strengthened at the year end, the option will be abandoned, with the cost of the premium having been paid by the company.

iii) It may be possible to change accounting policy if the auditors and the accountancy rules allow this, so that, instead of using year-end spot rates to convert the profits in the consolidated accounts, average rates for the year are used. In this case, likely exchange rates to be applied on consolidation of profits should be capable of a reasonably accurate estimate well before year end.

   Most accountancy conventions insist that assets and liabilities are translated at closing rates, but in some countries, for example the UK, average rates can be used for conversion of the annual profits. Auditors normally allow only occasional changes in the basis of consolidation of profits and companies will certainly not be allowed to chop and change at will, depending on which method proves more favourable each year.

iv) The company should undertake a serious public relations exercise to educate analysts to understand the effect of exchange rate movements on the profit stream.

v) For 'strong' companies, treating the investment community with respect and avoiding the use of a 'cash' hedge must be the preferred course, but this may not be possible for a company that is not considered to be a 'blue-chip' company, because of potential adverse reactions from shareholders, bankers and creditors.

3   Specific Examples of Translation Exposures on Balance Sheets

Example
A UK company has just acquired an American subsidiary at a cost of US $150m. The payment was funded by a sterling loan of £100m, which was converted to US $150m at the spot rate of 1.5. There was a net worth of £100m immediately before the transaction and no currency assets or liabilities existed until this acquisition. Immediately after the acquisition, the group balance sheet would look like this:

	Assets £m		Liabilities £m
(US $150m) Dollar Assets	100	Debt (Sterling)	100
Sterling Assets	100	Equity	100
	200		200

The gearing is 100% (Debt/Equity)
Net worth   £100m

In many loan agreements there are covenants under which banks require companies to meet certain financial conditions. In the documentation, financial targets may have to be met. Two of the most common are the 'gearing test' and the 'maintenance of net worth' or 'consolidated net worth' tests. Let us assume that the bank insisted that this company agreed to a loan covenant that requires a minimum net worth of £80m and a maximum gearing ratio (debt/equity) of 125%.

Let us now look at the year-end balance sheet in one year's time, making the unlikely but necessary assumption that the only change was the closing spot rate between the pound and the dollar.

There will be various alternative outcomes depending on the year-end spot rate:

Assumption one: All sterling debt and dollar rises to US $1 = £1.

	Assets £m		Liabilities £m
(US $150m) Dollar Assets	150	Debt (£)	100
Sterling Assets	100	Equity	150
	250		250

Gearing   67% (100 ÷ 150 x 100)
Net worth   £150m

Assumption two: Dollar falls to $2 = £1 and debt is all sterling

	Assets £m		Liabilities £m
(US $150m) Dollar Assets	75	Debt (£)	100
Sterling Assets	100	Equity	75
	175		175

Gearing   133% (100 ÷ 75 x 100)
Net Worth   £75m

What we find from this simple example is that the reported gearing and net worth of the company will be changed each year, depending on the exchange rate prevailing at the year end. As the company had agreed a 125% gearing covenant and a maintenance of net worth test at £80m, there would be a problem. This is all the worse because the movement in exchange rates may well only be temporary.

4 Use of Foreign Currency Borrowing to Hedge Balance Sheet Translation Exposure

In the above example, the solution to the net worth problem is straightforward. All that is required is to match foreign currency assets with foreign currency liabilities. In this case, both sides of the balance sheet will be equally affected, as shown in the following example:

We repeat, for convenience, the opening balance sheet of the previous example when the spot rate was $1.50 = £1

	Assets £m		Liabilities £m
(US $150m) Dollar Assets	100	(US $150 loans)	100
Sterling Assets	100	Equity	100
	200		200

Gearing	100%
Net Worth	£100m

Let us now examine the outcome if the borrowing had been denominated in US $ (150m at 1.50).

The next year's balance sheet assuming all conditions are as before (i.e. the only change is that the year-end spot rate is $1 = £1) (outcome 1).

	Assets £m		Liabilities £m
(US $150m) Dollar assets	150	(US $150 at $1 = £1)	150
Sterling assets	100	Equity	100
	250		250

Gearing	150%
Net Worth	£100m

Let us now see what happens when the closing rate at the next balance sheet date is US $2 = £1 (outcome 2).

	Assets £m		Liabilities £m
(US $150m) Dollar Assets	75	(US $150 at $2 = £1)	75
Sterling Assets	100	Equity	100
	175		175

Gearing	75%
Net Worth	£100m

This currency borrowing achieves the desired effect on maintenance of net worth, but gearing increases as sterling weakens (outcome 1), and reduces gearing as sterling strengthens (outcome 2). Thus, matching the net foreign currency assets of the company with foreign currency borrowings will stabilize the reported net worth, but will not stabilize the reported gearing. Treasurers should seek to negotiate loan covenants that will not be affected by translation exposures. Where these covenants are not available, seek covenants that relate only to net worth, or match the assets by 50% only by currency borrowing if there are gearing covenants (see examples below).

5 Managing Translation Exposures by Matching 50% Currency Borrowings and 50% Sterling Finance

Suppose the US $ assets of 150m shown in the previous three balance sheet examples had been originally matched with half sterling and half dollar debt when the spot rate was US $1.50. The balance sheet would have looked like this:

	Assets £m		Liabilities £m
(US $150m) Dollar	100	Loans	100
		(US $75 at 1.5 = £50 +£50)	
Sterling	100	Equity	100
	200		200

Let us now look at the outcome for the next balance sheet when $1 = £1, i.e. sterling has weakened.

	Assets £m		Liabilities £m
Dollar assets	150	Loans	125
		(US $75 at 1 = £75 + £50)	
Sterling assets	100	Equity	125
	250		250

Gearing	100%
Net worth	£125m

Now let us see the outcome when sterling has strengthened at the next balance sheet date to US $2 = £1:

	Assets £m		Liabilities £m
Dollar assets	75	Loans	87.5
		(US $75 at 2 = 37.5 + 50)	
Sterling assets	100	Equity	87.5
	175		175

Gearing   100%
Net worth   £87.5 m

Thus, it is possible to hedge translation exposures as regards net worth or gearing by currency borrowing. However, it is not possible to hedge both simultaneously by this method.

6   Considerations to Bear in Mind When Using Currency Borrowing to Hedge Translation Exposures

a)   Borrowing in the Currency of the Assets to Hedge Balance Sheet Exposures

The company can initially eliminate the translation net worth exposure by financing the overseas asset purchases with borrowings in the same currency. Thus, any increase in the asset value because of exchange rate movements will be matched by an increase in the domestic currency equivalent of the loan, and vice versa.

Although the initial purchase can be hedged in this way, this technique cannot entirely eliminate the exposure in future years. The net worth of the subsidiary in terms of local currency will increase or decrease because of profits, or losses and dividend or interest payments. It is difficult to predict year-end net worth in advance.

Some companies make monthly estimates of translation exposure, so they will not be 'caught out' by an unexpectedly large translations loss at the year end.

b)   Other Problems that Can Arise from Foreign Currency Borrowing to Hedge Translation Exposure:

i)   Foreign currency borrowings will have to be rolled over at maturity and the borrower will have to pay the current market rate of interest at the renewal date.

ii)   The borrowing may contravene local exchange controls.

iii)   If the foreign currency appreciates and the assets are sold, there will be capital gains tax to pay. In some tax jurisdictions, there will be no tax relief against the extra cost of the loan.

iv)   Servicing costs will be denominated in foreign currency, and this will create a transaction exposure unless the overseas assets are generating sufficient foreign currency to cover this servicing.

v)   Foreign currency borrowing facilities are not available in certain soft currencies.

vi)   If the asset does not require borrowings to fund its purchase, then borrowing to hedge translation exposures will artificially inflate the balance sheet and create unnecessary borrowing.

vii) If the asset is funded by an inter-company loan, there may be withholding tax complications.

7 Currency Swaps

a) The Use of Currency Swaps as an Alternative to Direct Currency Borrowing

We have already seen in Chapter 2 how banks utilize short-term currency swaps to cover their own exposures in connection with forward contract commitments. We now examine how, as an alternative to direct currency borrowing, longer-dated currency swaps can be used to effectively switch the currency in which a loan is denominated. A typical swap works as follows:

i) In a typical currency swap, two different currencies are normally exchanged at the outset.

ii) During the life of the currency swap, the counterparties agree to exchange interest payments on the principal amounts originally exchanged.

iii) At maturity, the principal amounts on the currency swap are re-exchanged at a rate agreed at the outset. This pre-set rate is often agreed as the same rate as applied to the original exchange.

Note

There may be subsidized rates of interest available (e.g. export finance from a government-backed export support scheme) and companies could borrow in their own currency from this source and swap into the desired currency.

b) Numerical Example of Currency Swap

A UK company, X plc, wants to borrow US $24m, repayable over 10 years to finance its US subsidiary. It is not well known in the USA and does not have a credit rating. However, the company is well known on the UK markets.

Let us assume that the company can issue a sterling debenture at 8%, fixed for 10 years, and that the following bank swap quote is available:

Rate US $	1.5 to £1
Interest on US $	5% fixed
Interest on £	8% fixed

The swap will operate as follows:

i) Day one: X plc borrows £16m in the market and swaps it for US $24m.

ii) Annual interest payments: X plc will receive £1.28m and will pay US $1.2m.

iii) At maturity: X plc will pay the bank US $24m and will receive £16m in exchange.

c)   Cash-flow diagrams
i)   Day one

To purchase subsidiary
US$ 24m

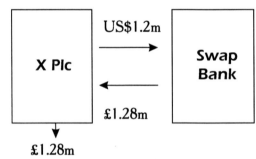

£16m
from debenture issue

ii)   Annual interest payments

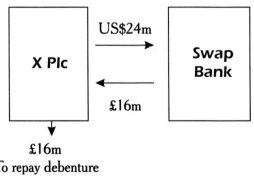

£1.28m
interest on debenture

Note
It is assumed that the subsidiary will generate US$ income to service the swap interest commitment.

iii)   Maturity

£16m
To repay debenture

The company has created a synthetic US $ loan in this case, but the rate of interest could well be much lower than that which would have been payable on direct US $ borrowing, if the company has access to subsidized export finance for its sterling borrowing, or if the company was a well-respected borrower on the sterling debenture markets.

At maturity, X plc will be obliged to use £16m sterling towards the purchase of US $24m. However, if X plc remains creditworthy, the bank will almost certainly extend the swap, using the interest rates ruling at the time of maturity as the basis of the subsequent interest rate exchanges.

Note
Particular care must be taken to obtain specialist tax advice and accounting advice to ensure that the sterling loan and currency swap are formally linked for tax and audit purposes.

8 Is It Necessary to Manage Translation Exposure?

Translation gains or losses do not result in any cash gain or loss. These changes are recorded in the reserves of the group and represent unrealized gains or losses on conversion of the net worth of overseas subsidiaries, or of other foreign currency denominated assets and liabilities. However, such gains or losses affect the reported gearing and net worth of the consolidated position and as such they affect the attitudes of lenders, creditors and investors. Thus, translation gains or losses can ultimately result in a cash effect if the behaviour of creditors, bankers and shareholders is changed.

For a strong company with a first-class international reputation the 'paper' gains or losses from translation exposure are not too important. Such companies can simply explain the true nature of the exposures to analysts and bankers, and there will be no adverse effects. However, companies that are not in the BP league need to take banker/market perceptions much more seriously.

In addition, truly world-wide multinational companies can afford to ignore translation exposure, because paper translation losses in some currencies will be offset by paper translation gains in other currencies.

Some companies do not attempt to manage translation exposure at all because:

● There is no cash inflow or outflow.

● The effect on the balance sheet can be likened to the effect of a revaluation of a factory in the balance sheet of a company with no foreign exchange commitments. If the factory is revalued, the increase in fixed assets in the published accounts is matched by an increase in reserves and a reduced gearing ratio. However, there is no change in the actual cash position of the company.

● If hedging techniques are used, companies are paying money to hedge what is purely an accounting exercise. Many writers feel that it is not in the shareholder's interest to hedge paper gains and losses.

- In addition, hedging techniques involve a cash inflow or outflow (e.g. the gain or loss on a close-out of a forward contract) which is not justified when the translation gain or loss is of a non-cash nature.

- Investing in overseas assets is essentially a strategic decision, and investors may have invested in a particular company to take advantage of its overseas investments. Any form of hedging would nullify that strategic exposure.

Indeed, when a company purchases assets in a country with a weak currency, it should ensure that the return on those assets is likely to be sufficient to compensate for the translation exposure.

The main argument for managing translation exposure is that, especially in the case of 'weaker' companies, changes in gearing or net worth, however caused, affect the attitudes of lenders, shareholders and creditors. This must ultimately affect the cash position. In addition, in many countries translation losses are not allowable for tax purposes. Thus, such losses can affect reserves by more than would the equivalent trading loss.

Whenever any hedging action is taken to cover translation exposure, always:

i) take specialist tax advice;

ii) make sure that the hedge is cost-effective. It is pointless spending precious management time in trying to construct a perfect translation exposure hedge. A hedge that approximately covers the translation exposure will be more cost-effective than a 'perfect hedge';

iii) In some countries, companies can now denominate their capital in currencies other than home currency if they wish. Hence, a major multinational could have part of its equity capital denominated in overseas currency to match overseas assets. However, there are major problems in having equity denominated in a cocktail of currencies:

    - There will be a need to explain and justify this, to the market

    - What happens if the currency base of assets changes?

    - The tax position is unclear

    - Separate dividend streams would be needed

    - Essentially, there would be separate companies for each type of equity;

iv) Hedging profit-and-loss translation exposure is always worthwhile in the following circumstances:

    - if the corporate has tight loan covenants covering reported gearing or reported net worth that might be breached because of translation losses;

    - if the Chief Executive has given a profit forecast to the share analysts for earnings that are exposed to translation fluctuations. It may be important to protect this commitment to retain credibility with the capital markets;

- if the company enjoys a high price-earnings ratio because of steady growth of reported accounting profits. This record may be an asset that is worth preserving, even though it means hedging a paper gain/loss with a cash gain/loss.

9 Economic Exposure

a) Overview

This arises from the structure of the business, the currency of competitors and the way in which costs and prices respond to change. A brief definition could be 'the risk that long-term movements in relative exchange rates will cause structural changes that undermine profitability'.

Foreign currency economic exposure risks are often not managed because they are:

a) not reported in the accounts;

b) difficult to quantify;

c) sometimes unhedgeable.

However, nowadays there are sophisticated computer techniques that can provide a logical and quantifiable analysis of economic exposure, but many large companies tend not to make full use of these developments.

When such computer techniques are not available, the treasurer can prepare a schedule showing the currencies to which the company is economically exposed.

However, major problems in trying to quantify economic exposure are:

i) In addition to forecasting exchange rate movements, it is necessary to forecast movements in relative inflation rates (or, better still, changes in input costs and output prices). If the move in exchange rates is caused by relative inflation differences, presumably the effect of the change of exchange rate will be cancelled out by way of increased or decreased costs or prices.

ii) It is not easy to know exactly what the currency of cost base is for competitors. For instance, Japanese car manufacturers have a sterling cost base to the extent that they manufacture some cars in the UK.

iii) It is even more difficult to ascertain whether and to what extent competitors have hedged their currency positions. Such hedging will nullify the effect of exchange rate movements for the amounts so covered.

b) General Points on Economic Exposure

A company that is entirely home-based and that makes all its payments and receipts in domestic currency can still have an economic exposure to foreign exchange risk if its market is subject to foreign competition.

A typical example could be a UK-based coal-mining operation with all its costs and revenues denominated in sterling. In the case of imports from Australia, the foreign currency economic exposure could arise if the Australian $ were to depreciate against sterling, without a corresponding change in relative price levels. In that situation, assuming the Australian's costs were denominated in Australian $ and assuming it did not hedge its sterling receipts, then there would be scope for a price reduction in £ sterling terms for Australian coal.

c) Minimization of Economic Exposure

The best methods are internal techniques such as:

- The company must have a high level of efficiency with good profitability. This makes the company less vulnerable to adverse economic changes.

- Diversification of suppliers, products, markets and countries of manufacture is essential. multinationals are well placed in this respect.

- There must be active research on new products and new materials to help to maintain diversity.

- The company may be able to exert political pressure to reduce competition via imports (e.g. by proving that the competitor's products do not meet safety standards).

- The company must not become over-borrowed, otherwise its room for manoeuvre is restricted.

- The company may be willing if necessary to switch its manufacturing location to match the cost base of its competitors. However, this would be a major strategic decision involving company policy in areas other than foreign currency management.

Note
External techniques could be used to manage economic exposure only if:

- the company can forecast its long-term future cash flows with reasonable accuracy;

- the competitors have a different currency of cost;

- the company cannot easily switch its own currency of cost.

10 Brown Construction: Case Study

Brown Construction plc is a UK-based company that specializes in undertaking major projects in the USA. Some three years ago the company acquired a subsidiary in the USA in order to help in overcoming the problems that can prevent UK firms from obtaining contract work in North America.

Recently the company purchased a quarry in the UK so as to be assured of a supply of raw materials which are required in the manufacturing process. The purchase cost, £10m, was funded out of a medium-term sterling loan at a fixed rate of interest.

In addition to the raw materials extracted from the UK mine, the company purchases raw materials from France and from other UK suppliers. The supplies from France make up about 20% of the company's costs of raw materials.

At the present time, there is strong competition from Japanese companies for the contracts in the USA.

The USA subsidiary has a current net worth of US $12m and the asset is translated into sterling for the purposes of Brown's accounts, using the closing rate method. The US $ has strengthened since acquisition, so the group treasurer has been content to leave the translation exposure unhedged. However, he would like to 'lock in' the existing translation gains.

Brown Construction have a policy of taking out forward contracts once firm commercial contracts have been agreed for USA sales.

Required

Assess the practical and theoretical issues that could be considered in connection with the management of foreign exchange exposures of Brown Construction.

11 Issues for Brown Construction to Consider

Practical Issues for Brown Construction

a) Transaction Exposure

It is assumed that the company is in a highly risky industry with large one-off payments. In addition, there will probably be a high ratio of fixed costs to variable ones. Because Brown Construction is certainly not a price maker, and as dollar receipts tend to be large 'lumpy' amounts, it cannot afford to take the risk of not hedging. Thus, a hedge-everything policy would seem wise.

Brown's should first of all try internal techniques:

- Possibly a larger proportion of the preparatory work could be switched to the USA to switch the cost base. This would be a major, long-term decision and strategic factors over and above transaction exposure would be involved in such decisions.

- Ascertain whether any UK suppliers will be prepared to invoice in US $. Some suppliers, for example, subsidiaries of USA multinationals, may be willing to cooperate. However, check that the dollar prices are still competitive in sterling terms.

- Obtain quotes for cross rates to convert some US$ receipts to euros, crediting the proceeds to a euro-denominated bank account. The benefit here is that euros credited to this account can cover the euro payments to French suppliers. In addition, the impact of the bank's bid/offer spread will be reduced, because it avoids converting dollars to sterling, and then converting sterling to euro to pay French suppliers.

After netting as far as possible by means of internal techniques, external techniques can be considered for managing the remaining transaction exposures.

- Use forwards for 'certain sums', then use options to cover potential, but not certain sums. Thus if 70% of the sales forecast was considered 'certain', forward contracts could be utilized. The remaining 30% could be covered by options.

- Hedge the pre-transaction exposure by way of options or seek other methods such as ECGD support (see Chapter 20 for a more detailed explanation of the problems of tender bonds and Chapter 18 for ECGD facilities).

b)   Translation exposures

The treasurer wishes to 'lock in' his translation gains that have arisen as a result of the appreciation of the US$. The past gains could be 'locked in' if the US$ asset were to be matched by a US$ liability. This switch could be achieved by borrowing US$ and converting the proceeds to sterling to pay off the sterling loan. However, a currency swap would be a more appropriate technique, because this leaves the existing sterling borrowing undisturbed and thus avoids any penalties for early repayment of the sterling loan (which in any case may well be at a subsidized rate for export finance).

If there are gearing covenants in the loan agreements, it may be wise to match around half the US$ assets with a currency swap. If net worth covenants apply, then consider matching the full dollar value of the subsidiary by means of a currency swap.

The US$ interest cost will help to hedge some of the US$ transaction exposure.

Take specialist tax advice to ensure the swap and the assets are matched for tax purposes.

Many academic writers consider that translation exposures should not be managed because they are merely 'paper' gains and losses. However, 'weaker' companies do need to monitor translation exposures, as the perceptions of bankers, creditors and shareholders could be affected.

If any profit forecasts have been made to market analysts, the company should take out a currency option to ensure credibility is not lost by adverse exchange rate movements. This will be less necessary if the average rate is used for consolidation of profits.

c)   Economic exposure

On the face of it, the relevant rates are £:US$ and Japanese yen:US$. If the yen depreciates faster than the £ against the $, and if there is no change in relative inflation, then the Japanese will gain a competitive advantage (vice versa if sterling depreciates faster).

However, in practice this economic exposure probably cannot be quantified. Brown's may not know the currency cost base of its competitor nor whether the competitor hedges.

In practice this exposure may not be hedged because it will not be reported in the published accounts.

Other Arguments to Support the Hedging of Exchange Rate Risks by Brown Construction

These arguments are summed up as:

i) Corporate hedging reduces the volatility of earnings and the volatility of future cash flows. This in turn reduces the risk of incurring the costs of financial distress.

ii) Lower risk should result in a lower cost of capital. The cost of capital (after some adjustments) is the basis of the discount rate applied to future cash flows when valuing the business; thus, the lower the discount rate the higher the value of the firm.

iii) Lower risk of financial distress may increase debt capacity for a hedged company.

iv) Managers and employees cannot hold a diversified portfolio of jobs. Good managers should be attracted to firms that manage foreign currency exposures because such firms are likely to be affected to a lesser extent by foreign exchange fluctuations.

v) The theoretical arguments against hedging (CAPM, PPP, market efficiency and self-insurance), even if valid in general terms, are all applicable over long periods of time. However, a single large loss on foreign currency could be enough to put Brown Construction into liquidation.

For more detailed explanation of points (iv) and (v) above, please see Chapter 7.

Other Matters Regarding Internal Controls

Strictly speaking these matters are outside the scope of this book, but a brief note is considered worthwhile.

The board of directors should ensure that there are clear written rules for the following internal aspects of currency management:

● hedging philosophy;

● which derivatives can be used;

● details of authority for company officers to transact derivatives business on behalf of the company (who is authorized, maximum amounts, which instruments and the extent to which the derivative must exactly match an underlying future cash commitment);

● separation of dealing, confirmation and settlement duties to avoid a 'Nick Leeson' situation;

● details of the banks with which derivatives business can be transacted;

● under Financial Accounting Standard 133 (FAS133) companies need to conform to strict rules as regards monitoring derivatives positions and reporting them in the published accounts.

9

METHODS OF INTERNATIONAL SETTLEMENT THROUGH BANKS

Objectives

On completion of this chapter, the student should be able to:

- Understand the dangers of money laundering in the context of transfers of funds abroad;

- Differentiate between nostro and vostro Accounts;

- Understand the book-keeping involved in funds transfer;

- Appreciate the different methods of international settlement, i.e. SWIFT, telegraphic transfer, mail transfer and bank draft;

- Understand the benefits of using a bank with an international branch network for overseas payments;

- Appreciate the importance of linking SWIFT to national domestic clearing systems;

- Appreciate the problems involved in the use of personal cheques for international settlement;

- Appreciate the issues set out in the EU directive on cross-border payments.

1 Money Laundering: Dangers of Fraud or Illegality When Transferring Money Abroad

Note

None of the following is intended as a detailed guide to the legal position on money laundering. Readers should refer any suspicions immediately to their compliance officer or to the ECU of NCIS (see below).

Under the Drug Trafficking Act 1994, The Criminal Justice Act 1988 and 1993, and under the Prevention of Terrorism Act (Temporary Provisions) 1989, banks must disclose to the authorities any suspicions regarding the location of funds that might be used for possible offences under these Acts. It is implied that banks making disclosures in good faith under the 'money laundering' provisions of these Acts will be protected from potential liability under the duty of secrecy to customers.

(a) What is money laundering?

Money laundering is the process whereby illegally obtained funds are integrated into the financial system, so that they apparently appear to be legitimate.

There are three stages:

● Placement, whereby illegally obtained cash is put into the banking system.

● Layering, whereby a series of complex transactions is undertaken with the intention of disguising the source of funds.

● Integration, whereby the monies are re-introduced into the financial system as apparently legitimate funds.

The main forms of offences in this area are:

● Assistance: helping another to obtain the benefit of the proceeds of criminal activity.

● Acquisition: possession or use of the proceeds of criminal activity.

● Concealment: concealing or transferring the proceeds of criminal activity.

● Failure to disclose: failing to disclose knowledge or suspicion of money laundering.

● Tipping off: disclosing information in order to prejudice an investigation.

In the UK, the main official bodies that fight money laundering are:

● The ECU of NCIS: The Economic Crime Unit of the National Criminal Intelligence Service.

● FSA: The Financial Services Authority which will work with the ECU of NICS.

To repeat, this section is not intended to act as a summary of the detailed legal position under money laundering; what it aims to do is to alert the reader to possible instances of money laundering and other fraudulent payments so that such suspicions can be reported to the appropriate person.

Generally speaking, prompt reporting of suspicions will be a suitable defence if all other actions in the matter have been in good faith.

(b) Typical examples whereby money laundering or fraudulent transfers of funds may take place

Many banks have a compliance office or a fraud office which is a central point, the function of which is to prevent fraud or illegal transfers taking place. It is important to identify examples of potential fraud and to refer them to the fraud office. Instances that could involve fraud are:

- large round amounts going abroad from a relatively new account, which is fed by many small payments coming in. Obviously, there may be legitimate reasons for the transactions but, where the account is new, its proprietors are not well known, and its business is not too clear, it may be worth a reference to the fraud office. It is important to take and follow up references on new accounts.

- attempts to transfer money in contravention of internationally agreed sanctions.

- unauthenticated instructions to make large sums available to a beneficiary abroad. Be particularly careful as regards messages via fax, telex or via a computer link that purport to authorize such transfers. It is essential that proper authority is held, by way of signatures or by way of computerized code.

- transfers that would contravene the laws of other countries, for example payments for exports which the exporter's government has banned by law. Involvement in such transfers could mean that the bank could be 'blacklisted' by the other government.

- status replies from other banks that are unauthenticated and cannot be verified as being genuine.

- requests from customers to pass messages to overseas businesses, usually by means of telex. Take care as to the wording of such messages and refer them to the compliance office if there seems to be any danger that the message could commit your bank in a way that may not be intended.

(c) Customer obligations

Under the Money Laundering Regulations 1993, and under the EU's Second Banking Directive, corporate treasurers have a duty to maintain proper verifiable records of the bank account details and have a duty to identify all counterparties with whom they may be doing business.

2 Nostro and Vostro Accounts

The word **nostro** means our and **vostro** means your.

From the point of view of a UK bank, a nostro account is its account in the books of an overseas bank, denominated in foreign currency. An example would be an account in the name of HSBC Bank, in the books of Chemical Bank New York, denominated in US $. HSBC is a customer of Chemical Bank.

From the point of view of a UK bank, a vostro account is an overseas bank's account with us, denominated in sterling. An example of a vostro account would be an account in the name of Chemical Bank maintained in the books of HSBC Bank. The account would be denominated in sterling and Chemical Bank would be a customer of HSBC.

When funds are remitted from the United Kingdom, nostro accounts are used if the payment is denominated in foreign currency, and vostro accounts are used if payment is denominated in sterling.

Banks treat their nostro accounts in the same way as any other customer would treat his bank account. The bank will maintain its own record of the nostro account, known as a mirror account, and it will reconcile the bank statements against these mirror accounts.

In order to maintain accurate records, the bank tries to **value date** all transactions. The bank estimates the date on which authorized transactions will actually be debited or credited to the nostro account, and it uses these dates in its mirror account.

3   Book-Keeping for Transfers of Funds

When a UK bank customer wishes to transfer funds denominated in sterling to the bank account of a beneficiary abroad, the book-keeping is as follows, assuming that an account relationship exists between the respective banks:

(a)   Debit the UK customer with the sterling amount, plus charges, and credit the sterling account of the overseas bank. This is a vostro account from the UK bank's point of view.

(b)   On receipt of the advice, the overseas bank will withdraw the sterling from the vostro account, convert it to currency, and then credit the beneficiary with the currency equivalent, less its charges.

If the transfer is denominated in foreign currency, the book-keeping is:

(i)   Debit the customer with the sterling equivalent, plus charges, of the required currency amount, and credit the currency to the nostro account. (If the UK customer maintains a foreign currency account, the appropriate currency amount can be debited to that account, and there will be no need to arrange for conversion into sterling.)

(ii)   Advise the overseas bank that it can debit the nostro account with the requisite amount of currency and credit the funds to the account of the beneficiary.

The various methods of settlement all involve the same book-keeping. The only difference is the method by which the overseas bank is advised about the transfer.

4   Mail Transfer and Telegraphic Transfer

There are many different names for the process of transferring funds abroad under bank-to-bank transfers. Traditionally, the two methods were called mail transfer and telegraphic transfer. Under each method, a remitter instructed his own bank to transfer funds to a beneficiary at a bank abroad. The difference was that the payment details were sent abroad by mail in the one instance and by telex or similar means in the other.

From the point of view of a UK remitter, the UK bank will need to know whether to credit the account of the beneficiary with a named bank (in which case it will request the bank account number) or whether it is instructed to request the overseas bank to advise and pay the beneficiary, if the beneficiary banks elsewhere. In the case of transfers of funds to a private individual, the overseas bank can be asked to pay the beneficiary on application and identification.

Please refer to the customer order forms (Figures I and 2).

On receipt of the customer's instructions, the book-keeping shown above will be applied. With a mail transfer, the UK bank will advise the overseas bank of the transaction by airmail, and the instruction must be signed by authorized signatories. In practice, paper-based mail transfers are becoming much less common with the advance of IT.

If a telegraphic transfer is used, the same procedure as for mail transfers is adopted. However, the instructions to the overseas bank are sent by cable or telex, and the overseas bank will require a special authenticating code word before it will act.

5 SWIFT (Society for Worldwide Interbank Financial Telecommunications)

SWIFT is a computerized method by which banks are able to remit messages using British Telecom or international lines. SWIFT is similar to cable or telex, except that it is a computerized link and is totally secure. Not all banks are in the SWIFT system.

Urgent SWIFT is an alternative to a telegraphic transfer. The accounting entries and procedures are identical for telegraphic transfer or for urgent SWIFT. The only difference is the method whereby the message is remitted to the overseas bank. These SWIFT transfers are sometimes known as 'express international money transfers'.

Ordinary SWIFT is used as an alternative to mail transfers. These transfers are sometimes-known as 'international money transfers'.

The distinction between 'priority' and 'non priority' SWIFT occurs in the speed of action undertaken by the overseas bank, not in the time it takes to deliver the message. For ordinary SWIFT, the UK bank will ask the overseas bank to value date the transaction forward to the date when an airmail instruction, sent at the same time, would be expected to arrive.

6 Application of Charges to SWIFT and TT and MT

The UK customer can instruct the bank as to who is responsible for charges.

This is best shown by an example. Suppose the transfer was for sterling £10,000, and the UK bank's charge was £20. The customer's authority would state who was responsible

| VPRPMT |
| To **HSBC Bank plc** |

Date
PLEASE PRINT OR TYPE IN BLOCK CAPITALS
AS PAYMENT IS TO BE SCANNED

HSBC ◆X◆
PRIORITY PAYMENT

Only Forms
bearing an
original
issuing till
stamp are
acceptable

PLEASE READ THE TERMS OVERLEAF

Method of Payment – *Please tick appropriate box*

	Payt. No.	**BANK USE ONLY**	**BANK USE ONLY**

☐ 1. Advise & credit account of beneficiary (Bank req'd)

☐ 2. Advise & pay beneficiary (Bene Address req'd)

☐ 3. Pay beneficiary on personal identification & application (Bank req'd)

Date Received		RC
Time Received		CX

Amount in words | Amount in figures | CH
| | CC
Name of currency | Value Date | Customer Ref. (SD) | TC
Exchange Rate (XER) | Sterling Equiv. in Figures £ | Forward Contract/Deal No. (FD) | PA
| | | CU
Remitter's Name and Address (OC) | | PB
Covering Agent Bank Use Only | PT
| PZ
Overseas Bank Code | CB
Beneficiary's Bankers | CT
Full Name and Address of Beneficiary (BC) | CO
| INPUT
Beneficiary Account No. | CHECKED
Message to Beneficiary Max. 140 characters (DE) |
Bank Message (BI) (Bank Use Only) | VA

SPECIMEN

| **CHARGES – PLEASE TICK APPROPRIATE BOX** | HSBC Bank charges to be paid by | (1) ☐ Remitter | (2) ☐ Beneficiary |
| | Foreign bank charges to be paid by | (3) ☐ Remitter | (4) ☐ Beneficiary |

Name

Please debit my
Account Number

Currency of Account

Account to be debited for charges
if different from above

Sort Code | 40 | - |

Signatures

To be signed in accordance with the Bank Mandate

1596-4 (2/98 UOI = 1 x Pk 50)

BANK USE ONLY

Branch Contact
Midnet No.

Payment Instruction authenticated
and authorised for payment

Payment Amount

Commission

Total

Authorised
Signature

Codeword

WATCHWORD – MPD PAYMENTS ONLY

Seq. No.						
Orig. S/C		
Area Code		
Date		
Curr. Amt.					
Ben. A/C No.					
Curr. Code		
Ben. Name					
MAC					

Figure 1

Terms & Conditions

SPECIMEN

Branch Issuing Stamp

Please note that whilst forms will not be accepted without the original stamp of the issuing branch, this stamp is for bank purposes and does not constitute confirmation that the payment has been made.

The Bank's responsibility

Reasonable care in the processing of payments will be exercised by the staff of the Bank and of its correspondents. Should such care not be exercised, the Bank will be responsible for any loss of a kind which would be ordinarily expected to occur. This includes interest but not loss of contracts or profits or other consequential loss.

In some jurisdictions (e.g. New York), payments may be made to a designated account number, whether or not this account number correctly identifies the intended beneficiary. The customer is, therefore, strongly urged to ensure that both the account number and the name of the beneficiary are correctly stated in the customer's instructions to the Bank. THE BANK DOES NOT ACCEPT LIABILITY FOR ANY KIND OF LOSS OCCASIONED BY THE CUSTOMER'S MISDESCRIPTION OF THE BENEFICIARY'S NAME OR ACCOUNT NUMBER IN ANY SUCH INSTRUCTIONS TO THE BANK.

Effecting Payment

Bankers can achieve same day value in a few financial centres, otherwise, customers can expect payments to been received by the beneficiary's bankers within 3 to 4 business days, (a business day being a day when banks are open for business both in London and in the financial centre where a payment is to be made). Value may, however, be delayed if there are complications in the routeing of payments or in overseas banking systems. In addition all banks apply cut-off times for the processing of payments to different parts of the world.

AS A RESULT, WE CAN GIVE NO GENERAL ASSURANCES ON THE ACHIEVEMENT OF VALUE DATES. CUSTOMERS ARE URGED TO DISCUSS THEIR NEEDS IN ADVANCE WITH THE BANK'S STAFF.

Cancellation of Payment

The customer is not entitled to cancel the payment. The Bank may, however, be willing to agree to the customer's request for cancellation and endeavour to retrieve funds on their behalf. Any refund of the amount retrieved will be made net of incidental expenses.

Expenses of Correspondents

Any expense incurred by the Bank in employing the payment services of correspondents may be debited to the customer's account, but only net of any prepayment the customer has made on account of this expense.

Other charges and expenses

A charge will be made for enquiries received in respect of both inward and outward payments where HSBC Bank has not made an error, e.g. refunds, cancellations, amendments, duplicate advices, fate of funds, copies of cleared payments etc. (A charge will be made per payment instruction).

Figure 2

for the charges. There are three combinations.

	UK Bank's Charges	*Australian Bank's Charges*
a)	Remitter	Beneficiary
b)	Remitter	Remitter
c)	Beneficiary	Beneficiary

a)   Account entries for remitter/beneficiary charges:

Debit UK customer	£10,020
Credit commission	£20
Credit vostro account	£10,000

The Australian bank will deduct its charges from the amount credited to the beneficiary.

b)   Account entries for all charges remitter:

Debit UK customer	£10,020
Credit vostro account	£10,000
Credit commission	£20

The Australian bank will credit its customer with the full £10,000, and will claim its charges from the UK bank who will debit the UK customer's account in reimbursement.

c)   Account entries for all charges beneficiary:

Debit UK customer	£10,000
Credit vostro account	£9,980
Credit commission	£20

The Australian bank will deduct its own charges from the £9,980 before crediting the beneficiary.

7 The Advantages and Disadvantages of TT, MT and SWIFT

All these systems are secure, in that the payments cannot be stolen in the same way as a cheque or bank draft could be. However, with mail transfer, there is always the danger that the instruction itself could be lost in the post.

The main disadvantage of TT or urgent SWIFT is that there is an extra cost involved for remitting an urgent message. However, the beneficiary can receive the funds much sooner, and this reduction in float time can save interest for both remitter and beneficiary. For large sums, TT or its equivalent will save far more in interest than will be lost by the extra costs.

8   Special Problems with Value Dating of TTs

Time-scale for effecting bank-to-bank payments

From the conditions shown on the reverse of the Priority Payment form shown previously, the reader can see that same-day value from a priority SWIFT transfer (beneficiary receives cleared funds on the same day as the remitter is debited) is possible in some financial centres. This will generally apply where both remitting and receiving banks are in a nostro/vostro account relationship, or where the remitting bank has links with the overseas clearing system, or where the remitting bank has a branch in the overseas country.

However, such situations are by no means the norm, and delays can arise due to complexities, such as early 'cut off times' and having to use more than one bank when there is not a direct nostro/ vostro relationship between the remitting and receiving bank. In addition, banks in a particular country may be closed on certain saints days or other special holiday days and this will inevitably delay the receipt of funds by the beneficiary.

The problem with value dating TTs is best illustrated by the following example.

Example

It is 9.30 a.m. your customer instructs you to transfer FRF50,000 to a beneficiary in Rouen, France, and US $50,000 to a beneficiary in Look out Mountain in Tennessee, both payments to be made by Telegraphic Transfer. The customer says that he telexed both beneficiaries the previous day and received replies from them. He therefore assumes that the funds will be received by the beneficiaries by close of business today.

(a)   Advise him whether it is likely that the beneficiaries will receive the funds today.

(b)   Are there any particular points that could help to speed up the transfer of funds?

Answer: Example part one
(a)   Many overseas banks have cut-off times, sometimes as early as 8.00 a.m. Any instructions received after this time are processed on the next working day.

(b)   It is most unlikely that the UK bank will have a nostro/vostro account relationship with the bank in Tennessee; likewise the French transfer will most likely have to be routed through a bank in Paris. The funds will therefore have to be transmitted through intermediary banks.

(c)   The messages between intermediary banks have to be authenticated, causing further delay.

(d)   On the Continent there are often local holidays where banks are closed on a particular saint's day. Hence there is no guarantee that funds will be received by the beneficiaries today.

Answer: Example part two

(a) Ask if there are any particulars that can be quoted, e.g. bank branch and account number of the beneficiary.

(b) The intermediary banks must be advised to remit all instructions by telex or telephone, or tele-transmission.

How major international banks can reduce the delays in receipt of funds by the beneficiary

In the previous example, there was no account relationship between the banks involved. However, there are instances where many of the delays seen in that example can be reduced.

A few global banks do have a major competitive advantage in funds transfer. These banks are members of clearing systems in many different countries, so when acting as remitting banks they can convert their customers' payment instruction into a form that will enable them to pass automatically into the clearing system of the country of the beneficiary.

This obviously saves time, and there is even greater benefit if the remitting bank has a branch in the overseas country where the beneficiary banks.

In other instances, banks in different countries have formed 'payment clubs', whereby bi-lateral systems are developed to speed up receipt of cleared funds by the beneficiary.

10   Settlement of Inward Payments to UK Beneficiaries

One possible cause of delay in the crediting of cleared funds into the account of a UK beneficiary could be the time taken between receipt of the funds from overseas by a London office of a UK bank and the transferring of those funds from that London bank to the branch bank of the beneficiary. The methods used depend on whether the payment is denominated in sterling or in foreign currency.

(i)   *Inward sterling payments*

Sterling will have been credited to the vostro account of the UK bank by the remitting overseas bank. Usually this vostro account will be maintained at the London office of the UK bank or at one of the major International Division branches in the provinces. Provided the beneficiary's bank account details as quoted on the incoming transfer show the account as being held at one of the branches of the bank holding the vostro account, there should be no problem regarding delays. The payment would normally be credited as cleared funds through the bank's internal systems on the date of receipt, or on the value date advised by the remitting bank.

Where the beneficiary's bank account details show a branch of a different bank, the CHAPS system could be used to transfer the funds on receipt of payment or on the value date quoted by the remitting bank. In theory CHAPS involves a same-day transfer of sterling funds between bank accounts in the UK. However, there are cut-off times after which the transfer cannot be effected until the next working day. Some banks have built an interface between SWIFT and their CHAPS gateways to facilitate rapid processing of international sterling payment instructions.

Usually payments of under £1,000 are made by banker's payment, which is, for all practical purposes, a cheque drawn on the Head office of the bank holding the vostro account. For transfers by this method, delay is inevitable both on account of postal time and on account of the time required to clear the banker's payment. Although such banker's payments are certain to be honoured if drawn on a reputable bank, there will be a delay before the payment is treated as cleared for interest purposes.

As an alternative to a banker's payment, the bank holding the vostro account may use the bank giro system to transfer the funds to the beneficiary's bank account. This method is superior to a banker's payment because the beneficiary will receive cleared funds on the second working day after the transaction has been initiated. Bank giro transfers can be for any amount.

Where the overseas remitting bank's advice merely quotes a name and address of the beneficiary, without bank details, the bank holding the vostro account will usually send a bank draft to the address shown. Once again, postal and clearing delays could apply.

(ii)   *Inward currency payments*

Initially such payments will be made into the nostro account in the name of the UK bank. Where the beneficiary banks at a branch of the same bank as that holding the nostro account, the relevant branch must be contacted for confirmation that the beneficiary requires the funds to be converted to sterling. Once that confirmation has been received, the currency will be converted to sterling, and the beneficiary will receive the funds in the same way as has already been detailed for the sterling funds in section (i) above.

Where the beneficiary banks at another bank, the bank holding the original nostro account would simply transfer the funds to the nostro account of the beneficiary's bank. That bank would then be responsible for transferring the funds into the relevant account of the beneficiary.

11   How a UK Beneficiary can Reduce Delays within the UK in Respect of Funds Received from Abroad

(i)   Always specify bank account details on the contracts and invoices sent to the buyer.

(ii) Whenever possible, insist that the buyer quotes the beneficiary's bank as the correspondent bank through which settlement is to be made by the remitting bank.

(iii) Where currency payments are to be received, the beneficiary should ensure that his bank is given clear instructions as to the disposal of funds. The bank should have been instructed in good time as to whether to convert the currency into sterling or whether the monies should be credited to a currency account in the customer's name.

(iv) The beneficiary should, whenever possible, insist that the buyer telexes the remitting bank's remittance reference. In the event of any delay in receipt of funds, the UK bank can be advised of this detail to help it to trace the payment.

(v) Whenever cash flow and interest considerations justify the expense, arrangements should be made to have all transactions advised by quickest possible means. This will ensure that internal UK transfers are made by CHAPS. However, for smaller amounts where the CHAPS fee is not justified, arrangements should be made for internal transfers to be made by bank giro, rather than by banker's payment.

12 The Disadvantages of the Buyer Using His Own Cheques in Settlement of Overseas Debt

This course of action is not to be recommended because:

(a) In some countries (but not in the United Kingdom) sending a cheque abroad may contravene the exchange control regulations of the buyer's government.

(b) The buyer's bank and the beneficiary's bank usually impose heavy charges for handling such cheques.

(c) There is an inevitable delay between the time the cheque is collected and the time funds are actually remitted by the buyer's bank. One method of speeding up the process of clearing cheques is to use a 'lockbox' facility and this system is particularly useful for UK exporters who sell to the USA and who are paid by the buyer's cheque. The buyer is instructed to post his cheque to a post office box address in the USA. A local bank opens the 'lockbox' at least once a day and initiates the clearing of the cheques. This process dramatically reduces the clearing time, because the cheque itself does not have to go from the USA to the UK and back again. UK banks can organize 'lockbox' facilities by making arrangements with correspondent banks abroad.

Lockbox facilities are also widely available within the EU. Arrangements can be made for the proceeds of the cheques collected via the 'lockbox' system to be held in a collection account with the overseas bank. The funds can then be drawn down as and when required to meet the local currency needs of the UK seller.

(d) From the beneficiary's point of view, there is no guarantee that the cheque will be paid.

13 Bank Drafts

A bank draft is in effect a cheque drawn by one bank on another. If sterling payment is required, the draft will be drawn on the vostro account; if currency payment is required, then the draft is drawn on the nostro account.

The UK bank will place sterling in the vostro account, or currency in the nostro account, to meet the drafts. The customer's account will be debited in reimbursement and charges will be passed.

The UK customer will forward the draft to the beneficiary who will pay it into his bank for credit to his account. Ultimately, the draft will be debited to the appropriate nostro or vostro account.

There are major disadvantages to the use of drafts for large transfers:

(a) The remitter is debited at the time the draft is issued, but there is a delay before the beneficiary can pay the draft into his bank account and obtain cleared funds.

(b) If the beneficiary does not bank at the bank on whom the draft is drawn, the funds will be treated as uncleared.

(c) The draft could be lost or stolen, and banks are reluctant to 'stop' a bank draft because it amounts to dishonour of the bank's own paper. In any case the bank will require an indemnity from the customer authorizing the bank to debit the customer's account if it should suffer any loss by stopping the draft and issuing a duplicate.

14 Developments within the EU Regarding Payments

(i) For some time now, corporate treasurers have been able to initiate CHAPS transfers from their own desk-top terminals. This facility is now available for international transfers by way of SWIFT or telegraphic transfer. In addition, the payment details of regular suppliers can be retained on computer so that the corporate treasurer merely needs to input the amount and value date to initiate a payment. Naturally, appropriate security procedures are laid down to cover direct payments.

(ii) The direct debit system has existed for many years in the UK. This has now been extended to international payments in parts of the EU. Thus a UK importer could authorize his bank to accept claims from his suppliers, subject possibly to maximum amounts and frequencies, at the debit of his account.

(iii) Strategic alliances of national clearing houses may well set up in competition with SWIFT.

(iv) Suppliers, purchasers and bankers are becoming linked in Electronic Data Interchange. This enables simultaneous real-time transfers to be made with automatic advice and reconciliation against invoice for the supplier (see also Appendix 2).

(v)   Lockbox systems can be used to speed up the collection of cheques.

(vi) Different giro systems are being linked in different countries to speed up international bank giro transfers.

(vii) Credit cards are being developed to facilitate person-to-person and person-to-company transfers.

(vii) Banks are increasingly seeking to develop new networks and links throughout the EU.

(viii) There are currency clearing systems in London whereby cheques drawn on foreign currency accounts by UK drawers may be cleared.

15 The European Parliament and Council Directive No. 97/5/EC 27 January 1997 and The European Central Bank (ECB) September 1999 report 'Improving Cross Border Retail Payment Services in the Euro Area – the Eurosystem's view'

The directive covers low-value cross-border payments (LVPs) and seeks to establish common rules aimed at reducing the price of cross-border credit transfers and at speeding up their execution. The ECB report says that 'the substantial disparities between domestic and cross-border payments ought now to be reduced, and should ultimately disappear'.

Currently there are problems in the implementation of the above ideals from:

● Different clearing cycles

● Different legal standards

● Different standards of prescribed formalities

It is anticipated that action will be taken to ensure that in future customers will know how long it will take to effect a cross-border payment and how much it will cost.

The improvement of cross-border payments systems is seen by many as being an important factor in the operation of a free market.

PART THREE

Introduction

You will recall that at the very outset it was claimed that students would find *Finance of International Trade* a stimulating and enjoyable challenge. In Part Two you applied sensible logical principles to practical aspects of foreign exchange and money transmission. No doubt you can now see that the claim made at the beginning of the book was perfectly valid.

In Part Three of this book we examine the documents used in international trade. The selection of documents is inexorably and logically linked with the shipping and payment terms agreed between exporter and importer, and this link is carefully analysed. Students should be aware that there are current developments to eventually replace many of these paper-based documents with electronic equivalents.

Finally, we consider the main methods of payment for exports, together with their attendant risks and methods of containing that risk. These methods of payment are analysed in detail purely from the point of view of the exporter and his bank. A detailed analysis of the considerations of importers and their banks will be given in Part Five.

10

TRANSPORT DOCUMENTS USED IN INTERNATIONAL TRADE

Objectives

On completion of this chapter the student should be able to:

● understand the basic meaning of open account payment terms;

● appreciate the role of the bill of lading in international trade;

● differentiate between transport documents that are documents of title and those that are not.

1 The Meaning of Open Account Payment Terms

When a buyer and seller agree to deal on open account terms, it means that the seller will despatch his goods to the buyer and will also send an invoice requesting payment. The seller loses control of the goods as soon as he despatches them. He trusts that the buyer will pay in accordance with the invoice. However, if the buyer does not pay, the seller is in a difficult position, because the goods are now in the buyer's possession.

Despite the problems from the exporter's point of view, open account terms are quite common, especially for trade within the EU. The role of documents as discussed in this chapter will relate solely to their use under open account payment terms. The changes that apply for documentary collection or documentary credit are described in Chapters 15 and 16.

2 Specimen Bill of Lading

A bill of lading normally embodies the following details, the numbers of which correspond to those on the specimen bill of lading (see Figure 1).

1 The name of the shipping company (sometimes known as the carrier).

2 The name of the shipper, who is usually the exporter, or the exporter's agent.

BILL OF LADING FOR COMBINED TRANSPORT SHIPMENT OR PORT TO PORT SHIPMENT

Shipper
Speirs and Wadley Ltd. ②
Adderley Road
Hackney
London E8 1XY
England

OVERSEAS ①
CONTAINERS
LIMITED

B/L No 45969648
Booking Ref 1234567
Shippers Ref Job 5678

DCL

Consignee
To Order ③   **SPECIMEN**

Notify Party Address
Woldal Ltd. ④
New Road
Kowloon
Hong Kong

Place of Receipt (Applicable only when this document is used as a Combined Transport Bill of Lading)
Speirs and Wadley Ltd.
Adderley Road
Hackney
London E8 1XY
England

Intended Vessel and Voy No
Cardigan Bay ⑤   0415

Intended Port of Loading
London

Place of Delivery (Applicable only when this document is used as a Combined Transport Bill of Lading)
Woldal Ltd.
New Road
Kowloon
Hong Kong

Intended Port of Discharge
Hong Kong ⑥

Marks and Nos. Container Nos ⑦	Number and kind of Packages, description of Goods	Gross Weight (kg)	Measurement (cbm)
WL 124 HONG KONG 1/5	5 Wooden Cases containing 400 ELECTRIC POWER DRILLS Model LM 425 2 Speed (900RPM/2400RPM) 425 Watt high-torque motor 2 chucks – 12.5mm and 8mm supplied with each drill ⑧	950	2.376

ABOVE PARTICULARS AS DECLARED BY SHIPPER

✱ Total No of Containers/Packages
Packages or pieces ⑨ 5

Movement
LCL. Depot/LCL. Depot

Freight and Charges (indicate whether prepaid or collect)
Origin zone transport charge   Prepaid
Origin Terminal Handling/LCL Service Charge   Prepaid
Ocean Freight   Prepaid ⑩
Destination Terminal Handling/LCL Service Charge Prepaid
Destination zone transport charge   Prepaid

ICS
CTB.I
April 78

Received by the Carrier from the Shipper in apparent good order and condition (unless otherwise noted herein) the total number or quantity of Containers or other packages or units, indicated✱, stated by the Shipper to comprise the Goods specified above for Carriage subject to all the terms hereof (INCLUDING THE TERMS ON THE REVERSE HEREOF AND THE TERMS OF THE CARRIER'S APPLICABLE TARIFF) from the Place of Receipt or the Port of Loading, whichever is applicable, to the Port of Discharge or the Place of Delivery, whichever is applicable, in accepting this Bill of Lading the Merchant expressly accepts and agrees to all its terms, conditions and exceptions whether printed stamped or written or otherwise incorporated, notwithstanding the non signing of this Bill of Lading by the Merchant When this document calls for Combined Transport it is a negotiable Combined Transport Document the terms of which are based upon the Uniform Rules for a Combined Transport Document (ICC Publication No 298)

Number of Original Bills of Lading
⑪ Two   (02)

Place and Date of Issue ⑬
London   01   08

IN WITNESS of the contract herein contained the number of originals stated opposite has been used one of which being accomplished the other(s) to be void

For the Carrier   A.J. S(ilhney) ⑫

COBRA B/L 2 9/831

Figure 1: Specimen Bill of Lading

3   The name of the consignee. If the word 'order' appears here, then the shipper (exporter) must endorse the bill of lading. When the bill of lading has been endorsed in this way, it is transferable by delivery. Once the goods arrive at their destination, they will be released to the bearer of one original bill of lading (see also item 11 below).

As an alternative to 'order', the name and address of the importer can appear as consignee. In such cases, the importer can obtain the goods, once they have arrived at their destination, by presenting an original bill of lading, together with identification.

Normally bills of lading are made out to order and endorsed by the exporter. It is unusual for the importer to be shown as consignee.

4   The notify party is the person whom the shipping company will notify on arrival of the goods. Usually this is the importer or his agent.

5   This is the name of the carrying vessel.

6   These are the two ports. In this case the goods are to be transported from Hong Kong port to the premises of Woldal Ltd in Kowloon, and thus a place of delivery is mentioned in addition to the two ports.

7   The marks and numbers will appear on the cases in which the goods are contained, so that it is quite clear which cases are covered by this bill of lading.

8   This gives a brief description of the goods.

9   This shows how many cases. In this particular shipment, the goods are packed into five cases.

10   This shows whether the freight costs have already been paid, as they have in this case, or whether payment of freight is due on arrival at the overseas destination.

11   This shows how many original bills of lading have been issued. An original bill of lading is one which is signed by the ship's master, or by an agent of the shipping company.

12   This bill of lading is an original, having been signed on behalf of the company.

13   This is the date on which the shipping company received the goods for shipment and/ or loaded the goods on board the ship.

3   How the Specimen Bill of Lading Would be Used in an Open Account Transaction

A UK exporter, Speirs and Wadley Ltd, has agreed to sell electric drills to Woldal Ltd, with Speirs and Wadley Ltd being responsible for all costs and risks until the goods are delivered to Woldal's premises in Kowloon.

The transaction will proceed as follows, assuming open account terms have been agreed:

a) Speirs and Wadley will pack the drills into cases and will arrange a contract with the shipping company to deliver the goods.

b) Speirs and Wadley will deliver the cases to Ocean Containers Ltd, who will issue two signed original bills of lading in exchange for the goods. The bills of lading will be given to Speirs and Wadley.

c) Speirs and Wadley will airmail one of the original bills of lading to Woldal Ltd, along with any other necessary documents. The other original will probably be sent by a later mail in case the first happens to go astray, although this is unnecessary if a courier is used.

d) When the goods arrive at Hong Kong port, Ocean Containers will notify Woldal, and will make arrangements to move the goods from the port, overland, to the Kowloon premises of the importer.

e) Ocean Containers will release the goods to Woldal only against an original bill of lading.

f) Woldal will then pay Speirs and Wadley in accordance with the arrangements they have made between themselves.

4 The Functions of a Bill of Lading

There are four main functions:

a) A bill of lading acts as a receipt for the goods from the shipping company to the exporter. Note the words 'received by the carrier from the shipper in apparent good order and condition' at the bottom right-hand part of the front of the specimen bill of lading.

   When there is no indication of damage to the goods, a bill of lading is said to be clean. The specimen bill is a clean bill of lading because the words 'received in apparent good order and condition' are not qualified in any way.

b) The bill of lading is evidence of the contract of carriage between the exporter and the carrier. In the specimen we can see the basic details of the journey (by the ship *Cardigan Bay* from London to Hong Kong and thence overland to Kowloon).

   The full contract details appear on the back of the bill of lading. A detailed knowledge of these conditions is not required for the purpose of this syllabus.

c) A bill of lading is a quasi-negotiable document. Any transferee for value who takes possession of an endorsed bill of lading obtains a good title to it, provided the transferor had a good title in the first place.

d) A bill of lading acts as a document of title for goods being shipped overseas. The goods will be released from the overseas port only against production of one of the original bills of lading.

Original bills of lading are usually issued in sets of two or three (the number of originals will be indicated on the bill of lading).

Because any one original bill of lading will enable the possessor to obtain the goods, possession of a complete set is required before control of the goods is assured. Shipping companies often issue unsigned copies of the bill of lading for record purposes. These unsigned copies are not documents of title.

5   The Different Types of Bill of Lading

There are many different types of bill of lading, but the main ones we need to consider are:

a)   Combined Transport Bills of Lading and Similar Documents

A combined transport bill of lading may evidence that goods have been collected from a named inland place and have been despatched to a port or inland container depot in the country of import.

Depending on the terms of the sales contract (known as Incoterms and explained in Chapter 12), the importer may have to make separate arrangements to have the goods collected from the port or inland container depot in his country and delivered to his factory or warehouse.

A through bill of lading is a similar document which may evidence despatch of goods to a named destination, for example the importer's warehouse. Strictly speaking, where the two parties agree that goods will be sent at the expense of the seller to the buyer's own premises, a through bill of lading should be used if any part of the journey is covered by a sea voyage.

In practice, combined transport documents are sometimes used in place of a through bill of lading, as can be seen from the Speirs and Wadley combined transport bill of lading (Figure 1). In this document, it appears that the delivery point is the warehouse of Woldal Ltd.

Finally, it must be noted that when we come to examine documentary credits, the words 'multi modal transport documents' may be used in certain circumstances.

b)   Transhipment Bills of Lading

These are used when the goods have to be transferred from one ship to another at a named transhipment port. Once again, the carrier has full responsibility for the whole journey, and these documents are usually considered to be documents of title if the appropriate **negotiable** wording appears.

c)   Container Bills of Lading

When goods are packed in containers, shipping companies issue bills of lading, which simply act as a receipt for a container. Container bills of lading can be issued to cover goods being transported on a traditional port-to-port basis, or they can cover transport from an inland container depot in the exporter's country to an inland container depot in the importer's country.

Palletized cargoes, and cargoes contained on **lash** barges which are loaded onto larger vessels, qualify for the issue of container bills of lading.

Once again the shipping company is responsible for the whole journey, and these bills of lading are considered to be documents of title, provided they contain the appropriate **negotiable** wording.

d)   Marine Bills of Lading or Conventional Ocean Bills of Lading

These bills of lading are issued when the goods are being transported from one port to another by ship.

e)   Short Form Bill of Lading

These bills of lading do not contain the full details of the contract of carriage on the back. However, they fulfil all the other functions of bills of lading and, in particular, they are considered to be documents of title.

f)   Liner Bills of Lading

These documents fulfil all the normal functions of a bill of lading, including that of document of title. The liner bill of lading indicates that goods are being transported on a ship that travels on a scheduled route and has a reserved berth at destination; thus the exporter can reasonably assume that his goods will reach the buyer's country by a set date.

An alternative name for these documents is 'bill of lading (liner)'.

g)   Charter Party Bill of Lading

A charter party bill of lading is issued by the hirer of a ship to the exporter. The terms of the bill of lading are subject to the contract of hire between the ship's owner and the hirer. Such bills are usually marked **subject to charter party.**

Because of the legal complexity involved, charter party bills of lading are not usually considered to be documents of title.

6   Sea Waybills

A sea waybill (sometimes known as a ship's waybill) is a transport document that can be issued by the shipping company as an alternative to bills of lading.

The functions of a waybill are similar to those of a bill of lading, except that a waybill is not negotiable and it is not a document of title. On arrival at their destination, the goods will be released by the shipping company to the named consignee against identification.

When exporters agree to sell on open account terms, it follows that the exporter should ask the shipping company for sea waybills rather than for bills of lading.

The objective with open account is for the goods to reach the importer with the minimum formality, and waybills can meet that objective. As soon as the goods reach their destination, the shipping company will notify the consignee, who will be the importer. The importer can then collect the goods, without the need to produce the waybill.

If bills of lading go astray, there are problems for the importer in collecting the goods, whereas it is immaterial to the importer whether or not he has possession of a waybill.

Sea waybills are very similar in scope to air waybills, a specimen of which we will examine at 10.7.

7 Specimen Air Waybill (also Known as an 'Air Consignment Note')

Air waybills are issued by airlines when goods are sent by air freight. There is no such thing as a bill of lading with air transport and the only transport document which can be issued is an air waybill.

Examination of the Air Waybill

The numbers correspond to those on the specimen air waybill (Figure 2).

1   This shows the names and addresses of the exporter (shipper), importer (consignee) and the carrier, Oriental Air. The words **not negotiable** indicate that this is not a document of title.

    In this particular example, the airline will notify the consignee, Woldal Ltd, when the goods arrive. Woldal will then be able to collect the goods without the need to produce this waybill.

2   This shows the names of the airports of departure and destination together with details of any special route.

3   This shows the declared value for customs purposes. A detailed knowledge of customs procedures is not required for this syllabus.

4   These marks fulfil the same function as the shipping marks on a bill of lading. The marks will appear on all the cases and on all other documents relating to this transaction.

5   This shows details of the freight charge.

6   This gives a brief description of the goods.

7   This shows whether freight is pre-paid, or whether it is payable at the destination.

8   The exporter or his agent signs here to confirm the certification shown above.

SPECIMEN

Shippers Name and Address		Not negotiable
Speirs and Wadley Ltd. Adderley Road Hackney London E8 1XY England ①		**Air Waybill*** (Air Consignment note) Issued by **ORIENT AIR** ①

Copies 1 2 and 3 of this Air Waybill are originals and have the same validity

Consignee's Name and Address	Consignee's account Number
Philmen Int. Longtown, California. ①	

It is agreed that the goods described herein are accepted in apparent good order and condition (except as noted) for carriage SUBJECT TO THE CONDITIONS OF CONTRACT ON THE REVERSE HEREOF THE SHIPPER'S ATTENTION IS DRAWN TO THE NOTICE CONCERNING CARRIER'S LIMITATION OF LIABILITY Shipper may increase such limitation of liability by declaring a higher value for carriage and paying a supplement charge if required Carrier is not liable for the goods until they are received at its town terminal or airport office

Issuing Carrier's Agent Name and City	Accounting Information
Brunswick Air London Airport, Gatwick	

Agent's IATA Code	Account No
93-5-2221	SW 123456

Airport of Departure (Addr of First Carrier) and requested Routing

Gatwick ②

to	By First Carrier		to	by	to	by	Currency	WT/VAL	Other	Declared Value for Carriage	Declared Value for Customs
							US$	PPD COLL	PPD COLL	N.V.D	N.V.D ③

Airport of Destination	Flight Date	Flight Date	Amount of Insurance	INSURANCE If shipper requests insurance in accordance with conditions on reverse hereof, indicate amount to be insured in figures in box marked amount of insurance
LONGTOWN ②	1-8-1986.		$8135	

Handling Information
5 cases
WL ④
124
LONGTOWN

No of Pieces RCP	Gross Weight	kg lb	Rate Class Commodity Item No	Chargeable Weight	Rate Charge	Total	Nature and Quantity of Goods (incl Dimensions or Volume) ⑥
5	950	k	4401	1000kg	0.80c ⑤	800.00	5 Wooden Cases containing 400 ELECTRIC POWER DRILLS Model LM 425 2 Speed (900RPM/2400RPM) 425 Watt high-torque motor 2 chucks – 12.5mm and 8mm supplied with each drill
5	950						

Prepaid	Weight Charge	Collect	Other Charges
800.00 ⑦			
	Valuation Charge		
	Tax		

Total other Charges Due Agent	
0.75	

Shipper certifies that the particulars on the face hereof are correct and that insofar as any part of the consignment contains restricted articles, such part is properly described by name and is in proper condition for carriage by air according to the International Air Transport Association's Restricted Articles Regulations

Total other Charges Due Carrier	
2.00	

M.J. Elly P.P. Brunswick Air ⑧

Signature of Shipper or his Agent

Total prepaid	Total collect
802.75	
Currency Conversion Rates	cc charges in Dest Currency

	1.8.	LGW ⑨	*M.J. Elly* ⑩ p.p. Brunswick Air
Executed on	(Date)		Signature of Issuing Carrier or its Agent

For Carriers Use only at Destination	Charges at Destination	Total collect Charges

ORIGINAL 3 (FOR SHIPPER)

Figure 2: Specimen Air Waybill

9   This shows the date on which the airline took custody of the goods.

10   This is the signature on behalf of the carrier.

8   Other Transport Documents

When goods are sent by rail or road haulage, the transport documents will be rail or road consignment notes, or truck/carrier receipts. These are not documents of title, and goods are released to the consignee (importer) on application and identification.

When goods are sent by post, the document evidencing postage is a parcel post receipt.

All forms of waybill/consignment note/parcel post receipt fulfil two of the functions of a bill of lading. They act as a receipt for the goods by the carrier, and give some evidence of the contract of carriage. However, these documents are not negotiable and are not documents of title. Usually the words **not negotiable** will appear on these documents to indicate that they are not documents of title, but that goods will be released to the named consignee.

11

DOCUMENTS OTHER THAN TRANSPORT DOCUMENTS

Objectives

On completion of this chapter the student should be able to:

● appreciate the important features of invoices;

● describe the various types of invoice that can be required in international trade;

● appreciate the open cover method of insurance of goods and understand the significance of the insurance certificate in this respect;

● understand the significance of the standard clauses of the Institute of London Underwriters;

● appreciate the importance of certificates of origin;

● be aware of other documents that may be encountered in overseas trade.

1   Specimen Commercial Invoice

A commercial invoice gives details of the goods, details of the payment and delivery terms, and a detailed breakdown of the monetary amount due. Invoices are prepared by the seller.

If we study the specimen document (Figure 1), we can see the main details that appear on invoices. The numbers correspond to those on the document:

1   Name and address of the exporter.

2   Name and address of the importer.

3   Reference number, tax point and place and date of issue.

4   Terms of delivery (sometimes called Incoterms, sometimes called shipment terms). These terms are discussed fully in Chapter 12.

5   Shipping marks. Note how these tie up with the marks on the specimen bill of lading and on the specimen air waybill.

SPECIMEN

INVOICE FACTURE RECHNUNG
         FACTURA FACTUUR

Seller (Name, Address, VAT Reg No)		C.C.C.N No
Speirs and Wadley Ltd ❶ Adderley Road Hackney London E8 1XY England		8505

Invoice No. and Date (Tax Point)	Seller's Reference
247 11 Aug ❸	Job No. 5678

Buyer's Reference	
124	

Consignee	Buyer (if not Consignee)
Woldal Ltd New Road Kowloon ❷ Hong Kong	

Country of Origin of Goods	Country of Destination
EEC United Kingdom	Hong Kong

Terms of Delivery and Payment
CIP Kowloon Hong Kong ❹

Vessel/Aircraft etc	Port of Loading
Cardigan Bay	London

Port of Discharge	
Hong Kong	

Marks and Numbers; Numbers and Kind of Packages, Description of Goods	Quantity	◉	Amount (State Currency)
WL ❺ 124 HONG KONG 1/5 ❻ 5 Wooden Cases containing 400 ELECTRIC POWER DRILLS ❼ Model LM 425 2 Speed (900RPM/2400RPM) 425 Watt high-torque motor 2 chucks - 12.5mm and 8mm supplied with each drill	400 ❾	£10.27	£4108

❿ TOTAL
£4108.00 Stg

Gross Weight (kg)	Cube (m³)
950	2.376

Freight £96.00 ❽
Insurance £12.00

Name of Signatory
J McDonald Chief Clerk

VAT Reg No. 241 8235 77

Place and Date of Issue
London 11 Aug ❸

Signature
⓫

It is hereby certified that this invoice shows the actual price of the goods described, that no other invoice has been or will be issued, and that all particulars are true and correct

380-1

Figure 1: Specimen Commercial Invoice

6 and 7

Description of goods.

8   Breakdown of the cost of freight and insurance. It is not always necessary for the seller to supply this information.

9   Quantity of goods, in this case 400 electric power drills.

10   Total amount payable by the importer.

11   Signature of the exporter, although signature is not strictly essential.

Note
For exports to other EU countries, the invoice must show the VAT number of the buyer to enable the exporter's goods to qualify for zero rating as regards VAT. This formality is unnecessary for exports outside the EU.

2   Other Types of Invoice

a)   Pro Forma Invoice

A pro forma invoice is very similar to a commercial invoice, except that it will not include any shipping marks, and it will be clearly stamped **pro forma**.

A commercial invoice is a claim for payment in connection with goods already shipped, whereas a pro forma invoice is an invitation to buy which is sent to a potential buyer. Once a definite order has been placed and once the goods have been shipped, an ordinary commercial invoice will be issued.

In some overseas countries there are exchange controls that restrict the remittance of funds abroad unless the Central Bank has given approval. Often a pro forma invoice is required by the Central Bank before approval can be given to pay for imports.

b)   Consular Invoice

This is required by some importing countries for customs purposes. The forms can be obtained from the embassy or the consulate of the importer's country. The exporter completes the details on the form and the document is then authenticated by the consulate of the importer. This consulate is located in the exporter's country.

The purpose of consular invoices is to certify that the exporter is not **dumping** goods at artificially low prices. Their other function is to provide information that forms the basis of the import duty to be paid on the goods.

Not all importing countries require production of consular invoices. However, those countries that do require such invoices almost always charge a fee for certification. When a consular invoice is not available, the consulate will authenticate the exporter's own invoice. This is known as a 'legalized invoice'.

3   Insurance of Goods

It is a matter for negotiation between the exporter and the importer as to who is responsible for insuring the goods during their journey from the exporter's premises to the importer's premises. In some transactions, it may be agreed that the seller will insure the whole journey and in others the onus may be on the buyer. It is also possible for the agreement to say that the seller must cover part of the journey, and the buyer must arrange cover for the rest. (The precise details of who does what are set out in **Incoterms**, covered in Chapter 12 of this book.)

For the moment, let us consider the position of an exporter who is responsible for the insurance of goods.

When an exporter sells goods on a regular basis, he will normally arrange an open policy of insurance to cover all his exports during a specific period. This provides insurance cover at all times within agreed terms and conditions. Each time a shipment is made, the exporter declares the details and pay a premium to the insurer. A certificate of insurance is then issued by the exporter, who sends one copy to the insurance company for its records.

The benefit of the open cover system is that it avoids the need to negotiate insurance terms each time a shipment is made, and it avoids the necessity of issuing a separate policy for each individual shipment.

If an exporter sells goods on a one-off basis, he will negotiate terms with the insurers and an insurance policy will be issued.

In the UK and in many other countries, an insured person must have a policy before he can take legal action against an insurer. A certificate alone is insufficient evidence on which to base a legal action. This legal problem is important only if the buyer needs to go to court because the insurance company has challenged a claim.

4   The Risks Covered by an Insurance Policy

The insurance cover is often based on the standard clauses of the Institute of London Underwriters. A detailed knowledge of these standard clauses is not required for this syllabus. However, exam questions sometimes mention the standard clauses in connection with risks.

There are three main standard clauses of the Institute of London Underwriters that refer to risk. Clause A begins:

This clause covers all risk of loss or damage to the subject matter below except as provided in clauses 4, 5, 6 and 7 below.

Clause A provides the fullest available cover against risks, and students should not be misled into believing that the **except** clause is detrimental. Buyers and sellers are generally satisfied that Institute clause A is perfectly acceptable cover against all risks.

Institute cargo clauses B and C also cover risks, but the extent of cover they provide is less than that provided by clause A.

5   Specimen Insurance Certificate

This insurance document (Figure 2) has been issued in connection with the Speirs and Wadley transaction (see 10.3). We have already examined various transport and invoice documents in connection with this sale.

Insurance documents usually show the following details, the numbers of which correspond to those on the document:

1   The name and signature of the insurer.

2   The name of the exporter (Speirs and Wadley, in this case).

3   The risks covered. As you can see, this information consists merely of a list of standard clauses that apply.

4   The sum insured. Normally this is expressed in the same currency as that of the invoice, and is normally for the invoice value plus 10%. The 10% is to cover an element of profit the importer would have made and any associated costs.

5   The description of the goods.

6   The place where claims are payable together with the details of the agent to whom claims are to be directed.

7   The signature of the exporter, which is required to validate the certificate. (The certificate forms are usually pre-signed by the insurer. The exporter must complete the details and then sign.)

8   The date of issue. This date should be the same as, or earlier than, the date on the transport document. If the date on the insurance document is later, indications are that the goods have been uninsured for a time.

6   Certificate of Origin

Some countries insist on certificates of origin before they will allow goods into the country. The exporter inserts the relevant details, and the form has then to be authenticated by an independent body, such as a Chamber of Commerce. The shipping marks on the certificate of origin should tie up with those on other documents such as the invoice or bill of lading.

ORIGINAL

(6) Lloyd's Agent at **Hong Kong**
is authorised to adjust and settle on behalf
of the Underwriters, and to purchase on
behalf of the Corporation of Lloyd's in
accordance with Lloyd's Standing
Regulations for the Settlement of Claims
Abroad any claim which may arise on this
Certificate.

(1) **LLOYD'S**

Exporters
Reference

THIS CERTIFICATE
REQUIRES ENDORSEMENT

Job No. 5678

SPECIMEN

Certificate of Insurance No. C 8700/**100051**

This is to Certify that there has been deposited with the Committee of Lloyd's an Open Cover effected by *Barclays Insurance Brokers International Limited* of Lloyd's, acting on behalf of *Speirs and Wadley Limited* with Underwriters at Lloyd's, dated the *First* day of *January, 19...*, and that the said Underwriters have undertaken to issue to *Barclays Insurance Brokers International Limited* Policy/Policies of Marine Insurance at Lloyd's to cover, up to *£100,000* in all by any one steamer or sending by air and/or road and/or rail and/or conveyance *Power Drills, other Interest held covered,* to be shipped on or before the *Thirty-first* day of *December 19...,* from any port or ports, place or places in *the United Kingdom* to any port or ports, place or places in *the World, other voyages held covered* and that *Speirs and Wadley Limited* are entitled to declare against the said Open Cover the shipments attaching thereto. (2)

(1)
for the Committee of Lloyd's

Conveyance	From	
Cardigan Bay	**London**	
Via/to	**To**	**INSURED VALUE/Currency**
Hong Kong	**Kowloon, H. K.**	**£4520 Stg.** (4)

Marks and Number

**WL
124
HONG KONG
1/5**

Interest

5 Wooden Cases
containing
400 ELECTRIC
POWER DRILLS
Model LM 425
2 Speed (900RPM/2400RPM)
425 Watt high-torque motor
2 chucks – 12.5mm and
8mm supplied with each drill (5)

(3) We hereby declare for Insurance under the said Cover interest as specified above so valued subject to the terms of the Standard Form of Lloyd's Marine Policy providing for the settlement of claims abroad and to the special conditions stated below and on the back hereof.

Institute Cargo Clauses (A) (1 1 82) or Institute Cargo Clauses (Air) excluding sendings by post) (1 1 82) as applicable
Institute War Clauses (Cargo) (1 1 82) or Institute War Clauses (Air Cargo) (excluding sending by Post) (1 1 82) or Institute War Clauses (sendings by Post) (1 1 82) as applicable
Institute Strikes Clauses (Cargo) (1 1 82) or Institute Strikes Clauses (Air Cargo) (1 1 82) as applicable
General Average and Salvage Contribution payable in full irrespective of insured or contributing values

Underwriters agree losses, if any, shall be payable to the order of Speirs and Wadley Limited on surrender of this Certificate.

(6) In the event of loss or damage which may result in a claim under this Insurance, immediate notice should be given to the Lloyd's Agent at the port or place where the loss or damage is discovered in order that he may examine the goods and issue a survey report.

(Survey fee is customarily paid by claimant and included in valid claim against Underwriters.)

This Certificate not valid unless the Declaration is signed by
SPEIRS AND WADLEY LIMITED
(2)

Dated at **London**   1 Aug 19 . (8)
p p *Speirs and Wadley Limited*

Signed **W. H. Mein** (7)

Brokers Barclays Insurance Brokers International Limited
India House 81/84 Leadenhall Street London EC3A 3DJ

14478/9

Figure 2: Specimen Insurance Certificate

7 Other Documents that are Found in International Trade

Black list certificate

A black list certificate will certify that the goods have no connection with certain countries, such as Israel. Many countries in the Middle East will insist on such a document before allowing goods to be imported. Recent political developments could reduce the use of such black list certificates.

Third-party inspection certificate

This is a certificate, issued by an independent third party resident in the exporter's country, stating that the goods conform to a certain standard. Sometimes the term 'clean report of findings' may be used.

Sometimes the buyer will insist that such a document is issued and this stipulation can form part of the terms of the sale contract.

Packing list/weight list

This gives details of the goods that have been packed and may also list the weight of individual items, together with a total weight.

Transport international routier (TIR) carnets

When goods travel overland across different frontiers outside the EU, a TIR carnet is necessary. This document certifies that the vehicle or container has been sealed by the customs authorities in the seller's country and ensures that no duty is payable in intermediate countries. When goods travel solely within the EU, the TIR carnet is unnecessary. TIR carnets usually accompany the goods on their journey. Bankers will not often see these documents and a detailed knowledge of their issue and procedures is unnecessary.

8 Automated Preparation of Shipping Documents

Efforts are constantly being made on a national and international basis to introduce methods of standardizing and simplifying export documentation procedures. In the UK, SITPRO (the Simpler Trade Procedures Board) is charged with carrying out this task.

The basic methods of simplification all have one common factor: All documents in a set will be prepared on the basis of one single input of information.

SITPRO has produced an aligned series of export documents whereby the whole set of documents (from invoice, bill of lading to insurance document) are produced by the single input of relevant data onto a master document. The relevant information from the master document is then transferred onto the individual documents, using overlays and masks. For example, if the SITPRO master had been used in connection with the invoice and certificate of insurance shown on the preceding pages, then the details of the quantity, unit price and amount would have been transferred from the master to the commercial invoice, but these details would not have been transferred onto the insurance certificate. Other details, such as the shipping marks, would have been transferred from the master onto both of the other documents.

An alternative method, using similar principles to those with the master document, is to use 'exportsets', which are 'self-carboned' paper formsets, which include a form for every document.

With the onset of computer technology, a single input of data into a computer can be used to provide the basic information for every document in a set. This technology will be basis of e-commerce – see Appendix 1.

Finally, SITPRO can provide a computerized system for preparing both the shipping documents and the relevant bank forms. For example, the SITPRO SPEX system can be used by exporters to prepare both shipping documents and documentary collection orders. (Documentary collections are covered in Chapter 15.)

12

INCOTERMS

Objectives

On completion of this chapter the student should be able to:

● understand the purpose of Incoterms;

● describe the obligations which the various Incoterms impose ;

● understand how Incoterms affect the documents that an exporter must produce;

● assess the cost implication of Incoterms.

1   The Purpose of Incoterms

In international trade there are likely to be three separate contracts of transport for the goods:

(a) From seller's premises to a transport operator within the seller's country.

(b) From the transport operator's premises in the seller's country to a named point in the buyer's country (e.g. a port, airport, or container depot).

(c) From the port, etc., in the buyer's country to the buyer's own premises.

It is vital to establish a clearly defined cut-off point to show where the exporter's responsibility ends and where the importer's responsibility begins. This cut-off point refers, in the main, to payment of freight and to insurance of the goods while in transit. Unless the demarcation of responsibility is clearly understood, it will be difficult for an exporter to price his goods accurately and for an importer accurately to calculate the full cost of the importation.

The problem in international trade is that different countries have different interpretations of the same contract wording, and this problem can be solved only by creating a set of internationally agreed terms.

The purpose of Incoterms is to provide such a set of standardized terms which mean exactly the same to both parties and which will be interpreted in exactly the same way by courts in every country.

Incoterms were drafted by the International Chamber of Commerce (ICC) and full details can be found in their publication number 560, which is entitled *Incoterms 2000*.

Incoterms are not incorporated into national or international law, but they can be made binding on both buyer and seller, provided the sales contract specifies that a particular Incoterm will apply.

Note

In the context of the examination, the words *shipment terms* or *terms of delivery* could be substituted for the word *Incoterms*. For exam purposes all these words and phrases are synonymous.

2   The 13 Incoterms

There are 13 different Incoterms, and each term sets out the obligations of the seller/exporter. It is not necessary to memorize the 13 terms, but it is necessary to be able to work out their implications, should such a term appear in an exam question.

Generally speaking, if Incoterms set out the obligations of the seller, by a process of elimination, any obligation that does not appear in a particular Incoterm must be the responsibility of the buyer.

In Chapters 10 and 11, we examined various documents relating to a sale by Speirs and Wadley Ltd of Adderley Road, Hackney, to Woldal Ltd of New Road, Kowloon. Table 1 explains the implications where appropriate for both parties of the different Incoterms that could be applied to such a sale. The various Incoterms are set out in a logical order, starting with the one that imposes least obligation on Speirs and Wadley and ending with the one that imposes most obligations.

Table 1			
Incoterm	*Standard ICC Abbreviations*	*Obligations of Speirs and Wadley Ltd (Exporter)*	*Responsibilities of Woldal Ltd (Importer)*
Ex Works (named place)	EXW	Make the goods available for collection from Adderley Road, Hackney by Woldal Ltd. Once collected by Woldal, all responsibility of Spiers and Wadley is ended. A commercial invoice or equivalent electronic message will be provided for Woldal. Goods will be suitably packaged unless it is the norm for the goods involved to be delivered unpacked.	Take delivery from Adderley Road. Make all arrangements at own cost to take goods to own premises. It is in Woldal's interests to arrange appropriate insurance to cover this journey. The obtaining of relevant export and/or import licences and also the completion of any customs formalities and payments for the export of the goods is the responsibility of Woldal.

Table 1 (continued)

Incoterm	Standard ICC Abbreviations	Obligations of Speirs and Wadley Ltd (Exporter)	Responsibilities of Woldal Ltd (Importer)
Free Carrier (named place) e.g. FCA Hackney Container Depot	FCA	Make the unloaded goods available to Hackney Containers at their Inland Container Depot on the exporter's means of transport. Note: If the goods were to have been made available at the exporter's premises, delivery would be incomplete until the goods had been loaded on the carrier's own transport. Advise delivery of the goods at Hackney Containers to Woldal. Complete export and customs requirements including obtaining any export licence and paying any costs, duties and taxes. Supply buyer with commercial invoice or its equivalent electronic message together with proof of delivery to Hackney Containers, e.g. multimodal transport document. Goods will be suitably packaged unless it is the norm for the goods involved to be delivered unpacked	Make all arrangements at own cost and risk to cover transport of goods to own premises from Hackney Containers Inland Container Depot. It is advisable to arrange appropriate insurance. Woldal should obtain any import licence and perform any customs requirements necessary for the import of the goods, including paying all costs, duties and taxes.

Table 1 (continued)

Incoterm	Standard ICC Abbreviations	Obligations of Speirs and Wadley Ltd (Exporter)	Responsibilities of Woldal Ltd (Importer)
Free Alongside Ship (named port of shipment) e.g. London	FAS	Complete export and customs requirements including obtaining any export licence and paying any costs, duties and taxes. Supply buyer with commercial invoice or its equivalent electronic message together with proof of delivery, e.g. transport document. Deliver goods to the quayside alongside the nominated vessel at the Port of London after which the exporter's liability basically ends. Goods will be suitably packaged unless it is the norm for the goods involved to be delivered unpacked.	Make arrangements with a shipping company for transport of goods by sea to Hong Kong. Notify Speirs and Wadley of the day and time that delivery is required at the Port of London and the name of the nominated vessel. Woldal is responsible for all risks from the quayside in London to the delivery of the goods to their final destination. It is therefore advisable to arrange appropriate insurance. Woldal should obtain any import licence and perform any customs requirements necessary for the import of the goods, including meeting all costs involved, duties and taxes.
Free On Board (named port of shipment) e.g. London	FOB	As for FAS but Speirs and Wadley's delivery liability does not end until the goods have crossed the ship's rail and have been loaded on board a named ship at London.	As for FAS, but with the exception of not being responsible for the goods until they have crossed the ship's rail in the Port of London.

Table 1 (continued)

Incoterm	Standard ICC Abbreviations	Obligations of Speirs and Wadley Ltd (Exporter)	Responsibilities of Woldal Ltd (Importer)
Cost and Freight (named port of destination) e.g. Hong Kong	CFR	Arrange and pay for transport of goods to Hong Kong port. Loading and unloading costs should be met where they form part of the charge for carriage. Complete export and customs requirements including obtaining any export licence and paying any costs, duties and taxes. Advise Woldal of delivery of the goods on board the carrying vessel and also details of the voyage. Supply Woldal with a commercial invoice or its electronic equivalent together with the relevant transport document, e.g. bill of lading. Goods will be suitably packaged unless it is the norm for the goods involved to be delivered unpacked. Speirs and Wadley are free of liability (for insurance purposes) once the goods have crossed the ship's rail in Hong Kong port.	Woldal should obtain any import licence and perform any customs requirements necessary for the import of the goods, including meeting all costs involved, duties and taxes. It is in Woldal's interests to arrange and pay for insurance of the goods from when they cross the ship's rail in the UK port. If unloading costs are not covered by charge for carriage, Woldal must also pay these.
Cost, Insurance and Freight (named port of destination) e.g. Hong Kong	CIF	As for CFR, but in addition Speirs and Wadley must insure the goods as far as the port of Hong Kong and supply the buyer with evidence of this, e.g. the insurance policy.	As for CFR, but insurance risk only falls on Woldal once the goods have crossed the ship's rail at Hong Kong.

Table 1 (continued)

Incoterm	Standard ICC Abbreviations	Obligations of Speirs and Wadley Ltd (Exporter)	Responsibilities of Woldal Ltd (Importer)
Carriage Paid To (named place of destination)	CPT	Similar to CFR, except that Speirs and Wadley must arrange and pay for transport to the named place of destination, which could be an inland container depot in Hong Kong as opposed to a port. It must advise Woldal of the name and address of the UK carrier into whose custody the goods have been given, so that Woldal can arrange insurance. Complete export and customs requirements including obtaining any export licence and paying any costs, duties and taxes. Supply buyer with commercial invoice or its equivalent electronic message together with a relevant transport document. Goods will be suitably packaged unless it is the norm for the goods involved to be delivered unpacked.	Woldal should obtain any import licence and perform any customs requirements necessary for the import of the goods, including meeting all costs involved, duties and taxes. It is in Woldal's interests to arrange and pay insurance for the goods from when they are delivered into the custody of the carrier in the UK. If unloading costs at place of destination are not covered by the charge for carriage, Woldal must pay them. Also it must pay all costs of transport from Kowloon Freight Yard to its own premises.
Carriage and Insurance Paid To (named place of destination)	CIP	Similar to CPT except that Speirs and Wadley must pay insurance charges during the carriage. The relevant insurance policy or document must be supplied to Woldal.	Similar to CPT except that Woldal does not have to arrange and pay insurance charges, which are met by Speirs and Wadley.

Table 1 (continued)

Incoterm	Standard ICC Abbreviations	Obligations of Speirs and Wadley Ltd (Exporter)	Responsibilities of Woldal Ltd (Importer)
Delivered at Frontier (named place)	DAF	This term is normally used when goods are in transit overland across a continent. Arrange and pay for transport of goods to a named point on the frontier of a country which may be the buyer's country but not necessarily so. It is in the interests of the exporter to insure the goods for the journey to the named place. Sufficient notice should be given to Woldal of dispatch of the goods so that the latter can make arrangements to take delivery of them. Supply a commercial invoice or its electronic equivalent together with a relevant transport document or delivery order to Woldal. Arrange issue of any export licence and complete customs formalities (including payment of all costs, duties and taxes). Goods will be suitably packaged unless it is the norm for the goods involved to be delivered unpacked.	Woldal should obtain any import licence and perform any customs requirements necessary for the import of the goods, including meeting all costs involved, duties and taxes. All costs and risks from the frontier point are the buyer's responsibility, including the costs of unloading the goods from the arrival means of transport at the frontier in order to take delivery .

Table 1 (continued)

Incoterm	Standard ICC Abbreviations	Obligations of Speirs and Wadley Ltd (Exporter)	Responsibilities of Woldal Ltd (Importer)
Delivered Ex Ship (named port of destination)	DES	Similar to CIF except that exporter's liability does not cease until the goods have been placed at the disposal of the buyer on board a vessel at the named port of destination. Theoretically, the exporter need not insure the goods but, in practice, the exporter would be wise to do so.	Similar to CIF. Importer's liability exists from the time when goods are placed at its disposal in the named port of destination.
Delivered Ex Quay (named port of destination)	DEQ	Deliver the goods on the quay or wharf at the named port of destination and pay unloading costs. Supply Woldal with commercial invoice or its electronic equivalent and transport document or delivery order. Arrange any export licence and complete export customs requirements, including payment of costs, duties and taxes. Arrange and pay for contract of carriage to the named port of destination. Advise Woldal of the expected time of arrival of the vessel carrying the goods so that arrangements can be made to take delivery. Theoretically, the exporter need not insure the goods on their voyage. However, in view of the exporter's liability for the goods, such action would be unwise. Goods will be suitably packaged unless it is the norm for the goods involved to be delivered unpacked.	Woldal should obtain any import licence and perform any customs requirements necessary for the import of the goods, including meeting all costs involved, duties and taxes. Accept delivery of goods at named port of destination. Importer liable for goods and costs from the time the goods are placed at its disposal on the quay or wharf.

Table 1 (Continued)

Incoterm	Standard ICC Abbreviations	Obligations of Speirs and Wadley Ltd (Exporter)	Responsibilities of Woldal Ltd (Importer)
Delivered Duty Unpaid (named place of destination)	DDU	Deliver the goods unloaded to the named place in the importing country and bear costs and risks involved in carrying the goods to the named place of destination. Advise the buyer of dispatch in sufficient time so that the buyer can make arrangements to take delivery of the goods. Arrange any export licence and complete export customs requirements including payment of costs, duties and taxes. Supply a commercial invoice or its electronic equivalent together with a relevant transport document or delivery order to Woldal. Goods will be suitably packaged unless it is the norm for the goods involved to be delivered unpacked.	Woldal should obtain any import licence and perform any customs requirements necessary for the import of the goods, including meeting all costs involved, duties and taxes. Woldal must take delivery of goods at named place of destination and is liable for all risks from then on.
Delivered Duty Paid (named place of destination)	DDP	Similar to DDU, except that the exporter is responsible for all import requirements and payments in addition.	Similar to DDU, except that the importer is not responsible for all import requirements and payments.

3 How Incoterms Affect the Documents that Exporters must Produce

One function of all documents in overseas trade is to act as proof that an exporter has fulfilled his obligations under a commercial sales contract. Since the Incoterm in the sales contract will determine where the exporter's obligations end, proof of fulfilment of the commercial obligations of the exporter will depend on whether the documents conform to the relevant Incoterm.

Examples of the documents that meet the requirements of the major Incoterms are set out in Table 2. Specific examples from the Speirs Wadley/Woldal sale will be given.

Table 2

Incoterm	Relevant transport document to be produced by the exporter Speirs and Wadley Ltd. covering overseas part of the journey	Relevant insurance document to be produced by the exporter Speirs and Wadley Ltd. covering overseas part of the journey
Ex Works (named place)	None. All that is required is a receipt from Woldal or their agents for the goods	None
Free Carrier (named place) e.g. FCA Hackney Container Depot	Receipt from Hackney Container Depot for the goods. Normally this would be a container bill of lading or a through bill of lading marked 'freight payable at destination'.	None
Free Carrier (named place) e.g. FCA Gatwick Airport	Air waybill showing Woldal as consignee, marked 'freight payable at destination'. The details of the flight must conform to those specified by Woldal. (If goods are sent by rail or road a rail consignment note or an international consignment note may be used showing the goods consigned to Woldal, marked 'freight payable at destination'.)	None

Table 2 (Continued)

Incoterm	Relevant transport document to be produced by the exporter Speirs and Wadley Ltd. covering overseas part of the journey	Relevant insurance document to be produced by the exporter Speirs and Wadley Ltd. covering overseas part of the journey
Free Alongside Ship (named port of shipment) e.g. FAS London	Clean bill of lading marked 'received for shipment' and 'freight payable at destination'. Details of the shipping line to conform to those stipulated by the buyer, and the port to be shown as London.	None
Free on Board (named port of shipment) e.g. FOB London	Clean bill of lading marked 'shipped on board' and 'freight payable at destination'. Details of the ship or shipping line to conform to the details stipulated by Woldal (e.g. the port must be shown as London).	None
Cost and Freight (named port of destination) e.g. CFR Hong Kong	Clean bill of lading marked 'shipped on board' and 'freight paid'. The destination of the ship must be Hong Kong.	None
Cost, Insurance and Freight (named port of destination) e.g. CIF Hong Kong	Same as for CFR.	Insurance policy or certificate covering journey from UK port to Hong Kong port. The date of the insurance document must be on or before the date of the bill of lading.
Carriage Paid To (named place of destination) e.g. CPT Kowloon Freight Yard	Clean container bill of lading marked 'freight paid', covering the journey to Kowloon Freight Yard.	None

Table 2 (continued)

Incoterm	Relevant transport document to be produced by the exporter Speirs and Wadley Ltd. covering overseas part of the journey	Relevant insurance document to be produced by the exporter Speirs and Wadley Ltd. covering overseas part of the journey
Carriage and Insurance Paid To (named place of destination) e.g. CIP Kowloon Freight Yard	Same as for CPT.	Insurance policy or certificate covering the journey from the exporter's country (UK) to Kowloon Freight Yard . The date of the document must be on or before the date of the bill of lading.
Delivered Ex Ship (named port of destination) e.g. DES Hong Kong	Clean bill of lading marked 'shipped on board' and 'freight paid' The destination of the ship must be Hong Kong.	None. However, the exporter will normally arrange insurance. The exporter is responsible for the goods up until the time they have been placed at the disposal of the buyer on board the vessel at the named port of destination.
Delivered Ex Quay (Duty Paid) (named port of destination) e.g. DEQ Hong Kong	Clean bill of lading marked 'freight paid'. The destination of the ship must be Hong Kong.	None. However, the exporter will normally arrange insurance for the voyage. The exporter is responsible for the goods until they have been placed at the disposal of the buyer on the quay or wharf of the named port of destination.
Delivered Duty Unpaid (named place of destination) e.g. DDU, New Road, Kowloon, HongKong	Clean combined transport document marked ' freight paid' and showing the destination as New Road, Kowloon, Hong Kong.	None. However, the exporter will normally arrange insurance of the goods for the whole journey to the named place of destination. The exporter is responsible for them up to that point.

Table 2 (continued)

Incoterm	Relevant transport document to be produced by the exporter Speirs and Wadley Ltd. covering overseas part of the journey	Relevant insurance document to be produced by the exporter Speirs and Wadley Ltd. covering overseas part of the journey
Delivered Duty Paid (named place of destination) e.g. DDP, New Road, Kowloon, HongKong	Clean combined transport document marked 'freight paid' and showing the destination as New Road, Kowloon, Hong Kong.	None. However, the exporter will normally arrange insurance of the goods for the whole journey to the named place of destination. The exporter is responsible for them up to that point.

Notes:

(a) Incoterms enable documents to be transmitted electronically using Electronic Data Interchange (EDI). Both seller and buyer must agree to such a method being used.

(b) Usually, it is assumed that transport of goods from the exporter's factory to his local port or airport, or container depot, is covered by his general insurance. Hence it would be unusual for an exporter to be asked for proof of insurance for the domestic part of the journey. For example, in the CIF Hong Kong contract, Speirs and Wadley would not normally be expected to produce documentary evidence of insurance of the goods from Adderley Road to the port of London. They would be expected to produce documentary evidence of insurance for the journey from the time the goods were taken by the shipping company (i.e. the date of the bill of lading), and this insurance should cover the goods on their journey from London to Hong Kong.

(c) CIF and CIP are the only Incoterms that stipulate responsibility for insurance. Under these the seller must arrange insurance for the buyer's benefit. Minimum cover is often arranged and if the buyer requires greater cover it must agree this with the seller. The latter will often be the case where manufactured goods are involved. Where other Incoterms are used, it is up to the parties concerned to agree who will meet the cost of insurance cover.

(d) Obviously the transport documents and the insurance document must describe the goods in the same way as they are described in the sales contract. Generally speaking, a brief general description, which is not inconsistent with the sales contract, will suffice.

(e) When bills of lading are used, the exporter must endorse them in blank if the consignee is shown as order.

(f) When waybills are used, the consignee must be the importer, or an agent of the importer who is specified in the sale contract. When bills of lading are used, the exporter must provide a full set of clean bills of lading, made out to order and blank endorsed.

(g)   When an insurance policy is required, it must be endorsed in blank by the exporter.

4   Why is Insurance for the Goods Necessary?

If goods are damaged in transit, the normal reaction would be to claim from the carrier. However, most transport contracts contain widely drawn clauses which, to a great extent, exclude liability on the part of the carrier unless damage is caused by the carrier's gross negligence. It is therefore necessary for either the buyer or the seller to take out insurance to cover the relevant parts of the journey.

One special form of insurance which an exporter can take out is transit insurance, or seller's interest insurance. While the buyer is responsible for arranging insurance for the sea voyage under an FOB or CFR contract, the exporter can, for a much reduced fee, take out his own seller's interest cover. This insures the exporter against loss or damage to the goods on the sea voyage when the importer has failed to fulfil his insurance responsibility. Naturally, the existence of such insurance is not disclosed to the buyer.

5   The Cost Implications of Incoterms for Exporters

Both exporters and importers need to know the precise financial implications of Incoterms so as to be able to set sensible prices and calculate costs.

It is unnecessary to set out the full implications of all 13 Incoterms, because the application of logic will provide the required information. A few examples from the most commonly used Incoterms will suffice. The examples refer to sales by UK-based exporters.

(a)   FAS Southampton

The exporter must take account of the following extra costs when setting his prices:

(i)   Insurance of the goods from the UK factory to Southampton.

(ii)   The cost of transport to Southampton.

(b)   FOB Southampton

In addition to the costs shown in the FAS example, the exporter must bear in mind the cost of loading the goods on board the ship.

(c)   FOB UK Port

The pricing implications of this term can be difficult to assess. The importer could specify any UK port as the port of loading. If the specified port were situated in a remote part of the country, the cost of transport and insurance could be very high.

6   The Cost Implications of Incoterms for Importers

The implications are the mirror image of those for exporters, and can be deduced by logical thought. The following examples, which relate to UK-based importers, will suffice.

(a)   FOB Antwerp

In addition to the sale contract price, the importer will have to pay all transport costs from Antwerp to his premises in the United Kingdom. The importer must pay the insurance for this journey, because any damage to the goods while in transit would be the importer's responsibility.

(b)   CIF London

In addition to the sale contract price, the importer will have to pay the cost of unloading the goods from the ship at London, and all freight costs from the port of London to his premises. The importer must also pay for insurance of the goods from the time they cross the ship's rail in London to his own premises, because any damage on this part of the journey would be the importer's responsibility.

13

An Overview of Terms of Payment

Objectives

On completion of this chapter the student should be able to:

- understand what is meant by terms of payment;

- distinguish between the four basic terms of payment;

- appreciate which terms of payment are more secure for the exporter and which terms are more favourable to the importer;

- understand the significance of the words 'terms of payment' in an examination context.

1   The Meaning of 'Terms of Payment'

Terms of payment reflect the extent to which the seller requires a guarantee of payment before he loses control of the goods. The more trustworthy and creditworthy the importer, the less will the exporter need to have payment guaranteed before he loses control of the goods.

There are four different terms of payment, which are:

a)   Open account;

b)   Documentary collection;

c)   Documentary credit;

d)   Payment in advance.

2   An Overview of the Four Terms of Payment

It is necessary for the exporter and importer to agree the terms of payment and incorporate the details in the contract of sale.

A detailed analysis of open account, documentary collection and documentary credit will appear in the remaining chapters of this part of the book. This chapter contains a brief overview of these three terms, with full coverage of payment in advance.

a)   Open Account

A brief description of this term has already been given at the beginning of this part of the book (see 10.1). However, to recap, open account terms mean that the exporter despatches his goods to the importer and invoices for payment. If there are any documents of title to the goods, these documents are sent directly to the importer.

The exporter loses all control of the goods at the time he despatches them, trusting the importer to pay.

Terms such as net cash on receipt of goods are sometimes used and they are synonymous with open account.

b)   Documentary Collection

The exporter despatches the goods, but instead of sending the documents of title directly to the importer, he uses the banking system.

The documents of title are usually sent via the following route:

a)   The exporter ships goods and obtains documents of title;

b)   The exporter sends documents of title to his bank with appropriate instructions;

c)   The exporter's bank sends documents of title to the importer's bank with the instruction that the documents can only be released:

   i)   On payment; or

   ii)   On acceptance of a bill of exchange (which for the moment we shall simply consider as being a legally binding undertaking to pay the exporter on a set or determinable future date);

d)   On payment or acceptance of the bill of exchange, the importer's bank releases the documents of title so that the importer can obtain the goods on their arrival in his country.

It can be seen that the exporter retains control over the goods under this method until either payment is made, or a legally binding undertaking to pay is given.

A full explanation of this method, including the procedures adopted when the transport documents are not documents of title, is given in Chapter 15.

c)   Documentary Credit

Briefly, a documentary credit is a guarantee of payment by the importer's bank, provided the

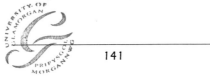

exporter presents specified documents within a stipulated period and conforms to the terms of the letter of credit.

If a documentary credit has been arranged, the exporter can despatch his goods in the knowledge that he is relying, not on the importer's integrity and creditworthiness, but on the reputation and creditworthiness of the importer's bank. Obviously, the exporter must fulfil the terms of credit if the guarantee is to be relied upon.

The procedure in brief is:

a) The exporter and importer agree on payment by documentary credit and incorporate the details in their sale contract;

b) The importer authorizes his bank to issue the documentary credit;

c) The importer's bank passes on the details to a bank in the exporter's country, which then advises the exporter of the existence of the credit;

d) The exporter ships his goods, obtains the documents required under the credit, presents these documents via the banking system, and is paid.

d)   Payment in Advance

'Payment in advance' means exactly what it says. The importer pays the exporter at some agreed stage prior to despatch of the goods.

Although full payment in advance is obviously most desirable for the exporter, he will only be able to obtain such terms when there is a seller's market, or occasionally when such terms are customary in that particular trade.

It is quite common for a sale contract to require partial payments in advance; for example the contract could stipulate, say, 20% payable on the signing of the contract with the remaining 80% payable after despatch of the goods under one of the other terms of payment.

3   The Order in which the Terms of Payment are Attractive to the Parties to a Sale

A moment's thought will show that from the exporter's point of view the order is:

most secure	-	payment in advance
then	-	documentary credit
then	-	documentary collection
least secure	-	open account.

The mirror image applies for importers:

most favourable	-	open account

then	-	documentary collection
then	-	documentary credit
least favourable	-	payment in advance.

4   Illustrative Examples

As this brief chapter serves merely to give an overview, we shall look at two illustrative examples that explain the significance of terms of payment in an examination context. A brief comment will follow immediately after each of the two questions.

Example 1

Your exporter customer has completed a sale contract with an overseas buyer, and it contains the following details:

> CIF Charleston. Payment in US $ by MT on terms. Net cash one month after receipt of goods.

Explain the possible risks to your customer in accepting the terms of payment that appear in this contract.

Comment

In this question you should describe the risks to an exporter under open account terms. You should **not** comment on MT because this is a method of settlement or a method of transfer of funds, and you should **not** comment on the exchange risk if the question simply refers to the terms of payment. The exchange risk would also apply if documentary collection or documentary credits had been selected as terms of payment.

Example 2

John Brown's Body Ltd are funeral directors. They have developed a business providing complete funeral services, including coffins, to British and American expatriates based in continental Europe, who wish to ensure that their deceased loved ones are returned to the UK or the USA for burial or cremation.

The company, which is sterling-based, has recently received orders for coffins from army units based in Germany. The terms of shipment will be either on a CIF Hamburg basis for shipments by sea, or on a CFR Frankfurt basis for air consignments. The cost of repatriation to the UK or the USA will be borne by the army groups outside the terms of the new orders.

As the customer has usually sold on an ex-works basis, a director asks you for an explanation of these terms of shipment and how they would affect the company.

You are informed that payments will be received in Deutschmarks, and that the company has no other foreign currency receipts or outgoings.

Required

Your explanation of:

i)   The terms of shipment mentioned, including the responsibilities of the contracting parties under these terms.

ii)   Any risks, other than the credit risks, that the company will incur by agreeing to accept the payments as indicated in the question.

Comment

i)   An explanation of the Incoterms ex works, CIF Hamburg and CFR Frankfurt is required, including the responsibilities of the parties;

ii)   An explanation of the exchange risk is required.

Note

Terms of payment refers to the credit risk, which is specifically excluded from this question, whereas the word **payment** refers to the fact that the sale is denominated in Deutschmarks.

In addition, the danger of damage to the goods on the journey to Germany could be mentioned along with the need to insure. Finally under CFR or CIF terms, the customer will need to ascertain the cost of transport to Germany.

14

OPEN ACCOUNT TERMS

Objectives

On completion of this chapter the student should be able to:

- appreciate the major risks that apply to exporters who sell on open account terms;

- appreciate how an exporter can reduce the risks inherent in open account terms;

- acquire an overview of the role of ECGD and NCM as insurers against bad debts on export sales.

1 Introduction

So far the book has covered matters from the point of view of both the exporter and the importer. Up to and including Chapter 20, we shall now concentrate on the subject matter **from the point of view of a UK exporter and of his bank**. Other providers of services to exporters will also be introduced where appropriate.

The position of importers and their banks as regards terms of payment will be covered from Chapter 21 onwards. Remember then that for these remaining three chapters we are looking at matters from a UK exporter's point of view.

2 The Major Risks that Apply to Exports on Open Account Terms

These risks can be classified under three main headings:

a) Buyer Risk

This is also known as the 'credit risk' and it covers the danger that the buyer may not pay for the goods because of insolvency or wilful default.

Remember that the exporter lost control of the goods at the moment he despatched them.

b)   Country Risk

The importer may be perfectly willing and able to pay, but the importer's government may introduce laws, often called exchange controls, which prevent payment from being made.

The reason for the imposition of exchange controls can be political. Alternatively, exchange controls can simply result from financial pressures, such as the Third World debt problem, which mean that the importer's country cannot afford to pay for imports.

c)   Transit Risk

Goods travel much farther in international trade than they do in a domestic deal, and therefore there is more danger of loss or damage to goods on their journey from seller to buyer.

Note
The exchange risk also applies if the exporter invoices in foreign currency, but the exchange risk will always apply in these cases, irrespective of the terms of payment between the two parties.

3   How an Exporter can Reduce the Risks under Open Account Terms

a)   Reduction of Buyer Risk

The exporter can obtain a status report on the buyer, and such reports should be updated at regular intervals. Alternatively, organizations such as the Department of Trade and Industry can supply more detailed reports on potential buyers. A favourable status report does not guarantee that the importer will pay his debts, but it does serve as a useful indication of his creditworthiness and integrity.

In addition, the exporter can insure against non-payment by the importer. See 14.4.

b)   Reduction of Country Risk

Most UK banks provide political and economic reports that comment on the situation in various overseas countries. These reports can give full details of current exchange control regulations in the overseas country, and can help the exporter to assess whether any additional restrictions are likely.

In addition, insurance can be taken out to cover loss because of newly imposed exchange controls.

c)   Reduction of Transit Risk

The obvious remedy is for appropriate insurance cover to be taken. If an Incoterm has been specified in the sale contract, it will be quite clear where the exporter's obligation ends and where the importer's obligation begins. In addition, the exporter can take out seller's interest insurance to cover himself against damage to goods if the importer has failed to insure under terms such as CFR.

Freight forwarders are firms that specialize in organizing overseas transport. Most freight forwarders are capable of arranging appropriate transport, insurance and documentation, if they are given a copy of the sale contract.

The exporter's bank can recommend suitable freight forwarders, and the bank can arrange appropriate insurance of the goods, if required.

4 Credit Insurance

Historically, credit insurance has been provided by the Export Credits Guarantee Department (ECGD), which is a government department. However, in 1991 the short-term credit insurance business arm (i.e. credit insurance for up to two years) was sold off to the Netherlands-based NCM Group, which is one of the largest providers of credit insurance in the world.

This has resulted in NCM Credit Insurance Ltd being the main provider of short-term credit insurance in the UK, although there are other notable providers, in particular, Euler Trade Indemnity. Euler Trade Indemnity provides cover against non-payment within the UK and also overseas. Insurers may be more interested in covering exports if the UK seller has a wide spread of domestic business which is also offered for cover.

ECGD still provides cover for terms in excess of two years. However, fiercer competition in the credit insurance market occurred with the arrival of the single European market, which enabled such credit insurers as HERMES from Germany and COFACE from France to increase their market base. There is also additional impact being made by other overseas companies, e.g. AIG of the USA which has opened offices in the UK.

5 NCM International Policy

The target market is exporters with an annual turnover of £5m or more who deal in cash or on credit terms of up to 180 days. In order to avail themselves of the lowest possible premiums, exporters should spread the risks over as many contracts as possible. Hence NCM are looking for exporters to cover all or most of their export turnover for at least one year and preferably for a longer period.

a) Risks Covered
● Buyer insolvency.

● The buyer's failure to pay within six months of the due date for goods accepted.

● Non-acceptance of the goods by the buyer, provided the goods conform to the contract.

Country risks including:

- Foreign government action that delays or prevents completion of the contract;

- Political, economic, legislative or administrative action outside the UK, which delays or prevents payment transfers;

- Delays in money transfer from the buyer's country;

- War, civil unrest or similar actions outside the UK that prevents completion of the contract (war between the five major powers is specifically excluded).

Export restrictions imposed after the date of the contract.

Non-renewal or cancellation of an export licence.

Where an importer is recognized by NCM as a public buyer, e.g. local or regional government. The exporter will be covered if the buyer fails to complete the contract.

b) Additional Available Cover

The policy normally covers the exporter from the date when the goods are sent to the buyer. By payment of an additional premium, cover can be provided from the date of the contract. This is known as covering pre-credit risk. It is of particular benefit to exporters who manufacture specialist one-off items that would have no other market if the underlying contract should fail.

Payment of royalties under franchising or licensing agreements.

Goods traded outside the UK, i.e. external trade.

Sales through overseas subsidiaries.

Services provided for foreign customers, e.g. maintenance contracts or professional services.

Sales carried out through overseas subsidiaries.

Sale of goods held overseas, including those exhibited at trade markets or exhibitions.

Goods invoiced in foreign currencies. NCM will also accept claims, within certain parameters, for any additional losses incurred in meeting forward exchange contract commitments (e.g. close-outs).

Where goods are sold on credit terms of more than 180 days but less than two years, or where their manufacture takes in excess of 12 months, an Extended Risk Endorsement can be added to the guarantee.

Insurance against unfair calling of bonds may be available.

c) Costs of Cover

Premiums are negotiable and tend to depend upon the spread of risks, the width of markets and the amount of cover involved. Obviously, if an exporter is negotiating business deals in a high-risk area of the world, premiums are likely to be higher than in other, more stable areas.

Costs normally include the following:

● Payment of an annual fee set according to the exporter's turnover.

● Payment of a monthly flat rate fee established according to the amount of business that is declared.

d) Amount of Cover Available

Risk Covered	Maximum % covered by NCM
Buyer insolvency	90
Buyer default	90
Non-acceptance of the goods by the buyer (provided goods conform to contract)	72*
Country risk	95

*In respect of non-acceptance of the goods by the buyer, the exporter must meet the initial 20% of the loss and NCM will meet 90% of the remaining balance, i.e. 90% of 80% = 72%.

e) Pay-out of Claims

● Buyer insolvency: immediately, provided that evidence of insolvency is furnished.

● Payment default by the buyer on goods accepted: six months after due payment date.

● Non-acceptance of the goods by the buyer: one month after resale of the goods.

● For the majority of the remainder of losses: four months after the due date.

NCM will assist the exporter in attempting to recover the debt and may be prepared to defray legal expenses incurred in the recovery action.

6   NCM Compact Policy

The NCM Compact policy is designed for expanding businesses with an annual turnover of £5m or less. It can cover both UK and overseas sales and has a fixed annual fee.

a) Risks Covered

● Buyer insolvency.

● Buyer default on payment.

Foreign government action that delays or prevents completion of a contract.

Foreign government action that delays or prevents payment.

Political action that delays money transfer from the buyer's country.

Legal statutes in the buyer's country that can release the buyer from a large proportion of his contractual payment obligations.

War or natural disasters that prevent completion of the contract.

Where an importer is recognized by NCM as a public (government-owned) buyer and fails to complete the contract.

This policy is marketed as being easy to use and enables smaller businesses to access credit assessment facilities from a database of around 6 million buyers, in addition to providing peace of mind.

7 ECGD Export Insurance Policy

In 1998 ECGD launched its Export Insurance Policy (EXIP) as a replacement for its Supplier Insurance Policy. It mainly supplies non-payment cover against commercial or political risks related to large-scale projects and the provision of capital goods and services. The EXIP is, however, flexible and, unlike its predecessor, can be a stand-alone policy specifically designed for an individual exporter's needs in addition to being used in conjunction with an ECGD Buyer Credit or Supplier Credit Financing Facility.

The EXIP covers the following risks:

a) Occurrences Outside the UK

Buyer or guarantor insolvency.

Default by the buyer or guarantor regarding payment within six months of its due date.

Default by the buyer or guarantor to meet a final judgment or award within six months of its date.

Default in payment or default in performance of the contract that prevents the supplier from carrying out his part of the contract.

Statutes introduced in the buyer's country that discharge the debt if it is paid in other than the currency of the contract.

Political or economic moves that prevent the transfer of contractual payments. This would include a general moratorium on debt repayment enforced by the buyer's government.

Any action by a foreign government that prevents the performance of the contract.

Any natural disasters, wars or civil strife that prevent the performance of the contract.

b)   Occurrences within the UK

- Non-renewal or cancellation of a supplier's export licence.

- Measures introduced after the contract date that hamper the performance of the contract.

- Withdrawal of finance by ECGD where ECGD has withdrawn cover on the buyer's country.

Additional cover is available for bonds risk. See Chapter 20.

The EXIP provides cover for 95% of the insured risk, with the exporter bearing the remaining 5%.

8   Additional ECGD Insurance Facilities

Tender to Contract Scheme

a)   Target market

Exporters who tender for contracts in foreign currency. These contracts must have a UK content of £5m or more.

b)   Risks covered

Losses incurred due to adverse exchange rate movements between the date of tender and the date of contract.

c)   Amount of cover

Cover is normally limited to between 1% and 25% of the contract price.

Should exchange rates move in the exporter's favour during the period covered, any gain must be paid to ECGD.

Cover can be arranged for tendering periods of up to nine months.

An additional facility to the normal tender to contract scheme is the Forward Exchange Supplement. It is designed for exporters who believe that they may have problems in arranging forward contracts for large sums over long time periods. If these forward contracts provide less sterling than expected, ECGD will make up the balance within the limits mentioned previously. This Forward Exchange Supplement can also be set up as a free-standing facility.

Project Participants' Insolvency Cover

a)   Target market

Members of UK consortia involved in overseas contracts valued at £20m or more.

b)   Risks covered

Where losses arise from the repercussions of the insolvency of a member of the consortium or a sub-contractor, they can be covered by this scheme. Cover can be extended to consortia, which include overseas consortia members or sub-contractors.

Overseas Investment Insurance Scheme

a)   Aim of the scheme

To encourage British investment overseas.

b)   Risks covered

Political risks for up to 15 years, including:

Expropriation, e.g. nationalization or other overseas government action to the detriment of the investor.

War or revolution.

Restrictions on remittance. This is to help investors overcome the potential problems that might arise if the transfer or return of funds to the UK is restrained or delayed.

c)   Target market

Companies carrying on business in the UK and their overseas subsidiaries. Insurance is available for new investments of equity capital in the form of cash, plant or knowledge; for loans to overseas entities where the repayment period is at least three years from the date of payment; and for some guarantees of loans that have been arranged outside the UK. The investor must apply for cover before committing himself to any investment. Cover may be arranged in some cases where there are some existing investments but this will be based on each individual case.

d)   Amounts available under the scheme

Equity investments: amount of investment plus retained profits up to a maximum of double the amount of the original investment.

Loan investments: the principal loan amount plus accrued interest.

e)   Payment of claim

Expropriation: one year following the commencement of the relevant action.

War: evidence of damage to physical assets; OR where the overseas entity has been unable to operate for one year; OR where the overseas entity has been operating, its inability to make profits for three consecutive years.

Restriction on remittance: inability for six successive months to repatriate currency.

With regard to loan investment, six months must have passed since the due date for an unpaid amount of capital or interest.

Any recoveries or compensation will be divided between the ECGD and the investor on the same basis as the loss was suffered.

9 ECGD Fixed-rate Finance Scheme (FRF)

In order to attract business, exporters sometimes have to be able to offer favourable interest rates to overseas buyers. ECGD supports this through its FRF scheme, which provides reimbursement to banks that are supplying funds at fixed rates where the actual cost of funds is greater than the fixed rate.

Commercial Interest Reference Rates (CIRRs) form the basis for this system of minimum fixed-interest rates. They are reviewed monthly. The advantage of the FRF scheme to exporters is that they can quote a firm fixed-interest rate to a potential buyer which can be maintained for up to four months pending the satisfactory completion of preliminary talks culminating in a signed agreement or contract.

15

DOCUMENTARY COLLECTIONS

Objectives

On completion of this chapter the student should be able to:

understand what is meant by bills of exchange;

appreciate the difference between sight drafts and term drafts;

describe the detailed operation of documentary collections;

appreciate the difference when air waybills make up the transport documents;

appreciate the significance of the various clauses on a collection instruction;

understand the meaning and purpose of Uniform Rules for Collections;

describe the checks which a remitting bank makes before it sends the documents abroad;

appreciate the difference between theory and practice as regards the timing of payments;

understand the risks to an exporter with documentary collections and how these risks can be reduced;

appreciate the difference in security between D/P and D/A.

1   Introduction

This introduction serves to remind you of the point made at the beginning of Chapter 14. The following chapter will consider documentary collections from the point of view of the exporter and his bank.

2   Definition of 'Bills of Exchange'

The definition of a bill of exchange can be found in the Bills of Exchange Act 1882. There are nine major aspects, which are as follows:

1   a bill of exchange is an unconditional order in writing;

2   addressed by one person (the drawer);

3   to another (the drawee);

4   signed by the drawer;

5   requiring the person to whom it is addressed (the drawee);

6   to pay;

7   on demand or at a fixed or determinable future date;

8   a certain sum in money;

9   to, or to the order of, a specified person (the payee) or to bearer. In the case of the specimen bills of exchange that follow, the drawer and payee are identical. The words our order indicate the order of Speirs and Wadley.

For convenience the above phrases are numbered to correspond to the reference numbers that appear on the specimen bills of exchange shown in Figures 1 and 2.

These specimen bills of exchange relate to an export sale by Speirs and Wadley to Woldal. Because the exporter is the person who requires payment from the importer, we can see that, in documentary collections, the exporter is the drawer and the importer is the drawee.

Please note that the word 'draft' is often substituted for 'bill of exchange'. The words are synonymous for our purposes.

3   Sight Drafts and Term Drafts

As you will have seen, the two specimen bills of exchange are identical, apart from item seven which relates to the due time for payment.

The bill that requires payment **at sight** is a sight draft or an on demand draft. The drawee, Woldal, should pay the bill as soon as it is presented, if the bill is to be honoured. Woldal will not need to sign the bill in any way. All that is required is for them to authorize payment via the banking system.

On the other draft, payment is due 90 days after sight. When the bill of exchange is presented to the drawee, the drawee should **accept** it if he wishes the bill to be honoured. Thus, Woldal would sign the bill of exchange on the front and insert the date of acceptance. Woldal would be legally bound to pay 90 days after the date of acceptance shown on the bill of exchange.

Drafts that are payable at a future date are called **term drafts**. Other descriptions which are synonymous are **tenor draft** and **usance draft**. When a term bill specifies the future date (e.g. if the specimen term draft had said on 1 January ...pay) there is no need for the drawee to accept the bill (although from the exporter's point of view it is better to have it accepted). However, when the words specify payment on a fixed period after sight, the drawee must accept the bill and insert the date of acceptance, otherwise it would be impossible to calculate the due date of payment.

SPECIMEN TERM DRAFT

£4,108

London
11 August 20

AT 90 DAYS AFTER DATE OF THIS FIRST OF EXCHANGE (SECOND OF THE SAME TENOR AND DATE BEING UNPAID) PLEASE PAY TO OUR ORDER THE SUM OF STERLING POUNDS FOUR THOUSAND ONE HUNDRED AND EIGHT ONLY FOR VALUE RECEIVED

To: Woldal Ltd
New Road
Kowloon
Hong Kong

For and on behalf of
SPEIRS AND WADLEY LTD

....
Director

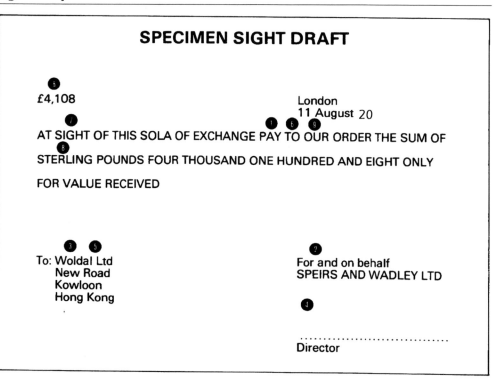

Figure 1: Specimen Term Draft

SPECIMEN SIGHT DRAFT

£4,108

London
11 August 20

AT SIGHT OF THIS SOLA OF EXCHANGE PAY TO OUR ORDER THE SUM OF STERLING POUNDS FOUR THOUSAND ONE HUNDRED AND EIGHT ONLY FOR VALUE RECEIVED

To: Woldal Ltd
New Road
Kowloon
Hong Kong

For and on behalf
SPEIRS AND WADLEY LTD

....
Director

Figure 2: Speciment Sight Draft

4   Operation of a Documentary Collection

(*Note* This example involves goods being transported by sea.)

a)   The exporter ships goods and obtains documents of title from the shipping line.

b)   The exporter, who is known as the principal, hands in the following documents to his bank (the remitting bank):

   i)   bill of exchange drawn on the importer;

   ii)   documents of title (i.e. a complete set of clean, shipped on board bills of lading, made out to order and blank endorsed), and other relevant documents (insurance policy or certificate if CIF);

   iii)   a collection instruction which contains the exporter's instructions to the remitting bank.

c)   The remitting bank completes its own collection instruction addressed to the importer's bank. This collection instruction contains the same instructions as the exporter's original collection order. This collection order is then sent to the importer's bank, along with the other documents.

d)   If the instructions are D/P (documents against payment), the importer's bank will release the documents to the importer only against payment.

   If the instructions are D/A (documents against acceptance), the importer's bank will release the documents against acceptance of the bill of exchange by the importer.

e)   If and when the bill of exchange is paid, the importer's bank sends the funds to the remitting bank for credit to the principal's account.

   The importer will require a bill of lading in order to obtain the goods from the overseas port. The bill of lading can only be obtained by payment of the bill of exchange (D/P), or by acceptance (D/A). Therefore, the importer cannot obtain the goods without paying or accepting the bill of exchange, and conversely an exporter retains control of the goods until payment or acceptance of the bill of exchange.

   When goods are sent by air freight, the airway bill could show the importer's bank as consignee. Once again, the importer must pay or accept a bill of exchange to be able to obtain the goods. Once the importer has paid or accepted the bill of exchange, the importer's bank will issue a delivery order. The delivery order is an authority, signed on behalf of the bank, authorizing the airport to release the goods to the named importer. An exporter should obtain the prior agreement of the importer and the importer's bank before he consigns goods to that bank. In practice, the importer's bank will not often agree to be named as consignee, unless its own customer is of major importance.

Notes

i)   When D/P terms are used, it is unnecessary to include a bill of exchange, because the overseas bank can release documents on payment of the invoice amount. However, sight drafts are usually included.

ii) In some overseas countries, there are heavy stamp duties on bills of exchange. In such situations it may be possible to use the banker's receipt instead of a bill of exchange to avoid these duties. The banker's receipt is used extensively in Italy and is known as a 'ricevuta bancaria'.

iii) Variations on traditional remittance methods for documentary collections.

iv) Some companies are now using on-line computerized collection instruction forms.

a)   Accelerated Bills Service Provided by UK Remitting Banks

The UK exporter completes a collection instruction, quoting from a pre-arranged series of reference numbers, but instead of submitting the collection to the remitting UK bank, the collection is sent by the exporter directly to the collecting bank abroad. A copy of the collection instruction is sent to the exporter's UK bank, or alternatively the exporter advises his UK bank by electronic means.

All subsequent correspondence is dealt with by the UK bank, and the UK bank maintains records of the position of all bills collected in this way. If the exporter is linked to his bank via a computer terminal network, the bank can advise the exporter of the position via this network.

The benefits to the exporter are:

● reduced bank charges;

● reduced processing time, which should mean quicker payment.

This method is useful when the exporter submits many collections to the same buyers over a period of time, because the UK bank can then preselect an appropriate collecting bank.

b)   Direct Collections

In some cases, exporters may simply send their collections directly to the overseas collecting bank, without involving their own UK bank in any way. The overseas bank would act as agent of the UK exporter in obtaining the proceeds. The benefits from the exporter's point of view are saving in time and saving of UK bank charges.

The drawbacks from the exporter's point of view are:

● all correspondence, including that for any follow-up action in the event of default, is made directly with the overseas bank;

● the exporter may find it difficult to trace payment of the bill proceeds without the benefit of a UK bank's reference number;

● the documents are not checked by the UK bank before being sent abroad.

5 The Collection Instruction

The specimen collection instruction (Figure 3) is a standard form of authority that enables the exporter to include specific instructions to his bank regarding the documentary collection.

The top third of the form is largely self-explanatory. Perhaps it should be stated that if the goods were sent by air, with the air waybill showing the overseas bank as consignee, the overseas bank would be shown as consignee with the importer as drawee.

You will see that specific instructions are required on the following points:

a) Release documents to the importer against payment (D/P) or against acceptance (D/A). Normally D/P will apply with sight drafts and D/A will apply with term drafts. It is, however, possible to arrange for D/P instructions to be given with term drafts and this can often arise in trade with the Far East.

b) If documents are not taken up on arrival of goods, instructions are required on whether to warehouse and insure the goods. This clause is known as a store and insure clause.

If the importer does not pay or accept the bill of exchange, he cannot obtain the goods. However, the goods will be at the docks or airport, or container depot, in the overseas country. If this clause is adopted, the overseas bank will be instructed to warehouse and insure the goods if documents are not taken up. The cost of this operation will be claimed from the exporter's bank, who will debit their customer, the principal. If the goods are warehoused and insured, they are protected, giving the exporter time to find an alternative buyer or to ship the goods back to the UK.

If waybills showing the importer as consignee are used, the **store and insure** clause will be superfluous.

c) The collection instruction will state whether bank and other charges have to be collected in addition to the face value of the bill of exchange. The exporter should complete the clause in accordance with the details agreed in the sale contract.

d) Specific instructions are required on whether or not to protest in the event of dishonour by either non-payment or non-acceptance.

If a bill of exchange is protested, a lawyer in the overseas country will undertake formal procedures whereby he asks the drawee the reason for dishonour and makes appropriate notes.

Again, it will be the overseas bank that instructs the lawyer to protest. The overseas bank will have to be reimbursed by the exporter's bank who will then debit their customer.

In some countries, the law requires a dishonoured bill of exchange to be protested within one working day, otherwise the drawer cannot sue on the bill.

e) Advice of dishonour, with reasons, should be given by airmail or cable. Cable is most desirable, but again the cost will ultimately be borne by the exporter.

Finance of International Trade

PLEASE COLLECT THE UNDERMENTIONED FOREIGN BILL AND/OR DOCUMENTS   A

Full Name and Address of Drawer/Exporter	For Bank Use Only	Date	I.S.B. Collection No.
	Drawers reference (to be quoted in all correspondence)		
	For Bank Use Only	Due Date	Correspondents Reference

Consignee - Full Name and Address	Drawee (if not Consignee) - Full Name and Address
	For Bank Use Only / Fate Dates

TO Barclays Bank PLC	Drawers Bankers Barclays Bank	Sorting Code No. 20-	Ref. No.

S.W.I.F.T. ADDRESS BARC GB22   Account No.

Subject to uniform rules for collections (1978 Revision) International Chamber of Commerce Publication No. 322.

PLEASE FORWARD DOCUMENTS ENUMERATED BELOW BY AIRMAIL. FOLLOW SPECIAL INSTRUCTIONS AND THOSE MARKED X

Bill of Exchange	Comm'l. Invoice	Cert'd./Cons. Inv.	Cert. of Origin	Ins'ce Pol./Cert.	Bill of Lading	Parcel Post Rec'pt	Air Waybill

Combined Transport Doc.	Other Documents and whereabouts of any missing Original Bill of Lading

RELEASE DOCUMENTS ON	ACCEPTANCE	PAYMENT	If unaccepted	Protest	Do Not Protest
If documents are not taken up on arrival of goods	Warehouse Goods	Do Not Warehouse	and advise reason by	Cable	Airmail
	Insure Against Fire	Do Not Insure	If unpaid	Protest	Do Not Protest
Collect ALL Charges	Yes	No	and advise reason by	Cable	Airmail
Collect Correspondent's Charges ONLY	Yes	No	Acceptance/Payment may be deferred until arrival of goods	Yes	No
Goods and carrying vessel.			After final-payment remit proceeds by	Cable	Airmail

For Bank Use Only

In case of need refer to	For Guidance	Accept their Instructions

SPECIAL INSTRUCTIONS 1. Represent on arrival of goods if not honoured on first presentation

Date of Bill of Exchange	Tenor	Amount of Collection

Bill of Exchange claused	Please apply proceeds of this collection as indicated with an 'X'	Credit us in Sterling	
		Credit our Foreign Currency Account No.	
		Apply to Forward Contract No.	

I/We agree that you shall not be liable for any loss, damage, or delay however caused which is not directly due to the negligence of your own officers and servants.

Any charges and expenses not recovered from the drawees, including any costs of protecting the merchandise, may be charged to us.

For Bank use Only	Date & Signature

371 (OC206) 1/85

Figure 3: Specimen Collection Instruction

f) When goods are transported by sea and documents go by air, it is quite common for the collection to be presented to the drawee before the arrival of the goods. If this clause is adopted, the overseas bank will be authorized to await the arrival of the goods before pressing the drawee for payment or acceptance.

g) The **case of need** referred to on the collection instruction is an agent of the exporter who is resident in the importer's country. The case of need can act in an advisory capacity or have **full powers**. The latter will allow the **case of need** to overrule the instructions contained in the collection schedule. If a case of need is named, the overseas bank will refer to him in the event of dishonour for guidance or instruction.

h) Finally, instructions as to the method of settlement are required. Obviously urgent SWIFT would be best from the exporter's point of view, but this is a more costly method than MT.

6   Uniform Rules for Collections (URC)

The URC form an internationally accepted code of practice covering documentary collections. (The rules are reproduced in Appendix 3.) URC are not incorporated in national or international law, but become binding on all parties because all bank authorities (especially the collection instruction) will state that the collection is subject to URC. URC will apply unless the collection instruction states otherwise or the laws in one of the countries concerned specifically contradict them. The rules do not extend to transactions which use EDI. The working party, which drew up the new rules, felt that there were too many legal problems for international rules to be drafted at that time. (See Appendix 1 for latest developments.) You must have a good knowledge of URC. Matters solely affecting the overseas bank and drawee are covered later.

7   Summary of the Provisions of URC

a) **Article 1** states that banks do not have to deal with collections but must advise the party, from whom they receive the collection, of their decision as soon as possible.

b) **Article 2** defines and differentiates between various terms:

   i)   Financial documents are the instruments used for the purpose of obtaining payment, e.g. cheques.

   ii) Commercial documents relate to the goods themselves, e.g. invoices, waybills.

   iii) Clean collections consist of financial documents that are not accompanied by commercial documents.

   iv) Documentary collections are commercial documents that may or may not be accompanied by financial documents.

c) **Article 3** identifies the main parties to a collection:

i) The principal, i.e. the exporter.

ii) The remitting bank. This is the bank to which the principal entrusts the collection, normally the exporter's own bank.

iii) The collecting bank. This is any bank, other than the remitting bank, which is involved with the collection. Usually, this will be a bank in the importer's country.

iv) The presenting bank. This is the collecting bank which notifies the drawee of the arrival of the collection and which requests payment or acceptance.

v) The drawee. This will normally be the importer to whom presentation will be made in accordance with the collection instruction.

The example given below will clarify the relevant positions of these parties in respect of a documentary collection:

An exporter (principal) hands in a documentary collection to his bank (Barclays – the remitting bank), drawn on an importer (drawee) in New York, USA. If the principal does not specify which collecting bank to use, Barclays will choose their New York office (collecting and presenting bank). However, if the importer banks at Chemical Bank, Barclays, New York may request Chemical Bank to attend to the actual presentation. In this latter case, Chemical Bank will be the presenting bank and Barclays the collecting bank.

d) **Article 4** mainly covers the constituent parts of a collection instruction. Additionally, it states that banks need not examine documents to ascertain instructions and can ignore any instructions from other than the party from whom the collection was received, unless the collection instruction states otherwise.

e) **Articles 5, 6, 7** and **8** discuss procedures relating to the presentation, release and creation of documents.

f) **Article 9** states that banks will act in good faith and exercise reasonable care.

g) **Article 10** excludes banks from responsibility or liability when goods are despatched direct to the address of a bank or consigned to a bank where prior permission has not been granted. Banks, in such circumstances, need not accept delivery of the goods.

h) **Article 12** obliges bank recipients of a collection instruction to advise the sender of this instruction of any documents that are not as listed or are not received without delay.

i) **Articles 16** to **19** cover payment procedures. An important point to note here concerns partial payments. In respect of clean collections, such payments can be accepted, provided that such an action is considered lawful in the place where payment is made. However, with regard to documentary collections, partial payments are permissible only where the collection instruction expressly allows them.

j) **Articles 20** and **21** relates to action to be taken by banks where payment of interest, charges and expenses is refused by the drawee.

k) **Article 24** states that a bank need not protest in the event of non-payment or non-acceptance unless expressly authorized to do so in the collection instruction.

l) **Article 25** indicates that a case of need (i.e. an agent of the exporter who is resident in the importer's country) must have his powers expressly stated in the collection instruction. In the absence of this, banks will not accept any instructions from the case of need.

m) **Article 26** imposes upon the collecting bank the duty of advising fate of a collection without delay to the bank from which the collection instruction was received.

Readers should note that this section of the chapter is merely a summary of the contents of URC. Full details of URC are contained in Appendix 3.

8 The Legal and Practical Positions Regarding the Duties of the Remitting Bank

Question

An exporter customer hands you a documentary collection. What is your bank's liability regarding examination of the documents and what other points would the bank check in practice?

Answer

The bank's legal liability is set out in the Uniform Rules for Collections. Banks must check that they appear to have received the documents specified in the collection instruction, but they have no liability to examine the documents in more detail.

However, in practice the remitting bank will make the following additional checks before it sends the documents abroad:

a) Make sure the bill of exchange is correctly drawn, signed and endorsed.

b) Ensure that the amount of the bill of exchange agrees with the invoice (and collection order if applicable).

c) If the bill of lading is made out to order, it must be endorsed in blank by the shipper (who is usually the exporter).

d) If bills of lading are used, a full set would normally be required. If any are missing, an explanation should be obtained and the collecting bank must be advised accordingly. (See Figure 3, Specimen Collection Instruction, other documents and whereabouts of any missing bills of lading.)

e) Ensure that the shipping marks tie up on all documents.

f)   If the invoice shows which Incoterms apply, check that the documents conform to it, e.g. with CIF, the bill of lading must be marked 'freight paid' and an insurance document should be present.

g)   Make sure that the instructions on the collection order are logical, e.g. release documents on payment with a sight draft.

h)   Check the bank's reference book to see if there are any special documentary requirements in the importer's country.

i)   Ensure that the customer signs the collection instruction.

Note

If the remitting bank does not make a thorough check of the documents, disaster can quickly result. For instance, there may be some special requirement in the importer's country. Failure to fulfil the documentary requirements could mean that the goods are physically present in the importer's country, but the importer cannot obtain possession. In this case, the exporter has lost physical possession of the goods but will not be paid for them. This problem will have been caused by the UK bank's failure to check that the documents are in the proper form.

If a remitting bank fails to take proper care, the exporter will soon transfer his account to one that does.

9   Payment under the Documentary Collection System: The Theory

The exporter should be able to make an accurate assessment of when payment can be expected. With sight drafts, the payment should be made as soon as the documents reach the presenting bank. The only additional delay will be if a **payment may be deferred pending arrival of goods** clause applies. There may be some delay while the importer is contacted by the presenting bank, but usually the importer will be eager to obtain the documents, and hence the goods, as quickly as possible.

The same timing considerations apply with term bills except that the period allowed after sight must be added.

10   Timing of Payments: The Practice

Some banks publish a list of countries with the average length of time that can be expected to elapse from:

a)   remittance of the collection from the United Kingdom when it is a sight draft;

b)   number of days after due date when it is a term draft.

Obviously, the time taken will depend on the method of remittance of proceeds (MT, SWIFT or TT).

A previous Chief Examiner has stated "Most experienced exporting companies appreciate that when they sell goods in a foreign country, a sight bill means, in effect, giving 20-30 days' credit, and similarly 20-30 days can be 'added on' to the due date of any usance bill. This is simply due to the delay in receiving funds."

11   Acceptance Pour Aval

This is an alternative to straightforward D/A. If the collection order states **release documents against acceptance pour aval**, it means that the bill of exchange must be accepted by the drawee and then guaranteed for payment at maturity by the drawee's bankers. Only then may the documents be released. The benefit to the exporter is that:

a)   the drawee's bank is liable on the bill, thus eliminating risk of non-payment if the bank is sound;

b)   funds will be remitted on the due date, thus reducing the 20-30 days' delay normally met.

The prior permission of the importers and their banks should be obtained before submitting such a collection.

12   Risks to Exporters Who Sell on Documentary Collection Terms

The risks are the same as for open account, i.e. buyer risk, country risk, and transit risk. As with all of the terms of payment, the exchange risk applies if the exporter invoices in foreign currency.

a)   Ways to Minimize the Risks

The country risk, exchange risk and transit risk are reduced by the same methods as those applying to open account (see 12.3).

The buyer risk can also be reduced by taking status enquiries and by insurance against bad debts.

b)   How to Further Reduce the Buyer Risk with D/P Collections

Provided that documents of title are used, the buyer cannot obtain the goods without paying the bill of exchange (or, where a bill of exchange is not included, paying the amount specified on invoice/collection instruction).

However, where a buyer refuses to pay, the physical goods are at the overseas port, in danger of being damaged or stolen and possibly incurring demurrage (demurrage means charges levied by port authorities for goods which are not collected).

To overcome this problem a **store and insure** clause should be incorporated on the collection schedule. The exporter knows the goods will then be protected until an alternative buyer can be found.

If the exporter has a reliable agent, he can insert details of a **case of need** on the collection instruction. If the agent is reliable, the collection instruction will give him full authority to sell the goods on behalf of the exporter.

With air freight, the airway bill could show that the goods are consigned to the presenting bank. The bank's prior permission is required, however, and this will not often be forthcoming.

c) How to Reduce the Risk with D/A Collections

The additional risk with a D/A collection is that the documents, and therefore the goods, are released on acceptance, with no guarantee that the payment will be forthcoming at maturity.

Once the bill of exchange has been accepted, the exporter is in no better position than under open account terms, except that there is an accepted bill of exchange on which he can sue the buyer if it is dishonoured at maturity.

However, if the exporter, importer and importer's bank agree beforehand, the collection order could stipulate **release documents against acceptance pour aval**. This means the importer's bank will accept the bill of exchange and hence guarantee payment.

16 A Set of Shipping Documents Being Sent for Collection

The illustrated examples that follow constitute a set of shipping documents presented by the drawer to his bank for collection. An examination of the documents will establish that they appear to be in order. Points to note are:

i) The drawee will be able to obtain delivery of the goods.

ii) He may claim from the insurers in the case of loss.

iii) The invoice and bill amount agree.

iv) The bill of exchange is properly drawn.

v) Bills of lading are marked 'freight paid' (CIF invoices).

vi) The insurance cover is at least the amount of the invoice.

vii) According to the reference books, no additional documentary requirements are necessary to satisfy the importing authorities.

viii) The instructions on the collection instruction form have been completed and are not contradictory.

FOREIGN BILL AND/OR DOCUMENTS FOR COLLECTION

Drawer/Exporter	Drawer's/Exporter's Reference(s) (to be quoted by Bank in all correspondence)
Power Woollen Company Limited P O Box 799 Bradford West Yorkshire BD1 1AA	34/ 18-5- 34/

Consignee	Drawee (if not Consignee)
Tulla AS HC Andersens Boulevard 18 Copenhagen Denmark	

To (Bank)	For Bank use only

FORWARD DOCUMENTS ENUMERATED BELOW BY AIRMAIL. FOLLOW SPECIAL INSTRUCTIONS AND THOSE MARKED X

Bill of Exchange	Comm'l. Invoice	Cert'd./Cons. Inv.	Cert. of Origin	Ins'ce Pol./Cert.	Bill of Lading	Parcel Post Rec'pt.	Air Waybill
1	3			1	2/2		

Combined Transport Doc.	Other Documents and whereabouts of any missing Original Bill of Lading

RELEASE DOCUMENTS ON	ACCEPTANCE	PAYMENT		Protest	Do Not Protest
		X	If unaccepted ————▶		
If documents are not taken up on arrival of goods	Warehouse Goods	Do Not Warehouse		Cable	Airmail
			and advise reason by		
	Insure Against Fire	Do Not Insure	If unpaid ————▶	Protest	Do Not Protest X
Collect ALL Charges		X		Cable X	Airmail
			and advise reason by		
Collect Correspondent's Charges ONLY			Advise acceptance and due date by	Cable	Airmail
Return Accepted Bill by Airmail			Remit Proceeds by	Cable	Airmail X
In case of need refer to				For Guidance	Accept their Instructions

SPECIAL INSTRUCTIONS: 1.   Represent on arrival of goods if not honoured on first presentation.

Date of Bill of Exchange 18 May 19	Bill of Exchange Value/Amount of Collection GBP 683.75
Tenor of Bill of Exchange SIGHT	
Bill of Exchange Claused:—	Please collect the above mentioned Bill and/or Documents subject to the Uniform Rules for Collections 1996 Revision I/We agree that you shall not be liable for any loss, damage, or delay however caused which is not directly due to the negligence of your own officers or servants.
	Date and Signature Bradford 18 May

Exhibit 1: Collection Instruction

INCORPORATING BILL OF EXCHANGE	ADDITIONAL COPY FOREIGN BILL AND/OR DOCUMENTS FOR COLLECTION

Drawer Exporter

Power Woollen Company Limited
P O Box 799
Bradford
West Yorkshire   BD1 1AA

Drawer's/Exporter's Reference(s) (to be quoted by Bank in all correspondence)

34/‾   18-5-   34/

Consignee

Tulla AS
HC Andersens Boulevard 18
Copenhagen
Denmark

Drawee (if not Consignee)

To (Bank)

English Banking Ltd
Mill Street
Bradford   BD1 1AA

For Bank use only

FORWARD DOCUMENTS ENUMERATED BELOW BY AIRMAIL. FOLLOW SPECIAL INSTRUCTIONS AND THOSE MARKED X

Bill of Exchange	Comm'l Invoice	Cert'd/Cons. Inv.	Cert. of Origin	Ins'ce Pol./Cert.	Bill of Lading	Parcel Post Rec'pt	Air Waybill
1	3			1	2/2		

Combined Transport Doc	Other Documents and whereabouts of any missing Original Bill of Lading

	ACCEPTANCE	PAYMENT			Protest	Do Not Protest
RELEASE DOCUMENTS ON		X	If unaccepted ⟶			
If documents are not taken up on arrival of goods	Warehouse Goods	Do Not Warehouse	and advise reason by		Cable	Airmail
	Insure Against Fire	Do Not Insure	If unpaid ⟶		Protest	Do Not Protest X
Collect ALL Charges		X	and advise reason by		Cable X	Airmail
Collect Correspondent's Charges ONLY			Advise acceptance and due date by		Cable	Airmail X
Return Accepted Bill by Airmail			Remit Proceeds by		Cable	Airmail
In case of need refer to					For Guidance	Accept their Instructions

SPECIAL INSTRUCTIONS   1. Represent on arrival of goods if not honoured on first presentation

447/490
Tear

SITPRO OVERLAYS 1979

Date of Bill of Exchange

BILL of EXCHANGE for   GBP 683.

At   Sight   Pay against this sole of exchange to our order the sum of   Six hundred and eighty three pounds 75.

⌐
Tulla AS
HC Andersens Boulevard 18
Copenhagen
Denmark
¬

⌐ DRAWEE ¬

Power Woollen Co Ltd
0274 4338

Richard King

FOR VALUE RECEIVED
Bradford 18 May

Signature

L   ⌐

Exhibit 2: Collection Instruction and Bill of Exchange

INVOICE	FACTURE FACTURA	RECHNUNG FACTUUR		

Seller (Name, Address, VAT Reg. No.)
Power Woollen Company Limited
P O Box 799
Bradford
West Yorkshire   BD1 1AA

C C C N No.
6003

Invoice No. and Date (Tax Point)
34/2   18-5-

Seller's Reference
34/

Buyer's Reference
345

Consignee
Tulla AS
HC Andersens Boulevard 18
Copenhagen
Denmark

Buyer (if not Consignee)

Country of Origin of Goods
United Kingdom

Terms of Delivery and Payment
FOB UK port. Plus freight and
insurance. Cash against documents
through English Banking Ltd.,
Mill St.. Bradford.

Vessel/Aircraft etc.
Charlotte

Port of Loading
London

Port of Discharge
Copenhagen

Marks and Numbers, Number and Kind of Packages, Description of Goods		Quantity	@ £	Amount (State Currency)
TUL 345 COPENHAGN 1/1	1 Carton - 1000 pairs woollen knee length stockings assorted colours Type 92	1000	.65 each	£650.00
	Freight			£30.00
	Insurance			£ 3.75

TOTAL
GBP 683.75

Gross Weight(=g)
60kg

Cube (m.3)
1.25m3

Name of Signatory
Richard King

Place and Date of Issue
Bradford 18 May

Signature

It is hereby certified that this invoice shows the actual price of the goods described,
that no other invoice has been or will be issued, and that all particulars are true and
correct

Exhibit 3: Invoice (three copies required for collection)

Exporter's Reference 34/.

Norwich Union Fire Insurance Society Ltd.
Maritime Insurance Company Ltd.

NORWICH HOUSE, WATER STREET, LIVERPOOL L2 8UP.

INSURANCE CERTIFICATE No. A.R. /   CODE No. 66/KK/

This is to Certify that
have been issued with an Open Policy and this certificate conveys all rights of the policy (for the purpose of collecting any loss or claim) as fully as if the property were covered by a special policy direct to the holder of this certificate but if the destination of the goods is outside of the United Kingdom this certificate may require to be stamped within a given period in order to comply with the Laws of the country of destination. Notwithstanding the description of the voyage stated herein, provided the goods are at the risk of the Assured this insurance shall attach from the time of leaving the warehouse, premises or place of storage in the interior.

Conveyance Charlotte	From London	
Via/To Copenhagen	To	Insured Value / Currency GBP 750 so valued

Marks and Numbers	Interest
TUL 345 COPENHAGN 1/1	1 Carton – 1000 pairs woollen knee length stockings assorted colours Type 92

SPECIMEN

CONDITIONS – ALL RISKS as per current Institute Cargo Clauses. (All Risks)
Subject to Institute Replacement Clause. (as applicable)
Including War, Strikes, Riots and Civil Commotions as per current Institute Clauses.
Refer to Clauses as over.

SURVEY CLAUSE – In the event of loss or damage which may give rise to a claim under this certificate, notice must be given immediately to to the undernoted agent/s so that he/they may appoint a Surveyor if he/they so desire.

Agents at .... are ....

CLAIMS In the event of a claim arising under this Certificate it is agreed that it shall be settled in accordance with English Law and Custom and shall be so settled in Liverpool or at ....
by ....

G. W. Unson
Liverpool Marine Underwriter

This Certificate Requires Endorsement.

Dated Bradford 18 May
Signed

The original Certificate must be produced when claim is made and must be surrendered on payment.

Exhibit 4: Insurance Certificate (front)

<u>IMPORTANT</u>

PROCEDURE IN THE EVENT OF LOSS OR DAMAGE FOR WHICH UNDERWRITERS MAY BE LIABLE

<u>LIABILITY OF CARRIERS, BAILEES OR OTHER THIRD PARTIES</u>

It is the duty of the Assured and their Agents, in all cases, to take such measures as may be reasonable for the purpose of averting or minimising a loss and to ensure that all rights against Carriers, Bailees or other third parties are properly preserved and exercised. In particular, the Assured or their Agents are required:—

1. To claim immediately on the Carriers, Port Authorities or other Bailees for any missing packages.

2. In no circumstances, except under written protest, to give clean receipts where goods are in doubtful condition.

3. When delivery is made by Container, to ensure that the Container and its seals are examined immediately by their responsible official.

   If the Container is delivered damaged or with seals broken or missing or with seals other than as stated in the shipping documents, to clause the delivery receipt accordingly and retain all defective or irregular seals for subsequent identification.

4. To apply immediately for survey by Carriers' or other Bailees' Representatives if any loss or damage be apparent and claim on the Carriers or other Bailees for any actual loss or damage found at such survey.

5. To give notice in writing to the Carriers or other Bailees within three days of delivery if the loss or damage was not apparent at the time of taking delivery.

NOTE.—The Consignees or their Agents are recommended to make themselves familiar with the Regulations of the port Authorities at the port of discharge.

<u>SURVEY AND CLAIM SETTLEMENT</u>

In the event of loss or damage which may involve a claim under this insurance, immediate notice of such loss or damage should be given to and a Survey Report obtained from the Office or Agent nominated herein.

In the event of any claim arising under this insurance, request for settlement should be made to the Office or Agent nominated herein.

<u>DOCUMENTATION OF CLAIMS</u>

To enable claims to be dealt with promptly, the Assured or their Agents are advised to submit all available supporting documents without delay, including when applicable:—

1. Original policy or certificate of insurance.

2. Original or copy shipping invoices, together with shipping specification and/or weight notes.

3. Original Bill of Lading and/or other contract of carriage.

4. Survey report or other documentary evidence to show the extent of the loss or damage.

5. Landing account and weight notes at final destination.

6. Correspondence exchanged with the Carriers and other Parties regarding their liability for the loss or damage.

The Institute clauses stated herein are those current at the date of printing of this certificate but where such clauses are revised the Institute clauses current at the time of commencement of the risk hereunder are deemed to apply.

Exhibit 5: Insurance Certificate (back)

Shipper Power Woollen Company Limited		COMMON SHORT FORM BILL OF LADING	UK Customs Assigned No. 6003	B/L No. 67

Shipper's Reference
34/

F/Agent's Reference

Consignee (if "Order" state Notify Party and Address)

Tulla AS

Name of Carrier
P. Bork Shipping Limited

Notify Party and Address (leave blank if stated above)

The contract evidenced by this Short Form Bill of Lading is subject to the exceptions limitations conditions and liberties (including those relating to pre carriage and on carriage) set out in the Carrier's Standard Conditions applicable to the voyage covered by this Short Form Bill of Lading and operative on its date of issue

If the carriage is one where the provisions of the Hague Rules contained in the International Convention for unification of certain rules relating to Bills of Lading dated Brussels on 25th August 1924 as amended by the Protocol signed at Brussels on 23rd February 1968 (the Hague Visby Rules) are compulsorily applicable under Article X the said Standard Conditions contain or shall be deemed to contain a Clause giving effect to the Hague Visby Rules Otherwise except as provided below the said Standard Conditions contain or shall be deemed to contain a Clause giving effect to the provisions of the Hague Rules

The Carrier hereby agrees that to the extent of any inconsistency the said Clause shall prevail over the exceptions limitations conditions and liberties set out in the Standard Conditions in respect of any period to which the Hague Rules or the Hague Visby Rules by their terms apply Unless the Standard Conditions expressly provide otherwise neither the Hague Rules nor the Hague Visby Rules shall apply to this contract where the goods carried hereunder consist of live animals or cargo which by this contract is stated as being carried on deck and is so carried

Notwithstanding anything contained in the said Standard Conditions the term Carrier in this Short Form Bill of Lading shall mean the Carrier named on the front thereof

A copy of the Carrier's said Standard Conditions applicable hereto may be inspected or will be supplied on request at the office of the Carrier or the Carrier's Principal Agents

Pre-Carriage by*	Place of Receipt by Pre-Carrier* Bradford
Vessel CHARLOTTE	Port of Loading LONDON
Port of Discharge COPENHAGEN	Place of Delivery by On-Carrier* Copenhagen

Marks and Nos; Container No.	Number and kind of packages; Description of Goods	Gross Weight	Measurement
TUL 345 COPENHAGN 1/1	1 Carton stockings	60Kgs	1.25m3

Freight Details; Charges etc.

RECEIVED FOR CARRIAGE as above in apparent good order and condition, unless otherwise stated hereon, the goods described in the above particulars.

IN WITNESS whereof the number of original Bills of Lading stated below have been signed, all of this tenor and date, one of which being accomplished the others to stand void.

GCBS CSF BL 1979 710	Ocean Freight Payable at Prepaid Number of Original Bs/L Two	Place and Date of Issue London 16.5. Signature for Carrier; Carrier's Principal Place of Business P. Bork Shipping Ltd London

Authorised and Licensed by the
General Council of British Shipping © 1979

*Applicable only when document used as a Through Bill of Lading

Particulars declared by Shipper

© GCBS 1979

Exhibit 6: Bill of Lading (full set of originals required for collection)

16

DOCUMENTARY CREDITS

Objectives

On completion of this chapter the student should be able to:

● give a clear and accurate definition of a 'documentary credit';

● explain briefly who the parties to a credit are, and describe their main responsibilities;

● understand the meaning of revocable/irrevocable and unconfirmed/confirmed;

● acquire an overview of how a documentary credit operates;

● understand the meaning of 'payment', 'acceptance', 'negotiation', and 'deferred payment';

● understand the meaning and purpose of Uniform Customs and Practice for Documentary Credits;

● understand the meaning and purpose of Uniform Rules for Bank-to-Bank Reimbursements under Documentary Credits;

● understand the benefits and drawbacks of documentary credits for exporters;

● appreciate the reasons behind the creation of Documentary Credit Dispute Expertise System.

1   Definition of and Parties to a Documentary Credit

A **documentary credit** can be simply defined as a conditional guarantee of payment made by a bank to a named beneficiary, guaranteeing that payment will be made, provided that the terms of the credit are met. These terms will state that the beneficiary must submit specified documents, usually to a stated bank and by a certain date.

However, before considering how documentary credits operate and the responsibilities of the various parties involved, it is important that students become familiar with the more detailed definition taken from the Uniform Customs and Practice:

Applicant

This is the buyer/importer who asks his bank, the issuing bank, to issue credit. The applicant is sometimes called the 'opener' or the 'accreditor'.

Issuing bank

The applicant is a customer of the issuing bank, and it is the issuing bank that gives the conditional guarantee in favour of the beneficiary.

Advising bank

This is a bank, usually domiciled in the beneficiary's country, that is requested by the issuing bank to advise the beneficiary on the terms and conditions of the credit. If the advising bank agrees to advise the credit, it must take reasonable care to check the apparent authenticity of that credit. If the advising bank elects not to advise the credit, it must inform the issuing bank without delay. If the advising bank is not able to establish the apparent authenticity of the credit, it must inform without delay the bank from which the instructions appear to have been received. In addition, the advising bank may, if it wishes, advise the unauthenticated credit, but at the same time must inform the beneficiary that it has not been able to establish the authenticity of that credit.

There is no liability on the part of the advising bank to honour the credit.

Beneficiary

This is the seller or exporter in whose favour the guarantee operates. Note that UK banks can issue letters of credit on behalf of UK clients in favour of UK beneficiaries, who may themselves be importing the goods.

Confirming bank

This is a bank which, at the request of, or with the permission of, the issuing bank, adds its own irrevocable undertaking to honour the credit if the issuing bank should default. Banks will only confirm irrevocable credits.

This undertaking is in addition to, and not in substitution for, that already given by the issuing bank. In effect, the beneficiary has the benefit of two bank guarantors. First recourse is to the issuing bank, and then to the confirming bank in the event of default. Naturally, there is no liability on the part of the confirming bank if the beneficiary has failed to comply with the terms of the credit.

Normally the advising and confirming bank are one and the same.

Obviously, a confirmed irrevocable documentary credit is the safest form of credit from the exporter's point of view, but it will be more costly than an unconfirmed credit because of the extra bank being involved.

Under Uniform Customs and Practice (see 16.4), branches of the same bank in different countries are considered to be different banks. Hence, for example, NatWest Bank in London could be asked to confirm a credit issued by one of its own overseas branches.

Revocable/irrevocable

All credits should state whether they are revocable or irrevocable and in the absence of any such indication, the credit will be deemed to be irrevocable. An irrevocable credit cannot be amended without the consent of all parties, whereas a revocable one can be amended or cancelled without the exporter's knowledge. For obvious reasons most credits are irrevocable.

2 Example of How a Documentary Credit Operates

Let us return to our old friends, Speirs and Wadley and Woldal Ltd. Let us now assume that these two companies have agreed that payment terms will be by way of an irrevocable, confirmed documentary credit.

The procedures that now occur are as follows:

a) Woldal ask their bankers, Downtown Bank and Trust Co., to issue an irrevocable credit and to request confirmation by Barclays Bank. Let us assume that Downtown Bank agrees.

b) Downtown Bank, the issuing bank, request Barclays to advise the beneficiary, Speirs and Wadley Ltd, of the details. Barclays are asked to confirm the credit, and we shall assume that they agree to this.

c) Barclays, as advising bank, now write to Speirs and Wadley, along the lines indicated in the specimen document (Figure 1).

Notes on the specimen advice letter

(These notes correspond with the numbers in the example.)

1   The type of credit (revocable or irrevocable);

2   The name and address of the exporter (beneficiary);

3   The name and address of the importer (accreditor);

4   The amount of the credit, in sterling or a foreign currency;

5   The name of the party on whom the bills of exchange are to be drawn, and whether they are to be at sight or of a particular tenor;

6   The Incoterm in the underlying sales contract;

7   Precise instructions as to the documents against which payment is to be made;

8   A brief description of the goods covered by the credit (too much detail should be avoided because it may give rise to errors which can cause delay);

9   Shipping details, including whether transhipments are allowed. Also recorded should be the latest date for shipment and the names of the ports of shipment and discharge. (It may be in the best interests of the exporter for shipment to be allowed *from any UK port* so that he has a choice if, for example, some ports are affected by strikes. The same applies for the port of discharge.);

10   Whether the credit is available for one or several shipments;

11   The expiry date and place for presentation of documents;

12   The credit is confirmed, as evidenced by the final sentence in the letter.

d)   Speirs and Wadley should immediately check that they will be able to produce the required documents at the appropriate time.

e)   Speirs and Wadley ship the goods, and obtain the necessary documents which are presented to Barclays Bank along with the bill of exchange.

As sight drafts are called for, and as Barclays are the drawee, Speirs and Wadley will receive immediate payment, provided they have complied strictly with the terms and conditions of the credit.

f)   Barclays send the documents to Downtown Bank and Trust Co., and claim reimbursement of the sterling funds paid to Speirs and Wadley from the vostro account in the name of Downtown.

g)   Provided Woldal have the funds. Downtown debit their account with the Hong Kong dollar equivalent of £4,108, and release the documents. (Even if Woldal do not have funds, Downtown are bound by the terms of the credit to honour the presentation.)

h)   The goods are delivered by the transport operator to Woldal's premises, and Woldal will be required to surrender an original combined transport document in exchange.

Note
Readers should be aware that there are current initiatives under way to replace paper-based documentary credits with electronic equivalents.

3   Types of Credit

Unless the credit states that it is available only with the issuing bank, all credits must nominate the bank that is authorized to pay, to incur a deferred payment undertaking, to accept or to negotiate.

If you examine the specimen advice letter from Barclays Bank to Speirs and Wadley (Figure 1), you can see that, while the drafts under this particular credit were to be presented to Barclays

BARCLAYS

Barclays Bank PLC
1 Union Court, London EC2P 2HP.

DOCUMENTARY CREDITS DEPARTMENT

date 20th July

SPECIMEN ①

IRREVOCABLE CREDIT No:- UTDC 65432
To be quoted on all drafts and correspondence

Beneficiary(ies) ②
Speirs and Wadley Ltd.
Adderley Road
Hackney, London E8 1XY

Advised through

Accreditor ③
Woldal Ltd.
New Road
Kowloon, Hong Kong

To be completed only if applicable

Our cable of

Advised through   Refers

Dear Sir(s)

In accordance with instructions received from The Downtown Bank & Trust Co.
we hereby issue in your favour a Documentary Credit for £4108
(say) Four thousand, one hundred and eight pounds sterling ④   available by your drafts
drawn on us ⑤

at sight
for the 100% c.i.f. ⑥   invoice value, accompanied by the following documents:-

1. Signed Invoice in triplicate.
⑦ 2. Full set of clean Combined Transport Bills of Lading made out to
   order and blank endorsed, marked 'Freight Paid' and 'Notify Woldal
   Ltd., New Road, Kowloon Hong Kong'.
3. Insurance Policy or Certificate in duplicate, covering Marine and
   War Risks up to buyer's warehouse, for invoice value of the goods
   plus 10%.

Covering the following goods:-
⑧
400 Electric Power Drills

⑨
To be shipped from   London   to   Hong Kong c.i.f. ⑥

not later than   10th August

Partshipment ⑩ not permitted   Transhipment ⑪ permitted

The credit is available for   presentation to us   until 31st August

Documents to be presented within 21 days of shipment but within credit
validity.

Drafts drawn hereunder must be marked "Drawn under Barclays Bank PLC 1 Union Court,
London   branch, Credit number   UTDC 65432   "
We undertake that drafts and documents drawn under and in strict conformity with the terms of this credit will be
honoured upon presentation.

Yours faithfully,

R.E. Daw

Co-signed (Signature No. 9347   )   Signed (Signature No. 10247   )

CRF 202 (replacing CRF 83, 606 series)   PLEASE SEE REVERSE

Subject to Uniform Customs and Practice for Documentary Credits (1983 Revision) ICC Publication No. 400

Figure 1: Specimen Document

for payment, the alternatives of negotiation or acceptance or of deferred payment could also have been applicable.

The four terms apply as follows:

Payment

The meaning of the term 'payment' is self-evident. The nominated bank will pay the beneficiary on receipt of the specified documents and on fulfilment of all the terms of the credit.

Sometimes the issuing bank nominates itself as paying bank, in which case payment will be made on receipt of the correct documents at their counters abroad. On other occasions, usually with confirmed credits expressed in sterling, the issuing bank will nominate the UK advising bank to pay. This is the position with our specimen documentary credit (Figure 1).

The term 'payment' applies only to sight drafts.

Negotiation

Sometimes the issuing bank will nominate the advising bank to negotiate a credit, or it may even make the credit freely negotiable, in which case any bank is a nominated bank.

If a bank negotiates a credit, it will advance money to the beneficiary on presentation of the required documents and will charge interest on the advance from the date of the advance until such time as it receives reimbursement from the issuing bank.

Such negotiation advances are said to be **with recourse**, so that if payment is not ultimately forthcoming from the issuing bank, the negotiating bank will be able to claim repayment from the beneficiary of the advance, plus interest.

However if the negotiating bank has confirmed the credit, the advance will be on a 'without recourse' basis, provided the terms of the credit have been complied with.

Acceptance

The term 'acceptance' can apply only when the credit calls for usance bills (term bills), i.e. bills of exchange payable at a specified time after acceptance by the drawee.

The acceptance credit is also referred to as a 'term credit' or 'usance credit', which means that the seller draws a draft on the nominated bank demanding payment at some determinable future date, e.g. **at 30 days' sight** instead of **at sight**, as shown in the specimen credit (Figure 1).

In practice, this means that instead of receiving immediate payment on presentation of the documents (at sight), the seller's draft is returned to him endorsed on the face with the nominated bank's acceptance. This acceptance represents an undertaking by the bank to honour payment of the draft on the due date.

Deferred payment credits

Normally the terms of a documentary credit will include an instruction to the beneficiary to draw bills of exchange, and the issuing bank will guarantee that such bills will be honoured, provided all the other terms of the credit are met.

However, in deferred payment credits, there is no need for the exporter to draw a bill of exchange. The issuing bank simply guarantees that payment will be made on a fixed or determinable future date, provided the other conditions have been fulfilled.

Although the exporter does not draw a bill of exchange, in all other respects these credits are identical to other documentary credits. Although bills of exchange are not drawn, in practice some banks will negotiate the documents providing they are entirely satisfied with the standing of the issuing bank.

One benefit of deferred credits is that they avoid the need for payment of stamp duty on bills of exchange. In some countries stamp duty is set at a low rate, or there may not be any stamp duty at all, whereas in other countries stamp duties can be much higher.

Currently, at least one major UK bank is seeking to end the use of drafts in documentary credits.

Wording of the credit as regards payment, acceptance, negotiation or deferred credit

All credits must clearly indicate whether they are available by sight payment, by deferred payment, by acceptance or by negotiation. All credits must nominate a bank (the 'nominated bank'), which is authorized to pay, incur a deferred payment undertaking, to accept drafts or to negotiate. When the nominated bank is a bank other than the issuing bank, then unless it is the confirming bank, nomination by the issuing bank does not constitute any undertaking by the nominated bank to honour the credit. However, if the nominated bank does honour the credit, then provided the credit terms have been fulfilled, the nominated bank is entitled to claim reimbursement from the issuing bank.

Thus, where the nominated bank is neither the issuing bank nor the confirming bank. the beneficiary must bear in mind that the nominated bank is not obliged to honour the credit unless that nominated bank has expressly agreed with the beneficiary that it will be liable.

4   Uniform Customs and Practice for Documentary Credits (1993 Revision)

The Uniform Customs and Practice for Documentary Credits (UCP) is a set of internationally accepted rules and definitions that cover the liabilities and duties of all parties to documentary credits. (The relevant provisions are reproduced in Appendix 4.) All bank authorities and advices of documentary credits will state that the credit is subject to UCP 1993. Where the terms of the credit contradict UCP, the terms of the credit will prevail and where national laws conflict with UCP, national laws will prevail.

The main provisions of UCP 1993, as they affect exporters and their banks, are as follows:

Article 3

Banks are concerned only with the documents presented under the credit. Even when the underlying sales contract is mentioned in the credit (e.g. where invoice stipulates the Incoterm), the bank's decision to pay depends solely on whether the documents presented conform to the credit.

Comment

The issuing bank should ensure that a credit is logical and workable when it is set up (e.g. if the sales contract is FOB, do not call for an insurance document) and beneficiaries should ensure that the credit meets their requirements as soon as it is advised to them.

However, once the credit has been set up, the bank's decision to pay or not depends solely upon whether the documents presented conform to the credit. The only way payment can be made against the wrong documents is if the applicant agrees to accept the documents despite the discrepancies and authorizes the issuing bank to debit the account.

Article 4

Banks are concerned only with documents, not goods nor the performance of the underlying contract.

Article 6

Credits should clearly indicate whether they are revocable or irrevocable. In the absence of any such indication, the credits are deemed irrevocable.

Article 7

The advising bank must take reasonable care to check that the credit is genuine, if it elects to advise the credit. If the advising bank cannot establish authenticity, it must inform the bank from which the instructions appear to have been received without delay. The advising bank may advise an unauthenticated credit but if it does so it must inform the beneficiary that authenticity has not been established. In all cases, there is no obligation on the part of the advising bank to advise a credit, but if it elects not to do so, it must inform the issuing bank without delay.

Comment

If a credit is received by the beneficiary directly from the issuing bank, the beneficiary should ask his own bank to check its authenticity.

Articles 13 and 15

Banks must examine all documents with reasonable care to ensure that on the face of it they appear to be in order. Documents which on the face of it appear to be inconsistent with one another will be considered as not appearing to comply with the credit terms. Any documents which are not called for by the credit will not be examined by banks.

Banks shall have a reasonable time, not to exceed seven banking days following the day of receipt of documents, to examine the documents and determine whether to take up or refuse the documents and to inform the party from which the documents were received of the decision.

If the credit contains terms and conditions without stating the document(s) to be presented in compliance with such conditions, banks will disregard the conditions.

Banks assume no liability for the genuineness of documents.

Article 20

Unless otherwise stipulated in the credit, banks will accept as an original document a document produced or appearing to have been produced by photocopier, carbon systems or computer, provided such a document is marked as original, and where necessary, appears to have been signed.

Any symbol executed or adopted by a party with the intention to authenticate should be accepted as a signature. One example of such a signature is the traditional chop mark used in Asia which is a legal and valid signature.

Unless otherwise stipulated in the credit, a condition calling for a document to be authenticated or certified will be satisfied by any signature, mark, stamp or label which appears to satisfy such conditions.

Articles 21 and 22

When documents other than transport documents, invoices and insurance documents are called for, the credit should stipulate by whom the documents are to be issued, and the required wording or data content.

If no such instructions are received, banks will accept such documents as tendered.

Banks will accept a document bearing a date of issue prior to that of the credit, subject to such a document being presented within the time limits set out in the credit and in other parts of UCP.

Article 23 – Marine/Ocean Bill of Lading

i) When a credit calls for a bill of lading covering port-to-port shipment, banks will accept the following unless otherwise stipulated in the credit:

- a bill of lading that indicates the name of the carrier and which has been signed or otherwise authenticated by the carrier, a named agent of the carrier, the ship's master or a named agent of the ship's master (the agents must indicate in what capacity they sign);

and which

- indicates that the goods have been loaded on board or shipped on a named vessel.

ii) The loading on board may be indicated by preprinted wording, in which case the date of loading on board will be deemed to be the date of issue of the bill of lading. Where the loading on board is evidenced by a notation on the bill, the date of shipment will be deemed to be the date of loading on board.

iii) If the credit calls for any signatures or initials to authorize the on-board notation, banks will have no duty to check the genuineness of such signatures or initials.

iv) A full set of bills of lading would be required unless the credit stipulates otherwise. Nowadays, some carriers issue only one original bill of lading in set, and in such cases that single bill would constitute a full set.

v) Transport documents that are subject to a charter party, for example charter party bills of lading, will be rejected unless specifically authorized by the credit.

vi) When a bill of lading indicates that transhipment will take place (that is the unloading and reloading from one vessel to another during the course of ocean carriage), such a transhipment bill of lading will be accepted unless prohibited by the credit.

Even if transhipment is prohibited by the credit, so long as the bill of lading indicates that the cargo is shipped in containers, trailers and/or LASH barges, transhipment is acceptable so long as the same bill of lading covers the entire ocean voyage.

vii) If the credit prohibits transhipment, a bill of lading that indicates the carrier reserves the right to tranship is still acceptable.

Article 24 – Non-negotiable Sea Waybill

This article contains similar provisions to those in Article 23 on marine/ocean bill of lading. The stipulations concerning transhipment, charter party bills and authentication are identical.

Article 26 – Multimodal Transport Document

i) When a credit calls for a transport document that covers at least two modes of transport, banks will accept a document that indicates the name of the carrier or multimodal transport operator, provided this is authenticated or signed by the carrier, multimodal transport operator or master or any named agent of these parties who must indicate in what capacity he signs.

ii) The document must indicate that the goods have been despatched, taken in charge or loaded on board. If this indication is pre-printed, then the date of issuance is deemed to be the date of despatch.

If the indication is by means of a stamp or some other additional notation, the date of despatch, taking in charge or loading is deemed to be the date of shipment.

iii) The position regarding transhipment and charter party is the same as that for marine/ocean bills of lading.

iv) Documents that bear names such as combined transport bills of lading or similar titles will be accepted.

Article 27 – Air Transport Documents

Banks may accept, unless stated otherwise in the credit, a document that indicates the name of the carrier and which has been signed or otherwise authenticated by the carrier or by a named agent of the carrier.

Article 30 – Transport Documents Issued by Freight Forwarders

Unless otherwise authorized in the credit, banks will only accept a transport document issued by a freight forwarder that:

● indicates the name of the freight forwarder as a carrier or multimodal transport operator and which appears to have been signed or otherwise authenticated by the freight forwarder as carrier or multimodal transport operator; or

● has been signed or otherwise authenticated by the freight forwarder as agent for a named carrier or multimodal transport operator.

Article 32 – Clean Transport Documents

A clean transport document is one that bears no clause or other indication which declares that the goods or the packing are defective. Where such clauses exist, banks must reject the documents, unless the credit specifically authorizes such clauses or notations.

Article 33 – Freight Payable/Pre-paid Transport Documents

Unless otherwise stipulated in the credit, banks will accept transport documents which state that freight or transport charges have still to be paid.

If the credit calls for transport documents that show freight paid, banks will accept a document clearly indicating that the charges have been paid even if such indication is simply by way of a stamp or other notation.

Articles 34 and 36

Insurance documents They must be expressed in the same currency as the credit, must cover CIF or CIP value plus 10%, must show cover effective from date of shipment (e.g. date on the bill of lading), must be issued by underwriters or their agents, and any certificates must be signed or authenticated by the shipper. Insurance certificates or declarations under an open cover policy, pre-signed by the insurers, are acceptable unless prohibited by the credit.

Brokers' cover notes are not acceptable unless specifically authorized.

Note

Where CIF or CIP value cannot be calculated, the bank will accept as a minimum amount 110% of the amount of the credit or 110% of the amount of the invoice, whichever is the greater.

Where the credit calls for an all-risks policy, any form of words covering all risks on the policy is acceptable, including the standard London Underwriters Cargo Insurance, **'all risks except...'**

Article 37

Invoices need not be signed.

The description of the goods in the commercial invoice must correspond exactly with the description in the credit.

In all other documents the goods may be described in general terms not inconsistent with the credit.

The invoice must appear to have been issued by the beneficiary and must be made out in the name of the applicant (except in the case of transferable credits which come under Article 48 and are covered in Part Four of this book).

Articles 39 and 40

The word **circa** or **about** or **approximately** indicates that a difference of 10% either way can be allowed.

Where the goods are described by volume or weight, a 5% tolerance in the amounts actually shipped is allowed, provided the monetary amount claimed is adjusted accordingly. Part shipments are allowed, unless the credit states otherwise.

Article 42

All credits must stipulate an expiry date and a place for presentation of documents for payment. Where a credit is freely negotiable, the implication is that the documents can be presented to any bank.

Article 43

Banks will reject any transport document presented more than 21 days after its date. Such documents are considered **stale**.

Article 44

When the expiry date of a credit falls on a non-business day, banks will accept presentation on the following business day. However, the transport document must be dated on or before the expiry date of the credit, or on or before the last date of shipment if the credit stipulates such a date.

5 Uniform Rules for Bank-to-bank Reimbursements under Documentary Credit

Documentary credit operations have increased and become more refined over the years. As already seen in 14.4, Uniform Customs and Practice for Documentary Credits (1993 Revision) is the main set of rules to which parties to documentary credits adhere and these have been regularly updated. Article 19 of these rules covers bank-to-bank reimbursements. However, it was felt that Article 19 did not cover the procedures in sufficient depth and that bank-to-bank reimbursement required its own set of rules to complement this article.

Inter-bank reimbursement procedures have to a great extent materialized out of practices considered acceptable at a local level in the major financial centres. The one exception to this has been in the USA, where rules have been specifically designed. In order to standardize international bank-to-bank reimbursement practices, a working party was set up in 1993 out of which has evolved ICC Publication No 525, Uniform Rules for Bank-to-bank Reimbursements under Documentary Credits (URBBR). It became operational in July 1996 and consists of 17 articles. Full details of these are contained in Appendix 5 and students and practitioners should ensure that they read these in order to appreciate their full implications.

6 The Importance of Documents in Documentary Credits

As can be seen from Article 4 of UCP, banks are concerned only with the documents in documentary credits. If the documents do not conform, the issuing bank is freed from liability under its guarantee. If the documents do conform, the bank must pay.

A common occurrence, which causes a problem for the beneficiary, arises when the buyer contacts the seller direct and requests a change in transport arrangements. If the transport document which is subsequently presented does not conform to the credit, presentation will be rejected by the banks. The fact that the buyer and seller have agreed to the change is immaterial, unless the buyer agrees to authorize the issuing bank to amend the credit.

7 Documentary Credits: Advantages and Problems

With a documentary collection, exporters retain a measure of control over the goods, either until they are paid or until the importer accepts a bill of exchange. Where D/P collections are used, importers can refuse to have anything to do with the collection, thus leaving the exporter with the problem of arranging an alternative sale while needing to pay the costs of storing and insuring the goods. With D/A collections, importers may not pay the accepted bill of exchange on the due date, thus leaving the exporter unpaid and without any control of the goods.

However, with a documentary credit, exporters know that they have a bank guarantee of payment provided they comply with the terms and conditions of the credit. Thus, on receipt of an advice of a documentary credit, exporters can confidently begin to assemble and ship the goods knowing that they hold a bank guarantee of payment.

The buyer risk is virtually eliminated, since an unknown buyer's agreement to pay is replaced by a conditional bank guarantee.

The transit risk does not really apply, provided the exporter produces the insurance document, if any, specified in the credit. Banks are concerned only with the documents, not the goods, and payment will be forthcoming against correctly tendered documents, irrespective of any damage that may have arisen to the goods themselves.

Problems that Can Arise for the Beneficiary

The country risk can still occur because the importer's government may prevent the issuing bank from making payment. In addition, there are certain areas of the world where banks are not as sound as they might be, and the issuing bank could possibly fail.

Finally, two problems that exporters often overlook are:

a)   If the credit advice is received direct from an unknown bank, there is a danger that it may be forged.

b)   The exporter may not be able to fulfil the terms of the credit, because it calls for documents he cannot provide.

8   How the Exporter Can Minimize the Problems

The actions the exporter can take are as follows:

a)   If the credit is received directly from an unknown bank, the exporter should ask his own bank to check the validity of the credit.

b)   If there is any doubt about the standing of the issuing bank, the credit should be confirmed by a bank in his, the exporter's, own country. Confirmation will also overcome country risk.

c)   Immediately on receipt of the advice, the exporter should check that he will be able to produce the required documents. If not, he should ask the importer to arrange for the issuing bank to amend the credit.

Note
UK banks must take care not to advise or confirm fraudulent credits sent by mail directly to UK exporters.

9 Alternative Course of Action When an Exporter has Presented Documents that do not Conform to the Credit

By far the best course of action is to have the documents corrected/amended locally, but it is not always possible to do this before the expiry date of the credit. When this amendment is not possible, the alternatives are:

a) The exporter could present the documents to the advising bank and ask that they be treated as a simple documentary collection.

   Where the exporter is sure of the creditworthiness and integrity of the importer, this is a reasonable step to take, but he must bear in mind that the issuing bank (and the confirming bank, if any) are freed from their guarantee.

b) Where the advising bank is nominated to pay or negotiate documents drawn under a credit, the exporter could request that bank to negotiate or pay despite the discrepancies. In these circumstances the advising bank would not be prepared to negotiate if there were discrepancies but would pay under reserve for their own customer or against a bank indemnity from the beneficiary's bankers.

   The advising bank would require the exporter to join in a suitable indemnity whereby the exporter undertook to reimburse the advising bank if payment were later refused by the issuing bank on account of the discrepancies.

   When the exporter is a customer of the nominated bank, the bank will consider creditworthiness before agreeing to pay under reserve against an indemnity. Where the exporter is a non-customer, the exporter's bankers will be required to join in the indemnity.

c) The bank could cable the issuing bank for permission to pay despite the discrepancies. The issuing bank will require the authority of the applicant before such permission can be granted. The cost of the cable will be charged to the beneficiary.

10 Documentary Credit Dispute Expertise System (DOCDEX)

Most documentary credits are found to have discrepancies on their first presentation. Many of these can be easily corrected. However, there have been a growing number of disputes between parties to documentary credits which have been difficult to resolve within the operative time period of the credits concerned.

Consequently, the ICC has set up DOCDEX, which is designed to expedite resolution of disputes by providing impartial and expert recommended solutions. The ICC's International Centre for Expertise oversees the operation of DOCDEX.

PART FOUR

Introduction

In the earlier part of the book, we examined foreign exchange, methods of settlement between banks, documents, Incoterms, and methods of payment.

Now that we have a sound understanding of the mechanics of foreign trade, we can proceed to study the remaining bank services for exporters. These services can be divided into financial and non-financial categories, and we shall see that in many cases there is a link between the terms of payment and the relevant service.

The syllabus for the examination, quite rightly, requires an understanding of the services that are offered by non-bank competitors, and it is in this part of the book where this aspect is of most relevance.

Finally, please remember that this part of the book is in no way connected with importers. The services that banks and others provide for importers are covered in Part Five.

17

SHORT-TERM FINANCE FOR EXPORTS

Objectives

At the end of this chapter the student should be able to:

- understand what is meant by 'short-term finance';

- distinguish between 'pre-shipment' and 'post-shipment' finance for exporters;

- appreciate the significance of 'with recourse' and 'without recourse' finance;

- describe the various forms of short-term finance that clearing banks and their group affiliates can provide.

1   The Definition of 'Short-term Finance'

No legal definition of 'short-term finance' exists, but for our purposes we shall consider any facility that would normally be repaid within two years to be of a 'short-term' nature.

Facilities that cover a two-to-five year period are usually classed as 'medium-term' facilities and any period in excess of five years is normally classed as 'long-term'.

Usually, exporters of consumer goods require short-term finance because importers do not expect long periods of credit. Exports of capital goods are often sold on medium- or long-term credit.

2   The Difference Between Post-shipment and Pre-shipment Finance

Post-shipment finance is money required to finance the exporter between despatch of goods and receipt of payment. Usually this period is longer for exporters than for businesses that sell purely in the domestic market, and special schemes have been developed to meet the needs of exporters.

Pre-shipment finance is the money required to finance the business between the commencement of the manufacturing process and the despatch of goods. This period will be identical for the exporter and the non-exporter.

3 With Recourse and Without Recourse Finance

If finance is provided with recourse then the exporter is legally responsible for repayment of that money.

4 An Overview of the Short-term Facilities Available to Exporters from Banks and their Group Affiliates

Table 1

Name of facility	Exporter/importer payment terms which are appropriate	Credit period	With or without recourse	Special facilities
Loan or Overdraft.	Open account or documentary collection.	Up to two years.	With recourse.	-
Loan or over-draft secured by an assignment of the exporter's credit insurance policy.	Open account or documentary collection.	Up to two years.	With recourse.	-
Banks' special export finance schemes.	Open account or documentary collection.	Up to two years.	With recourse.	-
Negotiation of collections.	Documentary collection.	Usually short-term, say, maximum six months.	With recourse.	-
Bill advance.	Documentary collection.	Usually short-term, say, maximum six months.	With recourse.	-
Acceptance credit.	Usually documentary collection.	Six months is the usual maximum.	With recourse.	Minimum trans-action usually £100,000.

Table 1 (continued)

Name of facility	Exporter/importer payment terms which are appropriate	Credit period	With or without recourse	Special facilities
Negotiation of bills drawn under documentary credits.	Documentary credit.	Usually short-term, say, maximum six months, but longer periods can apply.	With recourse if the credit is unconfirmed. Without recourse if it is confirmed.	-
Assignment of proceeds of documentary credit.	Documentary credit.	Provides pre-shipment credit.	See detail in Section 7.	-
Red clause documentary credit.	Documentary credit.	Provides pre-shipment finance.	With recourse to the issuing bank only.	-
Export factoring invoice discounting.	Open account (or sometimes documentary collection).	Usually six months maximum.	Usually without recourse.	-

Note

Hire purchase, leasing, forfaiting and export-house type facilities may be for both short- and medium-term credit periods. For convenience, these facilities are covered in Chapter 18.

If finance is provided **without recourse**, it means that the lender has agreed to look to someone other than the exporter for repayment.

With recourse finance must be shown on the customer's balance sheet as a liability, whereas, subject to the agreement of the company auditors, **without recourse** will not appear there.

5 Loans, Overdrafts, Use of Credit Insurance Policies as Security and Specialized Bank Exporter Schemes

a) Loan or Overdraft to be Repaid from the Export Sale Proceeds

These facilities can be secured or unsecured, and the bank's considerations are the ones that apply to any lending proposition. (Lending criteria are examined in one of the specialized option papers and a detailed knowledge of credit assessment is not required for this examination.)

The customer benefits of an overdraft facility are its simplicity and flexibility. Interest is charged only on the debit balances actually outstanding on a day-to-day basis.

Loan accounts and overdrafts for export or import finance are completely exempt from the Consumer Credit Act 1974.

b) Loan or Overdraft Secured by an Assignment of a Credit Insurance Policy

This is a traditional type of facility that has formed the basis of many of the specialist schemes covered in (c) below.

The exporter signs a standard assignment form which instructs the insurance company to allow the lending bank to take over the exporter's rights to:

i) Any claim against the policy; or

ii) Any claim against a particular buyer; or

iii) Any claim against any buyer from a particular country.

This assignment is useful backing to the bank if an exporter cannot repay because a particular buyer has defaulted. The bank will be able to stand in the shoes of the exporter, and eventually will be able to receive the proceeds (if any!) of the claim from the insurance company.

Some students mistakenly believe that this form of security is absolutely safe, but this is not the case. The bank's rights are no better than the exporter's. Thus, if the exporter's claim is refused by the insurance company, the bank's assignment will be worthless.

An exporter's claim under his credit insurance could fail because:

i) The exporter did not fulfil the commercial contract;

ii) The exporter did not declare the shipment and pay the premium;

iii) The amount outstanding from the buyer who defaulted exceeded the credit insurance limit for that buyer.

In addition, the maximum percentage of risk covered by the policy is 95%.

Nevertheless, for a commercially reliable exporter, such an assignment is a very useful security for a lending bank, and some banks would charge a slightly lower rate of interest than would apply to an ordinary unsecured overdraft.

c) Individual Banks' Short-Term Export Finance Schemes

Major banks over the years have provided off-the-shelf schemes for exporters where the latter have acceptable credit insurance (either their own policy or under the umbrella of the banks' policy).

However, in recent times, the banks have suffered losses in respect of these schemes. These have arisen for a number of reasons. The first has been the inability of exporters to meet the conditions laid down in the relevant insurance policies, either deliberately or by accident. Another has been the provision of funds for one-off export situations which naturally have a higher risk factor. There has also been a growth in fraudulent activity in respect of the presentation of documentation.

Consequently, the banks are nervous about the provision of short-term export finance schemes. Students should, therefore, ascertain what schemes are currently being offered by their banks and make a note of their salient points.

In general, banks have had two main schemes on offer. The smaller exports scheme is aimed at businesses with annual export turnover of under £1m. The finance for exports scheme has a target market of businesses with an annual export turnover of more than £1m.

Both these schemes are marketed as 'without recourse' facilities, which is not technically true. If the exporter has failed to fulfil the terms of the credit insurance policy, or the terms of the underlying commercial contract, or has reneged on the payment of the credit insurance premiums, the schemes are considered to be 'with recourse' to the exporter. However, in respect of non-payment of premiums and contravention of credit insurance conditions, some banks have agreed with the credit insurers that the latter will cover such risk.

i)   Smaller exports scheme

The smaller exports scheme provides post-shipment finance for up to 100% of the invoice value for up to 180 days' credit.

The customer's exports are covered under a bank's own credit insurance policy. This will normally cover up to 95% of the invoice amount with the remaining 5% of risk being stood by the bank itself. Facilities are only offered subject to status.

The scheme is appropriate for exporters who trade on open account or who use promissory notes or bills of exchange.

The scheme operates as follows:

- The exporter will furnish the bank with a copy of the buyer's order, relevant invoice and evidence of despatch/shipment, e.g. bill of lading together with the appropriate lodgement form.

- In respect of open account trade, details of the payment terms must be given to the bank, together with confirmation that such payments will be forwarded direct to the bank. With regard to bills and notes, the relevant bill and note will be given to the bank.

- The exporter's bank then sends the relevant documents to the buyer's bank on a collection basis via its Bills Department.

- Payment will then be forwarded by the buyer's bank on the due date through the banking system to the exporter's bank.

- As stated above, in the event of buyer payment default, the bank will seek restitution under its credit insurance policy for up to 95% of the invoice amount, with the remaining 5% of risk being stood by the bank itself.

ii)   Finance for exports scheme

The main differences with this scheme, as opposed to the smaller exports scheme (apart from the difference in annual export turnover), are as follows:

- Credit periods can be for up to two years;

- Finance is normally only available for up to 90% of the invoice amount;

- Exporters participating in this scheme can hold their own credit insurance, although if they do not do so, the exporter and the bank can become joint policyholders on an appropriation policy, subject to the credit insurer accepting the exporter (and bank) as such.

6   Negotiations of Documentary Collections, Bill Advances and Acceptance Credits

a)   Negotiation of Documentary Collections

When a customer sells on documentary collection terms, he may be able to arrange a negotiation facility with his bank. A negotiation facility is a lending facility, and normal lending criteria apply.

The facility works as follows:

i)   The exporter submits the normal documentary collection items to his bank, but instead of signing a collection instruction, he signs a **negotiation request**, which is very similar to the collection instruction. This form requests a negotiation facility and gives the exporter's bank the right to deal with the documents in any way it thinks fit, to ensure repayment. By negotiating, the bank is in fact buying the bill of exchange and documents from the exporter and therefore collects the proceeds in its own name. The advance is therefore for 100% of the bill amount.

ii)   If the bank agrees to the facility the procedure is as follows:

- If the bill of exchange is drawn in sterling, the bank immediately credits the customer's current account with the full face value. If the bill is drawn in foreign currency, the bank credits the current account with the sterling equivalent at the bank's spot buying rate, assuming the customer does not maintain an account with the bank denominated in that currency.

- The bank debits a negotiation account with the face value of the bill of exchange. If the bill is drawn in sterling, there is a sterling amount debited to the negotiation account, and if the bill is drawn in foreign currency, then a foreign currency account is debited.

iii) The exporter's bank then sends the collection to the collecting/presenting bank in the usual way. The standard customer authority gives the exporter's bank the right to vary the customer's instructions on the collection order, should it so wish. Generally speaking, the collecting bank will wish to include **protest** instructions, even if the customer prefers not to do so. As far as the collecting/presenting bank is concerned, the collection is received and dealt with in the same way as any other documentary collection. The exporter's bank completes its own standard collection order, so the collecting/presenting bank will not know of the negotiation facility.

iv) On receipt of the proceeds, the negotiation account is cleared. Interest is calculated, and then debited to the current account.

If the negotiation account is denominated in foreign currency, then the interest is calculated in that currency and the customer's current account is debited with the sterling equivalent at the bank's spot selling rate. Naturally, the rate of interest will be based on the inter-bank rates for the relevant currency.

v) If the bill of exchange is dishonoured, the exporter's bank has rights against:

- the exporter, because this finance is with recourse;

- the drawee, provided he has accepted the bill of exchange;

- the goods, provided they have not been released to the importer. Under a D/P collection, goods will not have been released, but under D/A terms, the goods will have been released to the importer on acceptance.

vi) The bank's basic considerations when asked to grant a negotiation facility are:

- creditworthiness of exporter:

- creditworthiness of importer;

- existence of exchange control regulations in importer's country;

- saleability of goods if D/P terms;

- whether the terms are D/P or D/A, D/P being much more secure;

- whether credit insurance is held, and if so whether it is assigned to the bank;

- whether there is an agreement for **acceptance pour aval** on D/A terms;

- whether the documents give full control of the goods.

b) Bill Advance

This method works in exactly the same way as the negotiation facility, except that the bank advances only a percentage of the amount of the bill, instead of lending the full face value. The bank then collects the proceeds on behalf of the exporter.

Bill advances will apply:

i)   When the exporter does not need to borrow the full face value; or

ii)   When the bank does not feel justified in lending the full face value; or

iii)   When the bank is not entirely satisfied with the status of the importer or his country.

Note

With a negotiation, the bank has recourse only in the event of dishonour, whereas with a bill advance the bank can recall the advance at any time.

c)   Acceptance Credit

These facilities are available only for transactions of £100,000 minimum, and thus only large, established customers can use them.

The exporter's bank allows the exporter to draw a bill of exchange on the bank itself, and the bank accepts that bill of exchange. Since this bill is a bank bill the exporter can discount it in the discount market at a fine rate, which may be below base rate.

As security, the exporter's bank usually obtains authority to take over all rights to a documentary collection, which it submits on the exporter's behalf. For undoubted customers, the bank may agree to grant an acceptance credit facility when the exporter sells on open account terms.

Traditionally, acceptance credits have been made available only by merchant banks, but nowadays clearing banks are active in this market.

7   The Special Facilities Available in Connection with Documentary Credits

a)   Negotiation of Bills of Exchange Drawn under Documentary Credits

This facility operates in the same way as the negotiation facility described at 17.6 (a) except that the bill of exchange is always drawn on the issuing bank. Provided the issuing bank is sound and the credit terms have been fulfilled, the bill will be accepted by the issuing bank and honoured at maturity. Thus the exporter's bank will look upon such facilities as being risk-free.

Such finance is with recourse, unless the lending bank has confirmed the credit.

b)   Discounting of Bills of Exchange Drawn under Documentary Letters of Credit

Bills of exchange that have been drawn on and accepted by banks and are drawn for a period of 180 days' sight or less are called **eligible bills**. The rates of discount are much lower on eligible bills. The term **fine rate of interest** is used to indicate that a bill is an eligible one which qualifies for lower rates.

When the credit calls for sterling bills at a tenor of below 180 days, the UK bank will be nominated as the accepting bank. Hence, such bills will automatically become eligible bills once the UK bank has accepted them.

Finally, exporters should remember that it may be possible to persuade the importer to pay the costs of negotiating/discounting bills of exchange drawn under documentary credits. If such an agreement is made, the details should be incorporated in the credit at the time of issue.

c)   Assignment of the Proceeds of a Documentary Credit

This is a means of obtaining pre-shipment credit with the cooperation of the exporter's bank. The exporter's bank, acting on its customer's authority, issues a letter of comfort to the exporter's local suppliers indicating:

i)   That the exporter is the beneficiary of a documentary credit;

ii)   That the bank is authorized to pay over, direct to the supplier, a certain sum from the proceeds (if any!) of the credit when received.

This letter of comfort may persuade the exporter's local suppliers to grant pre-shipment and post-shipment credit to the exporter.

d)   Red Clause Documentary Credits as a Form of Pre-Shipment Finance

A red clause documentary credit contains an instruction from the issuing bank for the advising bank to make an advance to the beneficiary prior to shipment. When the exporter subsequently presents the documents, the amount of the advance, and interest, will be deducted from the full amount of the credit.

The advance can be in two forms:

i)   Conditional, whereby the beneficiary must sign an undertaking to use the money to help him assemble the goods referred to in the credit. In some cases the beneficiary may have to produce receipts for specified goods/raw materials before the advance can be made;

ii)   Unconditional, whereby the beneficiary merely signs a receipt for the money.

In either case, the issuing bank will be responsible for reimbursing the advising bank if the exporter should subsequently fail to present the documents called for under the credit. (The issuing bank will then seek reimbursement from its customer, the applicant.)

8 Export Factoring and Invoice Discounting Compared

1 The bank's customer sends his invoices to the factor (most factoring companies offer invoice discounting services).	1 The bank's customer sends his copy invoices to the factor.
2 For approved debts, the factor will advance up to 80% of the invoice at once. The factor then collects the debt himself.	2 The factor will advance up to 80% of the invoice value. The customer collects the debt himself.
3 The debtor receives an invoice from the factor and sends his remittance to the factor.	3 The client's debtor pays the client in the usual way.
4 The factor then pays over the balance to the exporter, less interest and charges.	4 The client settles with the factor when the debtor's remittance is received.
5 The factor takes over the sales ledger administration of the exporter.	5 The exporter is responsible for sales ledger administration.
6 Factoring is disclosed to the debtor.	6 Invoice discounting is not disclosed to the importer.
7 Charges are between 1% and 3% of turnover, plus interest on any advances.	7 Interest is charged on amounts advanced. The administration fee is relatively small, because the factor is not involved in any sales ledger administration.
8 The factor will deal with every invoice of the exporter. In other words, the factor takes over the sales ledger administration.	8 With invoice discounting the factor only deals with invoices against which an advance is required.
9 Factoring would be applicable if the exporter does not have the personnel to handle sales ledger administration.	9 Invoice discounting is applicable when the customer wishes to continue to handle sales ledger administration himself.
10 Usually bad debt insurance is included as part of the package, and the facility is without recourse.	10 Usually bad debt insurance is included as part of the package, and the facility is without recourse.

Conditions that would Apply

1   Both facilities are applicable to fast-growing companies with good-quality debtors. The minimum annual turnover varies between factoring companies.

2   The terms of trade must be simple, with no complex documentary requirements. With factoring, normally only open account terms will apply, although documentary collection would be appropriate for invoice discounting.

3   The factor must approve the debtors. Debtors should be well spread, and the factor may be more keen to cover the export business if the UK exporter has a good spread of domestic business which is offered as well.

Customer Benefits of Factoring

1   Sales ledger administration. (With overseas debtors the factor can handle correspondence in the language and even in the dialect of the overseas debtor.)

2   Protection against bad debts is available for an extra fee.

3   The client has the benefit of the factor's computerized credit reference system.

4   Cash flow is more predictable because the client knows that he can claim up to 80% as an immediate advance against his invoices.

5   Debtors settle more quickly because the factor is more efficient at collecting the debt. Some clients use the factor purely for this reason and do not utilise the right to advances against the invoice.

6   Saving in management time. All overdue debts are 'chased' by the factor.

7   Advice on trading terms in export markets.

8   Local collections and assistance with the resolution of disputes.

9   Protection against exchange risk when invoicing in foreign currency.

10   Swifter transfer of funds to the UK.

11   Expert local knowledge of overseas buyers' creditworthiness.

12   Financial facilities available in sterling or major currencies.

Note
UK factors will provide factoring facilities to overseas exporters who sell to UK buyers. The overseas exporter sends his invoices to the UK factor.

Customer Benefits of Invoice Discounting

1   As for factoring, except that the client must run his own sales ledger administration.

2   Invoice discounting is not disclosed to the debtors of the factor's client.

3   Useful if the client has an efficient sales ledger team of his own.

4   This is a very fast-growing service for exporters.

Conclusion Regarding Export Factoring and Invoice Discounting

Using these export services means that the exporter can spend more time developing a positive sales relationship with export customers. He can adopt a more aggressive approach to his marketing in the knowledge that collection problems and bad debts will be taken care of.

Export factoring/invoice discounting is particularly suitable for exports to the USA or to the EU. These facilities are not always appropriate for exports to Third World countries.

18

MEDIUM- AND LONG-TERM FINANCE FOR EXPORTS

Objectives

On completion of this chapter the student should be able to:

- distinguish between supplier and buyer credit;

- understand the role of ECGD guarantees in the provision of medium- and long-term finance;

- know how forfaiting operates and appreciate its customer benefits;

- understand the various ways in which hire purchase and leasing can provide finance for exports;

- appreciate the services offered by members of the British Exporters' Association.

1 Introduction

There are several specialist forms of longer-term export finance available. It is vital that the student can distinguish between these different facilities, since the examiner often sets practical problems to which only one of the various types of finance is applicable. If the student chooses an inappropriate facility, he will receive no marks because, in the real world, this would be of no help whatsoever to the customer.

2 Supplier Credit and Buyer Credit

In Chapter 17, we considered the terms 'pre-shipment finance' and 'post-shipment finance'; in this chapter our two major definitions are 'supplier credit' and 'buyer credit'.

Supplier credit involves the exporter's bank in the lending of money to the exporter, to provide post-shipment finance. The onus is on the exporter to repay the bank.

Buyer credit facilities involve a loan from a UK bank to enable the buyer to pay the full cash price of the export on shipment. (The loan can be made directly to the overseas buyer, or via an intermediary organization in the importer's country.) There is no recourse to the exporter if the buyer defaults, because it is the buyer who has borrowed the money, not the exporter. Buyer credit facilities turn the export sale into a cash on shipment sale from the exporter's point of view.

3 ECGD Supplier Credit Financing Facility

The ECGD Supplier Credit Financing Facility (SCF) enables exporters to obtain credit for between two and five years usually, although this upper time limit can be extended where the surrounding circumstances warrant it. The SCF is principally used by those exporters dealing in semi-capital or capital goods. The minimum value of contracts under this scheme is £25,000. There is no obligation on the exporter to cover all his export business, as cover under the facility can be provided on a contract-by-contract basis. It also has the added benefit to the exporter of being on a 'without recourse' basis for the most part. It is only in a relatively few cases that ECGD will insist upon the exporter having a recourse responsibility, such as where there are complicated or substantial contract obligations. Such a recourse responsibility would normally be limited in value to a maximum of 15% of ECGD's total liability under the contract. Finance under the facility is not purely limited to sterling and is available in a range of currencies for up to 85% of the contract price.

Operation of the SCF Facility

Banks offering finance under the scheme will have joined in a Master Guarantee Agreement (MGA) with ECGD. This details the terms and conditions under which the banks can provide the finance and the SCF facility. The exporter can approach any bank in the scheme and must obtain approval for the transaction to be covered by ECGD. Initially, however, the exporter will require to know the likely premium for the facility and the interest rate. It is possible to obtain a commitment from ECGD on the credit terms and interest factor for up to four months prior to the signing of the commercial contract. This is of great help to the exporter when concluding negotiations with the overseas buyer.

Interest rates will normally be at Commercial Interest Reference Rates (see Chapter 14).

If the exporter wishes to go ahead under the scheme, an application must be made via the bank. It is at this time that the exporter must apply for pre-finance insurance cover under the ECGD Export Insurance Policy, if required (see Chapter 14 for details).

ECGD will then make an offer of finance and an Export Insurance Policy (if requested). This will be accepted by the exporter and the bank which will complete declaration and acceptance forms and forward the required premium.

The exporter will then receive an ECGD 'Certificate of Approval', a copy of which will be forwarded to the bank. (The exporter will also receive an ECGD Export Insurance Policy, if it has been requested.)

Once the exporter has carried out his obligations under the commercial contract, the 'Certificate of Approval' should be presented to the bank together with the following:

- Bills of exchange or promissory notes, which have been guaranteed/avalized, normally by financial institutions.

- Documentary evidence of delivery of the underlying goods or of performance of the services contracted for.

- A confirmation warranting that the terms agreed between the relevant parties have been met.

- Any other documents that may have been stipulated by the bank.

The bank will ensure that the documents are in order and will then purchase the bills or notes from the exporter for their full value. If the buyer were to default, the bank is not at risk. It would initially seek restitution from the avalizer/guarantor and if payment was not forthcoming, the bank would then look to ECGD for repayment.

Under the SCF, bond insurance is an additional facility that is available (see Chapter 20).

Note:
It is necessary to arrange for a third party (bank or government) to avalise or guarantee payment of the bills of exchange before the UK bank can advance the funds.

4 ECGD Buyer Credit Facility

a) Operation and Availability

The ECGD buyer credit facility is usually available where the contract value is for a minimum of £5m. The exporter and his bank should contact the ECGD before commercial negotiations begin, to see if the facility will be available. Certainly the exporter should be aware of the ECGD's attitude and likely conditions before he submits any tender or quotation to the overseas buyer.

Normally the overseas purchaser makes a down payment of about 15% of the contract value, and the UK bank lends the buyer the remaining 85% so that he can pay cash for the exports.

b) Position if the Buyer Defaults

The loan from the UK bank to the buyer is guaranteed in full by the ECGD. There is no right of recourse by the ECGD if the buyer defaults on the loan, unless the exporter is in default on the commercial contract. Hence, two particular advantages of buyer credit facilities for the exporter are:

i)   **No contingent** liabilities need appear in his balance sheet because there is no right of recourse;

ii) There is no need to take out any form of ECGD insurance because, from the exporter's point of view, the sale is on cash terms.

c) Other Advantages to the Exporter from Buyer Credit Facilities

i) The exporter does not have to pay interest on the loan, because the loan is made to the buyer.

ii) The interest rate, payable by the buyer, is fixed. Commercial Interest Reference Rates apply in exactly the same way as for the ECGD SCF facility.

iii) ECGD may be prepared to grant bond support. This aspect is covered in Chapter 20.

d) The Disadvantages of Buyer Credit Facilities

i) There is usually a minimum contract value of £5m.

ii) Complex documentation, which takes a long time to finalize.

iii) The buyer may object to having a loan from a UK bank and paying interest and charges to a UK bank. (This is usually for political reasons.)

e) Procedure

i) The exporter, importer, UK bank and ECGD agree in principle that buyer credit guarantees are suitable.

ii) Four agreements are made simultaneously:

- Supply contract – the commercial contract of sale.

- Loan agreement – UK bank to overseas buyer.

- Guarantee ECGD – the UK bank.

- Premium agreement - exporter – ECGD.

iii) The money covered by the ECGD buyer credit facility is paid directly to the exporter by the lending bank, against presentation of documents specified in the loan agreement and in the supply contract. Legally, this transaction amounts to a transfer of loaned funds on the buyer's instructions, and the buyer becomes liable to repay.

5 ECGD Lines of Credit

a) Common Principles that Apply to all Types of Lines of Credit

From the UK exporter's point of view, lines of credit operate in a similar way to buyer credit. The lines of credit cover loans to buyers to enable them to pay on cash terms for UK exports of capital, semi-capital goods and associated services.

Common factors that apply to both buyer credits and to lines of credit are:

i) Commercial Interest Reference Rates apply in exactly the same way as for the other two facilities already described.

ii)   The buyer must pay a percentage of the contract value from his own resources.

iii)   Being a buyer credit facility, there are no contingent liability problems.

iv)   Because there is no recourse to the exporter, he does not require any ECGD insurance of the debt, but must contribute towards the overall cost of the ECGD cover given to the lending bank.

v)   Details of all lines of credit are available from the specialist export finance departments of the banks, or from the ECGD.

How then does a line of credit differ from buyer credit? The basic difference is as follows: from the individual exporter's point of view, the minimum amount, although varying with different lines of credit, can be as low as US $25,000, as opposed to the usual £5m minimum contract value of a buyer credit.

b)   Project Lines of Credit

This facility is useful for major projects where a number of UK suppliers are nominated by the overseas buyer to provide goods and services in connection with a single project.

The ECGD will guarantee a loan from the UK bank to the overseas buyer or procurement agent. The buyer can split up the loan using it to pay various UK suppliers on individual contracts which may be as low as US $25,000 each. The total amount lent to the overseas buyer will normally exceed £3m, but, as already shown, this sum can be divided to cover individual contracts of US $25,000 minimum, with credit periods of two to five years.

c)   General Purpose Lines of Credit

In this case the UK bank lends a sum normally in excess of £3m to an overseas financial institution, as opposed to the overseas buyer. The overseas financial institution can use this money for loans to the individual overseas buyers to enable them to pay on cash terms for approved UK exports.

The UK exporter and overseas buyer can negotiate a commercial contract knowing that up to 85% of the contract price can be lent to the buyer. Again, individual contracts for as low as US $25,000 can be financed in this way, with credit periods of two to five years.

d)   Lines of Credit to Overseas Banks

From the UK exporter's point of view, the differences between these lines of credit and general-purpose lines of credit are merely academic.

From the point of view of the ECGD, the difference is that the ECGD is concerned solely with the repayment of the loan to the UK bank by the overseas financial institution. If the individual overseas buyer defaults on the loan from the overseas institution, the ECGD is in no way liable. Thus, the ECGD can set up these facilities very quickly, because it does not need to see the individual commercial contracts.

6 Forfaiting

The forfaiting service provides finance to exporters who grant credit periods of between 180 days and seven years. Usually the total minimum value of a forfaiting deal is £50,000 or the equivalent in foreign currency. Forfaiting deals, however, tend to be flexible and credit periods of ten years are seen.

a) How Forfaiting Operates

i) The importer finds a bank or other first-class institution that is willing to guarantee his liabilities. The institution is not resident in the exporter's country (and in fact would normally be resident in the importer's country). However when the buyer is resident in a Third World country, the guarantor institution may well be a European bank.

ii) The method of guarantee can take the following forms:

- An aval, whereby the guarantor endorses bills of exchange drawn on the importer, thus becoming liable on them.

- A separate form of guarantee of the importer's liabilities. This usually applies when promissory notes are signed by the importer, as opposed to bills of exchange being used.

- When the guarantor is a bank from the USA, the guarantee takes the form of a stand-by letter of credit whereby the American bank undertakes to honour bills of exchange drawn in the prescribed way.

iii) The form of the guarantee is unimportant, provided the guarantee is legally binding. What matters is the status of the guarantor institution.

iv) Provided the guarantor is undoubted, the exporter's bank, known as the forfaitist, will discount the bills or promissory notes, i.e. will pay the exporter the face value less the discount charge. If the importer is undoubted, then the forfait facility could be provided without the need of a guarantee from another institution. It is rumoured that a UK football club was able to obtain forfait finance for the transfer of a UK soccer star to Italy. The forfaitist did not require a guarantee because the Italian club was probably more creditworthy than its bank.

b) Benefits of Forfaiting to the Exporter

i) The facility is flexible. The documentation can be set up in a matter of hours, whereas ECGD buyer credit facilities can take up to three months to arrange. In suitable cases. the forfait facility can cover the full amount of the contract price.

ii) The rate of discount applied by the forfaitist is fixed, and subsequent changes in the general level of interest rates do not affect the discount.

iii) The finance is without recourse, so there is no need for any contingent liability on the exporter's balance sheet. Forfaiting does not affect any other facilities, e.g. overdraft.

iv)   All exchange risks, buyer risks, and country risks are removed.

v)   The exporter receives cash in full at the outset.

vi)   The finance costs can be passed on to the buyer if the exporter is in a strong bargaining position.

vii) Administration and collection problems are eliminated.

c)   Disadvantages of Forfaiting

i)   Costs can be high, and there is no interest rate subsidy.

ii)   It may be difficult to find an institution which will be prepared to guarantee the importer's liabilities. Sometimes the guarantor institution may charge a high commitment fee if the buyer is not considered to be undoubted.

7   Leasing and Hire Purchase

Leasing of goods that are exported operates in much the same way as the leasing of goods traded within the domestic market. The leasing company (the lessor) buys the goods outright from the supplier and then leases them to the ultimate buyer, who has the use of the goods for an agreed period, subject to payment of the agreed rent to the lessor. There are various taxation complexities in connection with leasing, but these are not in our syllabus.

The system can work in one of two ways:

a)   by arranging for a lessor in the exporter's country to buy the goods and to lease them to the overseas buyer. This is known as **cross-border leasing;** or

b)   by arranging for a lessor in the buyer's country to act.

UK commercial banks all have subsidiary or associate leasing companies that can provide cross-border leasing facilities. These companies are also able to arrange for overseas lessors to act, where appropriate.

The benefit to the UK exporter is that the sale is in effect a cash sale and that there is no recourse unless he has defaulted on the commercial contracts.

Most forms of plant and machinery, vehicles or office equipment can be leased. Hire purchase performs a similar function to leasing, but the buyer may be required to pay a deposit from his own resources. Once again the legal differences between leasing and hire purchase are outside the scope of the syllabus.

8   The Traditional Role of Members of the British Exporters' Association

These organizations are well-known firms in the City of London who specialize in providing four main forms of service:

a)   Export Merchants

An export merchant buys goods from a UK manufacturer and then sells them abroad. As far as the UK manufacturer is concerned, the sale is a domestic sale. All normal export risks are eliminated, because the manufacturer receives sterling payment from an undoubted UK organization in accordance with the terms agreed. The disadvantage is that the UK manufacturer can tend to become out of touch with his market. In addition the export merchant will pay a lower price than would be received if the manufacturer sold to the overseas buyer directly.

b)   Manufacturers' Export Agents

In this case, a UK manufacturer employs the organization to act as an agent for the purpose of obtaining overseas orders. A period of credit is agreed for the overseas buyer. The manufacturer then ships the goods, and the export agent pays as soon as the goods have been despatched. The overseas buyer then pays the manufacturer's export agent in accordance with the agreed credit terms.

The finance is in effect without recourse, post-shipment finance. Although the sale contract is between the UK manufacturer and the importer, the manufacturer's export agent stands the credit risk.

c)   Confirming Houses

They act in exactly the same way as manufacturers' export agents, but it is the buyer who employs them. Hence a confirming house's fees are paid by the buyer whereas a manufacturers' export agent's fees are paid by the exporter.

d)   Export Finance Houses

Export finance houses provide finance for semi-capital or capital goods on a non-recourse basis. This will be supplied over the total period of credit granted to the importer for up to 100% of the total amount due.

Export finance houses tend to be flexible in their outlook. Although their primary objective is to supply finance for large capital projects, they will also finance smaller deals. They will also arrange finance for bank consortia where huge projects and joint ventures are being contemplated. Finance can be provided on a one-off basis or to cover a number of orders, or even through a line of credit arranged with an overseas bank in the importer's country.

Major UK banks have established subsidiaries that have infiltrated the traditional market of the export houses. New innovative services are being continually marketed by these companies. Students should therefore make enquiries as to how subsidiaries of their own banks have broken into this market and what services they currently offer.

9   Pre-shipment Finance

The foregoing sections have all covered what is essentially post-shipment finance. Pre-shipment finance can be available from a number of sources:

- Assignment of documentary credit (see 17.7). Red clause documentary credit (see 17.7).

- ECGD buyer credits generally provide post-shipment finance, but can be structured to include stage payments prior to actual physical export of goods, where the exporter's contract allows such payments.

- Buyers may agree to avalize bills of exchange prior to shipment and these bills could then be discounted.

- Forfaiting of avalized bills which the buyer has made available prior to shipment, probably for part only of the contract value.

- Overdraft or loan, possibly secured by a debenture.

- Bridgeover facility, whereby the bank provides pre-shipment finance, which will be cleared from, say, post-shipment buyer credit or forfaiting. Much depends on the standing of the exporter, the ultimate buyer and the terms of the sale contract. Documentary credits can also be used by the exporter to persuade the bank to grant pre-shipment finance on a bridgeover basis.

19

NON-FINANCIAL SERVICES FOR EXPORTERS

Objectives

At the end of this chapter the student should be able to:

● describe the various types of travel facility available and understand their advantages and disadvantages;

● appreciate the considerations a business must bear in mind when deciding whether or not to enter the export market;

● describe the non-financial services that banks can provide for new exporters;

● appreciate the services that are available to new exporters from sources other than banks;

● understand how joint ventures operate;

● appreciate how international licensing and international franchising can assist exporters.

1   Introduction

This chapter will cover all the non-financial services available to exporters, except for countertrade, bonds and standby letters of credit (which are covered in Chapter 20).

2   Travel Facilities

'Travel facilities' constitute a service that can be used by export salesmen when they visit overseas countries on sales tours. For convenience, the travel facilities that apply to holidaymakers are also covered in this chapter, because in many cases the needs and requirements of both export salesmen and holidaymakers are very similar.

The main forms of travel facilities, together with their advantages and disadvantages, are described below. These comments relate to travellers who are leaving the UK to travel abroad.

a) Sterling Notes

There are no government restrictions on how much cash is taken out of the UK, but only relatively small amounts should be taken, to cover:

i)   Sundry payments on board planes, ships or ferries and at UK airports;

ii)   Payment of taxi fares and expenses for the homeward journey from the UK port or airport to home.

The disadvantages of relying entirely on sterling notes are:

i)   Danger of loss or theft;

ii)   Inconvenient because of bulk;

iii)   Poor rates of exchange may be given for sterling notes;

iv)   The traveller runs the exchange risk if he converts his sterling notes into local currency;

v)   There may be restrictions imposed by the overseas exchange controls on the amount of sterling notes allowed into or, more vital still, out of the country.

b) Foreign Currency Notes

It is a good idea to take a small number of foreign currency notes to meet initial expenses on arrival in the overseas country.

Once the traveller has acquired the notes, he has eliminated the exchange risk, unless he has surplus cash on his return which has to be reconverted to sterling. The disadvantages which apply if the traveller relies entirely upon taking foreign currency notes are:

i)   Danger of loss or theft;

ii)   Inconvenience because of bulk;

iii)   The overseas government may impose exchange controls limiting the amount of cash a traveller can take into or out of the country;

iv)   At the end of the trip, any surplus foreign coins cannot normally be converted into sterling;

v)   Exchange risk applies to any surplus notes that are reconverted to sterling at the end of the trip.

c) Sterling Traveller's Cheques

Sterling traveller's cheques are purchased and paid for before the traveller leaves the UK, and they can be cashed at most banks throughout the world, or can be used to pay bills in certain hotels, shops or restaurants.

The UK bank makes a charge when the traveller's cheque is first issued, and a charge may be made by the organization which cashes the cheque abroad.

Advantages of sterling traveller's cheques:

i)   There is a refund service available if the traveller's cheques are lost or stolen;

ii)   Traveller's cheques can be purchased in high denominations (e.g. £100), and hence may be less bulky than sterling or currency notes;

iii) The purchaser does not have to have an account to buy traveller's cheques from a bank. Payment can be made in cash if necessary;

iv)   Traveller's cheques issued by well-known banks can be used to make purchases in a variety of establishments, such as restaurants, shops, hotels.

Disadvantages of sterling traveller's cheques:

i)   The travellers run the same exchange risk as with sterling notes;

ii)   Sterling traveller's cheques are not always readily encashable abroad (for example travellers should always take dollar traveller's cheques to the USA).

d)   Foreign Currency Traveller's cheques

Foreign currency traveller's cheques have all the advantages of sterling traveller's cheques, and in addition the exchange risk is eliminated if the traveller's cheque is cashed in the country of the currency in which it is denominated. The traveller usually obtains a better rate of exchange if he buys his traveller's cheques in the United Kingdom.

The only disadvantage is that the traveller runs the same exchange risk as applies to foreign currency notes, i.e. any unused cheques will be reconverted to sterling at the end of the trip at the rate of exchange ruling on that date.

e)   Eurocheque Scheme

Most banks now offer a special eurocheque card and a pack of special uniform eurocheques. The eurocheques can be used at any outlet at home or abroad where the **EC** symbol is displayed.

In most countries the traveller will write out his eurocheque in local currency, and each cheque is guaranteed up to the equivalent of approximately £100 when used in conjunction with the eurocheque card. If the amount required exceeds the sterling equivalent of £100, two or more eurocheques can be used.

Eurocheques are issued at the discretion of the branch manager, the criteria being similar to the conditions for the issue of a domestic UK cheque card. There is a fee for the issue of the eurocheque card itself, and usually the eurocheques are issued free of charge.

The advantages of eurocheques are as follows:

i)   They do not require any initial cash outlay (apart from the fee mentioned above) as opposed to the facilities previously mentioned which are paid for in full before the journey begins. Thus the traveller saves on interest and the bank loses the 'float time' which applies to traveller's cheques.

ii) They are flexible, and this is particularly useful for travellers who are country hopping around Europe or the Mediterranean.

iii) Employers can arrange for eurocheques to be purchased on the firm's account to cover the business expenses of employees.

iv) Eurocheques can be cashed at more than 250,000 bank branches. (This figure will increase as time goes by.)

v) Eurocheques can be used to make purchases at four million retail outlets such as shops, garages and hotels in over 40 countries, including the USA. (This figure will probably increase as time goes by.)

vi) With some banks the eurocheque card performs a double function. As well as being a cheque guarantee card, it can act as a cash card to obtain money from cash dispensers located overseas.

vii) Eurocheques avoid the need to carry large amounts in notes or traveller's cheques.

viii) Eurocheques can be used to pay motorway tolls on the continent.

The disadvantages of eurocheque cards are that:

i) There are a limited number of cheques in each eurocheque book.

ii) Cheques are written in local currency, and are usually converted to sterling at the spot rate ruling on the date of presentation to the United Kingdom. There is thus an exchange rate risk of a few days' duration.

iii) The eurocheque card or eurocheques could be stolen. Cases of loss or theft must be reported to the issuing bank at once.

f) Credit Cards

Credit cards operate abroad in much the same way as they operate domestically, and the traveller can use them at any outlet displaying the appropriate symbol. Advantages and disadvantages are much the same for the eurocheque scheme, apart from the following additional benefits:

i) Credit cards, as the name implies, give the holder the opportunity of enjoying a period of up to eight weeks' credit before paying off the amount owing on the card. (Eurocheques are debited to the customer's account as soon as they are presented for payment.)

ii) There is much greater flexibility than with the eurocheque system because there is no need to take sufficient eurocheques. A single plastic card will cover any number of transactions, provided the traveller keeps within his credit limit.

iii) Credit cards usage can help the holder to benefit from incentive schemes such as air miles or free travel insurance.

g) Debit Cards or Charge Cards (Travel and Entertainment Cards, e.g. Diners Card)

Such cards operate in a similar way to credit cards except that:

i)   there may be an annual subscription;

ii) there is no period of credit allowed beyond the date of the account settlement, which must be made in full, usually by cheque, or by the favoured direct debit.

Bank publications quote that their charge cards and credit cards are accepted in more than nine million shops, hotels and restaurants all over the world.

h) Open Credit

Open credit involves a similar arrangement to a domestic UK open credit facility. The traveller's bank sends a specimen of the traveller's signature to a nominated bank branch abroad, and the overseas bank branch is instructed to cash the traveller's own personal cheques up to a stated amount.

Advantages of open credits are:

i)   no risk of loss or theft;

ii) cash can be drawn as required. There is no loss of interest as applies to traveller's cheques and float time.

The disadvantage is that encashment is restricted to a named bank branch.

With the advent of credit and debit cards, the use of open credits should diminish.

i) Company Credit Card

Company credit cards are suitable for business customers who are limited companies, partnerships, associations, sole traders and other groups of particular individuals. The company is given an overall limit by the credit card company, and it then issues company credit cards to individual employees who travel abroad. Each individual's card can have an individual limit programmed on it.

Advantages to the company are:

i)   The credit cards can be used throughout the world. Most airlines, restaurants and hotels accept payment by credit card.

ii) The company card scheme enables a company to simplify its expense accounting system yet still maintain a complete record of all transactions. Cash flow is improved, since expenses are debited once a month, instead of being debited at unpredictable times.

iii) The company receives a detailed statement for each executive together with a summary statement and payment invoice. Overseas transactions are converted and shown in sterling on the statements.

Advantages to the employee are:

i)   The fact that he has a company credit card can give him status in the eyes of his overseas counterparts.

ii) The employee is not required to use his own funds to meet company expenses, nor does he have the problem of claiming reimbursement from the company.

j)   Emergency Cash

If a traveller finds himself without cash, money can easily be provided from his own bank, provided there are sufficient funds available. Many banks now have dedicated help lines or fax numbers to help in emergencies, especially when these are caused by the loss or theft of a credit card or traveller's cheques. The traveller will be asked to supply the following:

i)   Full name.

ii) Full address of where the traveller is currently residing.

iii) The amount of money required.

iv) If possible, the name and address of a local bank to which the funds should be remitted. Generally speaking the funds will then be made available against passport identification.

3   Should a Business Enter the Export Market?

A business must bear in mind the following considerations when deciding whether or not to enter the export market:

a)   Is there a market for the product?

b)   If there is a potential market, what selling price could be set?

c)   What additional costs must be incurred, for example in packaging, shipping and insurance?

d)   Is it possible to deliver the product overseas? Are there any import tariffs or quotas, or any onerous customs problems to solve? (Please refer to Chapter 1 for details of how GATT, WTO and SMP have reduced these problems.)

e)   How is the exporter to sell the goods? Does he require an agent or will the exporter sell direct to a distributor?

f)   The exporter will almost certainly need to visit the potential buyers, to ascertain whether there is any prospect of firm orders.

g)   The potential exporter must decide, in the light of the above, whether it would be profitable to export his product.

h)   Buyer and country risk.

i)   Exchange controls.

j)   Competition.

4   How the Bank Can Help New Exporters

The following list of services will help exporters to answer the questions posed in Section 3 above.

a)   **Status reports** on potential buyers and agents abroad.

b)   **Political and economic reports** on various overseas countries to help the exporter to decide upon the economic prospects and on the likelihood of country default.

c)   **Trade development departments** which give advice on technical problems affecting the export marketability of products. Some departments also offer a service that involves obtaining several contacts for an exporter in a particular market.

d)   Details of any **trade fairs** being held overseas, where the customer could benefit from renting a stand. The bank may have its own representative present at such events and he can help to arrange on-the-spot introductions to the exporter.

e)   **Letters of introduction** to overseas banks which may have detailed knowledge of the market and which could arrange introductions with buyers and agents. The UK bank could arrange for copies of the exporter's brochures and price lists to be forwarded.

f)   **Registers of potential buyers** for the customer's product.

g)   Recording the details of the exporter's' product on **registers** that are made available to potential overseas buyers.

h)   **Travel facilities** for export salesmen on their travels abroad.

i)   Advice on matters in general that affect the exporter, e.g.:

    i)   Overseas documentary requirements, overseas tariffs, quotas and import requirements.

    ii)   Information on any exchange control restrictions on payments by overseas governments.

    iii)   Advice on the meaning and significance of Incoterms. Arrangement of appropriate insurance for terms such as CIF.

    iv)   Advice on the significance of the various methods of payment for exports (open account, documentary collection, documentary credit, payment in advance), with an explanation of the risks and means of reduction of such risks. In areas such as the USA and the EU, open account trading is the usual method of payment.

    v)   Advice on the exchange risk, together with appropriate methods of reducing the risk (forward contracts, currency borrowing, currency options and foreign currency accounts if there are receipts and payments in the same currency; bear in mind that currency options may not be appropriate for **new** exporters).

vi) The bank can recommend, without responsibility, a freight forwarder which would normally be a member of the British International Freight Association

vii) Introduction to other providers of export services such as the Chamber of Commerce.

viii) The bank can provide information on trade missions that are supported by British Trade International (see 5 below) .

Note

Normally new exporters will be too small to become involved in the bank's confirming house operations.

5 Services Available from Non-Bank Sources

a) The UK's National Trade Strategy

Since May 1999, British Trade International has had lead responsibility within government for trade development and promotion on behalf of British business. It brings together the work of the Foreign and Commonwealth Office and the Department of Trade and Industry in support of British trade overseas.

The strategy provides a series of commitments on behalf of Britain's firms. They include:

- a pledge to make all basic sector and market information available electronically by the end of year 2000;

- special emphasis on helping smaller companies to develop their exporting skills;

- a planned national information gateway to help firms to access the help available;

- further work to identify the markets and sectors where government help can add most value to British firms;

- new customer feedback arrangements for firms to comment on performance;

- benchmarking of Britain's export services against those provided by some of the key international competitors.

The aim of British Trade International is to help UK firms to take full advantage of overseas business opportunities, by providing support, information, advice and assistance throughout the exporting process.

The British Trade International network comprises Country Helpdesks and other teams providing export information services in its London headquarters, the commercial sections at more than 200 British Diplomatic Posts overseas, more than 70 core Business Links throughout England, Scottish Trade International, The National Assembly for Wales, and Trade International Northern Ireland.

British Diplomatic Commercial Officers are always willing to meet business people visiting the market to provide general advice or to discuss particular opportunities. In some cases, they can arrange a programme of visits to potential business contacts for UK exporters. These officers can brief exporters on local business etiquette and business practices.

Examples of the help available are the Market Explorer and the Trade Fair Explorer schemes for first-time or inexperienced exporters focusing on Western Europe.

The purpose of Market Explorer is to give potential exporters their first taste of a possible export market and focuses on those countries such as the Republic of Ireland, the Benelux countries and the Nordic countries which offer the best opportunities for new exporters.

Trade Fair Explorer concentrates on giving exporters access to the international trade fairs in France, Germany, Italy and Spain. This gives firms the opportunity to see at first hand the marketplace for their products.

Note
As situations change, the government-backed support systems also change. Readers are advised to consult the web site www.brittrade.com/all/ to keep abreast of developments. The authors have made extensive use of this and other related websites to obtain details of the current support systems.

b) Chambers of Commerce and Business Links

Chambers of Commerce usually specialize in the products of the local area. The Chambers often advise on technical requirements of local products exported to particular markets and, in appropriate circumstances, the Chamber of Commerce can issue **third-party inspection certificates** showing that the exporter's goods meet the specifications of the importing country.

Most Chambers of Commerce now work within the Business Link system and can advise on how to access the various services of British Trade International.

A typical example of the facilities (over and above those shown above) available from a local Chamber of Commerce/Business Link system is:

- Company information (financial and other) on potential buyers.

- Directories and Trade Journals with details of potential customers and of new trends in the market.

- Translation facilities.

- Specialist help with technical documentation in areas such as those involving legal or medical terminology.

The aim of the Chamber of Commerce/Business Link system is to act as a local first point of contact for exporters. Where applicable, the full services of British trade International can be accessed in this way.

c) Business Libraries

Many such libraries can provide useful information. For example details of the rate of inflation in Germany over the last five years, or details of the exchange rate changes between the £ and dollar over such a period of time. Such libraries often use Datastream or similar computer-based information sources.

6 Bank Assistance for UK Manufacturers that Wish to Set up Joint Ventures with Overseas Distributors

a) What is a Joint Venture?

Sometimes high import duties make the exporter's product uncompetitive in the overseas country. One means of avoiding such duties is to set up a joint venture with the local distributor. Such an operation can overcome import quotas as well.

The UK exporter will usually take a small cash stake in the joint venture, and will provide the expertise, and possibly some specialized plant and machinery, to help to set up the manufacturing operation. Once the operation is on stream, the UK manufacturer will provide some of the specialized components, but the joint venture company will assemble the product locally.

The product will then be sold in the overseas country, and the UK exporter will be entitled to payment in accordance with agreed financial arrangements.

Joint ventures can be seen in reverse if we look at Japanese car operations in the UK.

b) How Can a UK Bank Assist in a Joint Venture?

i) The bank can provide travel facilities for executives who visit the overseas country. (Small amounts of local currency, traveller's cheques for short stays, and credit cards for longer journeys.) Company credit cards can also be arranged.

ii) The bank, through the expertise of its international division, can advise:

- Whether an equity stake or a loan capital injection is better. Some overseas countries tax interest more favourably than dividends, and vice versa.

- Whether there are any overseas exchange controls that could affect remittance of dividends or capital back to the UK.

- What is the likelihood of expropriation or country default. (Bank political and economic reports.)

iii) If this information is not available at the international division, the division could obtain the details from the local office of the bank, if there is one in the area. Otherwise a correspondent (agent) bank will be asked to assist.

iv) The bank will provide letters of introduction to:
- a reputable local lawyer;
- a reputable local accountant.

v) All financial arrangements and other agreements should be drawn up, if possible, subject to English law.

c) Help with Local Banking Arrangements when the Joint Venture Begins

i) The UK bank can open an account at the local branch of the bank if one exists. Failing that, it could provide a letter of introduction to a local correspondent bank.

ii) If there is a local branch office, the UK bank can arrange overdraft facilities.

iii) If a correspondent bank is used, the UK bank could agree to guarantee the joint venture's overdraft with them.

7 International Licensing and International Franchising

a) What is International Licensing and International Franchising?

International licensing is an arrangement whereby an exporter who is the owner of exclusive rights gives permission for someone overseas to use the rights. The **exclusive rights** could be a brand name, product, process or service.

The exporter, who is known as the **master licensor**, will grant the overseas business, the **master licensee**, the right to use the product or service in a specified territory for a given period. The master licensee must pay a licence fee or royalty or both.

International franchising is similar to licensing, but the overseas business, the franchisee, is subject to much stricter controls in the use of the product or service. The franchisee becomes, in effect, a controlled outlet of the franchisor. Financial arrangements vary, but usually the franchisee pays a lump sum up front and then pays a royalty on subsequent sales.

b) Examples of Products and Countries which would be Suitable for Licensing or Franchising

Any uniquely British products would be suitable, for example:

i) specialist quality clothing;

ii) food and drink;

iii) specialist cosmetics (e.g. Body Shop).

Countries with a similar cultural background are most suitable, for example, Commonwealth countries, Western Europe and North America. (Examples of franchising in reverse are MacDonald and Wimpey. Here the franchisor is American and the franchisee is in the United Kingdom.)

c) Advantages of Franchising or Licensing from the Point of View of a UK Exporter

i) Greater commitment on the part of licensees than is found among traditional agents or distributors.

ii) Greater control over presentation and pricing of products.

iii) Lower start-up costs compared with joint ventures or traditional selling techniques.

iv) Closer involvement with the overseas marketplace.

d) Bank Assistance to UK Exporters

Some banks already have specialist departments, and others are about to follow. The bank can advise on:

i) Market research to test suitability.

ii) Financial projections to cover cost of setting up the arrangements and the potential revenue.

iii) Legal matters to ensure the licensee is committed to payment of fees and proper treatment of the product.

iv) Exchange controls in overseas countries.

v) Promotions to find potential licensees and franchisees.

vi) Advice on differences between the home market and the overseas market.

Note

Licensing applies only to well-established products or services. Do not suggest licensing or joint ventures for small firms just starting.

Joint ventures apply more to capital goods, whereas licensing/franchising is applicable mainly to consumer goods or services.

8   Types of Agents and Types of Distributors

a)   The Difference between Distributors and Agents

The exporter appoints a distributor who is usually based in the importing country. The exporter sells goods to the distributor who then sells these goods on his own account.

When an exporter appoints an agent, that agent may enter into a contract with the buyer on the exporter's behalf, or the agent may introduce the buyer to the exporter.

b) Sole Agents and Exclusive Agents

Sole agents

The exporter cannot appoint another agent in the sole agent's agreed territory. However, the exporter may obtain orders directly from buyers in the agreed territory without having to pay commission.

Exclusive agents

Not only is the exporter barred from appointing another agent in the agreed territory, but the exporter is also barred from obtaining orders directly from that territory or, if such orders are obtained, then commission must be paid to the exclusive agent.

EXPORTERS SHOULD TAKE SPECIALIST LEGAL ADVICE BEFORE APPOINTING AGENTS OR DISTRIBUTORS BECAUSE THERE MAY BE COMPLEX LEGAL OBLIGATIONS INVOLVED

20

BONDS, STAND-BY LETTERS OF CREDIT AND COUNTERTRADE

Objectives

On completion of this chapter the student should be able to:

  understand the role of bonds in international trade;

  describe the various types of bonds;

  appreciate the function of a stand-by letter of credit and ISP 1998;

  distinguish between *on demand* and *conditional* bonds;

  describe the procedures for issuing bonds;

  appreciate the problems that bonds cause for exporters;

  understand how these problems can be reduced;

  describe the various forms of countertrade;

  appreciate the role of banks and others in promoting countertrade.

1   The Role of Bonds in International Trade

A bond is issued by a guarantor, usually a bank or an insurance company, on behalf of an exporter. It is a guarantee to the buyer that the exporter will fulfil his contractual obligations. If these obligations are not fulfilled, the guarantor undertakes to pay a sum of money to the buyer in compensation. This sum of money can be anything from 1% to 100% of the contract value.

If the bond is issued by a bank, the exporter is asked to sign a counter-indemnity which authorizes the bank to debit his account with any money paid out under the bond.

Bonds are usually required in connection with overseas contracts, or with the supply of capital goods and services. When there is a buyer's market, the provision of a bond can be made an essential condition for the granting of the contract. Bonds are commonly required by Middle Eastern countries, but nowadays many other countries also require them. Most international aid agencies, such as the World Bank or the European Development Fund, and most government purchasing organizations in the developing world, plus major purchasers of goods and services in the North Sea oil sector now require bonds from sellers.

2   Types of Bond

The various types of bond are set out below:

a)   Tender or Bid Bonds

A tender or bid bond is usually for between 2% and 5% of the contract value, and will guarantee that the exporter will take up the contract if it is awarded. Failure to take up the contract results in a penalty for the amount of the bond. In addition, the tender bond usually commits the exporter and his bank to joining in a performance bond if the contract is awarded. Tender bonds serve to prevent the submission of frivolous tenders.

b)   Performance Bonds

Performance bonds guarantee that the goods or services will be of the required standard and a stated penalty is payable if they are not. The amount payable will be a stated percentage of the contract price; often it is 10%, but sometimes more.

c)   Advance Payment Bonds

Advance payment bonds undertake to refund any advance payments if the goods or services are unsatisfactory.

d)   Warranty or Maintenance Bonds

Warranty or maintenance bonds undertake that the exporter will maintain the equipment for a period of time.

e)   Retention Bonds

Retention bonds enable retention monies, which would otherwise be held by the buyer beyond the completion of the contract, to be released early. These bonds guarantee the return to the buyer of these retention monies in the event of non-performance of post-completion obligations by the exporter.

f)   Recourse Bonds

Recourse bonds are sometimes demanded by the ECGD to cover the potential recourse by the ECGD under buyer credits.

3 'On Demand' Bonds and Conditional Bonds

a) 'On Demand' Bonds

These bonds, sometimes known as 'unconditional bonds', can be called at the sole discretion of the buyer. The bank must pay if called upon to do so, even in circumstances where it may be clear to the exporter that the claim is wholly unjustified. UK courts have often ruled that the bank must honour claims under on demand bonds.

If the bank has to pay under the bond, it will debit the customer's account under the authority of the counter-indemnity. The exporter will then be left with the unenviable task of claiming reimbursement in the courts of the buyer's country.

It must be stressed that banks never become involved in contractual disputes. If payment is called for which conforms to the terms of the bond, the bank must pay.

b) Conditional Bonds

Conditional bonds can be divided into two types:

i) conditional bonds requiring documentary evidence;

ii) conditional bonds that do not require documentary evidence.

Conditional bonds requiring documentary evidence give maximum protection to the exporter. Payment can be called for by the buyer only against production of a specified document, such as a certificate of award by an independent arbitrator. Unfortunately, this type of conditional bond is often unacceptable, particularly in the case of Middle East buyers.

On the other hand, conditional bonds which do not require documentary evidence are little better than on demand bonds from the exporter's point of view. Such bonds often specify that payment must be made **in the event of default or failure on the part of the contractor to perform his obligations under the above-mentioned contract**. This terminology is so vague that banks are often obliged to pay a simple on demand claim if one is received.

4 The Procedure for Issuing Bonds

If the UK bank is satisfied that joining in a bond is justified, it would prefer to issue its own bond direct to the importer. However, in certain countries, notably in the Middle East, local laws or customs prevent importers from accepting bonds issued directly by UK banks. In these circumstances, the UK bank will instruct a bank domiciled in the buyer's locality to issue a bond against the UK bank's own indemnity.

At the same time as the bond is issued, the exporter will complete the counter-indemnity to authorize the bank to debit the account with the cost of any payments under the bond. The bank will make a suitable charge for the service, usually a stated annual percentage of the bond's value. This percentage usually varies between 0.5% and 1.5% a year, payable quarterly in advance. In addition, if a local bank is involved, it will charge between 2% and 3% per annum.

5 The Problems that Bonds Cause for Exporters

a) The Effect of Bonds on the Credit Rating of the Exporter

Banks treat the issue of bonds in exactly the same way as they would treat any lending facility. If payment is called for within the terms of the bond, the bank must pay, irrespective of whether its customer has funds to honour the counter-indemnity. Hence banks would normally wish to reduce a customer's maximum borrowing facilities pound for pound by the same amount as the bond.

Tender bonds involve the worst problems. The average success rate is often said to be one in eight for tenders, so the average contractor may at any one time have eight tenders outstanding. If each of these tenders involves a tender bond of, say, 2%, then the exporter's total potential borrowing facilities are reduced by 16% of his overall tender volume.

b) Unauthorized Extension of Bonds

Some countries, such as Syria, have laws that prevent the local bank from cancelling the bond without the importer's specific authority. This prohibition applies even if the bond contains an expiry date.

Sometimes the local bank will threaten to call for payment unless the bond is formally extended. The usual result is that the local bank is able to persuade the UK bank to extend the bond, and that the annual bank charges continue to be levied by both banks.

Sometimes tender bonds are not cancelled, even when the contract has been awarded and a performance bond has been issued.

c) Unfair Calling of Bonds

The buyer may call for payment, even when such a call is unjustified. If the call conforms to the terms of the bond, the bank must pay and will debit the exporter's account under the terms of its counter-indemnity. The exporter can be left with the task of claiming reimbursement from the buyer via the overseas courts.

There is also a danger that advance payment or retention bonds could be called, even though the advance payment or retention monies have never been paid over to the exporter in the first place.

6 How an Exporter can Overcome or Reduce the Problems of Bonds

a) Effect of the Bond on the Exporter's Credit Rating

ECGD Bond Insurance Policy

Where bonds have to be provided as part of a commercial contract, the ECGD Bond Insurance Policy can cover 100% of the liabilities involved. For 'on demand' bonds this cover also includes unfair calling of bonds. In order to avail itself of the benefits of this policy, the exporter must already have some basic cover provided by ECGD, e.g. Export Insurance Policy, Buyer Credit facility.

ECGD is normally willing to transfer the bond support from the exporter to the bank that issues the guarantee. This means that from the bank's point of view the issue of the bond is risk free, since in the event of a claim, the bank will pay out and be reimbursed by the ECGD. ECGD will only claim against the exporter if the bond has been called with justification, and there will be no recourse if the bond has been called unfairly. Thus, whatever the justification for the claim, the bank will be reimbursed for the full amount by ECGD.

b) Other Insurers

Some private sector insurers, such as NCM, may also be prepared to grant appropriate indemnities. The issue of bonds that are covered by such insurers' indemnities should not affect the bank's credit assessment, provided the indemnity is assigned to the bank, and provided the insurer does not have recourse to the bank if the bond is called with justification. However, in many cases private sector insurers will pay out only if the bond has been called unfairly. In such situations, the bank would only rely on the insurance as 'comfort', and would normally treat the bond as a credit facility.

c) Unauthorized Extension of Bonds

i) If the bond can be issued directly by the UK bank, standard wording can be incorporated to ensure that the bond has an expiry date and that the bond will be governed in accordance with English law. In such cases the bond cannot be extended without the exporter's agreement.

ii) If (i) above is not possible, the UK bank may agree to insert a clause in the counter-indemnity which specifies that the exporter's liability is limited to the period stated in the bond, and that any extension must be approved by the exporter.

Obviously this concession transfers the risk of an unauthorized extension from the exporter onto his bank, and the bank will only agree to this for important customers.

iii) When a tender bond stipulates that a performance bond must be issued if the contract is awarded, the performance bond should be worded so that it is only effective when the tender bond has been returned to the UK bank for cancellation.

d) Unfair Calling of Advance Payment Guarantees and Retention Money Guarantee

Ensure that the bond incorporates a reduction clause. This should state that the guaranteed value can be reduced in line with performance of the contract. An operative clause should also be included. This will ensure that the bond is effective only on receipt by the exporter of the advanced payment.

7 Other Precautions that an Exporter Can Take When Required to Provide Bonds

In addition to the suggestions made earlier, the exporter can take the following precautions:

a) Information

The exporter should obtain the most detailed commercial and financial information on the prospective buyer and the market. Banks can assist in this matter, along with the British Trade International or the Chamber of Commerce.

b) Agent

He should consider employing a good local agent in markets where there are many contracts that require bonds. An agent can be particularly useful in obtaining the return of an expired bond so that formal cancellation can be effected. Many foreign banks continue to charge commission on bonds that have been issued against an indemnity from a UK bank even though the expiry date has passed. Only on formal return and cancellation do they cease to charge. In addition, the UK bank must consider the contingent liability to continue to apply on such bonds, pending formal return of the document. Thus an agent who could obtain the return of a bond on its expiry date would be very useful in reduction of liabilities and charges.

c) Build Cost into Price

The cost of bonding can be built into the contract price. When tender bonds are required, a price escalation clause in the commercial contract could avoid situations where the contract has become uneconomic due to delayed adjudication. If this arises, the exporter has the unenviable choice of completing an uneconomic contract or declining the contract and being made to pay under the tender bond.

d) Sub-contractors

Ensure that if the exporter acts purely as a sub-contractor, any bond relates only to the part of the work for which he is sub-contracted.

e) Insurance

The exporter should also consider ECGD or private-sector insurance against unfair calling of the bond, where available.

8   Stand-by Letters of Credit

a) Stand-by Letters of Credit as an Alternative to Bonds

An alternative to the bond is a stand-by letter of credit issued in favour of the beneficiary, promising to pay a given amount against specified documents, usually a formal default claim.

There are various types of stand-by letters of credit, the main ones being linked to the various types of obligations covered by bonds. Thus the main stand-by credits are called:

- Bid/tender bond standby credits
- Counter standby (to support the issue of a performance standby if a commercial contract is awarded which had a bid/tender standby included)
- Performance standby
- Advanced payment standby

As a generalization, the applicant of such a credit would be the equivalent of the person who applied for a bond/guarantee and the beneficiary would be the same as the beneficiary of a bond/guarantee. Thus in the equivalent of a bid, counter and performance bond situation, the applicant would be the exporter/seller and the beneficiary would be the importer/buyer.

However, the use of standby credits is not necessarily restricted to the above situations and there are many instances where a documentary credit promising to pay a given amount against specified documents such as a formal default claim would be appropriate.

b) International Standby Practices 1998 (ISP 1998)

The choice of which rules govern a stand-by letter of credit are determined by the applicant/ beneficiary. Standby letters of credit can be issued subject to Uniform Customs and Practice for Documentary Credits (1993 revision) or subject to International Standby Practices 1998. The ISP are set out in ICC publication number 590.

ISP 98 has the same purpose as UCP in that it aims to simplify and standardize the drafting of stand-by letters of credit. Provided the credit is stated to be 'subject to International Standby Practices 1998' or, subject to ISP 1998', these provisions will apply.

Under Rule 1.02 it can be seen that these rules will supplement national laws, and so will apply unless there is anything in the law of the country concerned that contradicts them.

Under Rule 1.06 it can be seen that the normal position on documentary credits applies, so that what determines whether payment can be enforced is whether the documents on the face of it conform to the terms of the credit.

Rule 9.01 states that all stand-by letters of credit must have an expiry date.

Perhaps the key rule is Rule 3 which defines how documents are to be presented and authenticated. Specific provisions covering electronic generation and presentation are included here.

The rules have been carefully drafted to make them as 'watertight' as possible because stand-by letters of credit can often apply in a dispute situation. The rules are written to provide guidance to judges and lawyers.

From a bank's point of view, a stand-by letter of credit is better than a bond because it will be subject either to Uniform Customs and Practice for Documentary Credits (1993 revision), or to the International Standby Practices 1998, instead of being subject to complex legalities. In addition, a stand-by letter of credit will always have a definite expiry date which can overcome one of the main problems for issuers of bonds. It is anticipated that the bulk of stand-by letters of credit in future will be drawn subject to ISP 1998, since these rules are more appropriate than the traditional UCP for a bond type situation. The new rules make stand-by letters of credit even more attractive as an alternative to bonds.

9 Countertrade

a) What is Countertrade?

There is no one accepted definition of countertrade and the term is used by different specialists to describe different operations. Nevertheless, most participants would find the following definition acceptable:

Countertrade is an international trading transaction where export sales to a particular market are made conditional upon undertakings to accept imports from that market.

It is thus a form of bilateral trade which has continued to grow despite its condemnation by some international agencies because of its limiting effect on free trade and therefore multilateral trade.

There are two basic reasons for the development of countertrade:

i)   Some countries do not have the cash or credit facilities to pay for imports, so countertrade has become their only means of arranging deals;

ii)   Some developing countries wish to build up their manufacturing exports. Brazil, for example, one of the leading exponents of countertrade outside Europe, countertrades manufactured goods rather than raw materials such as coffee or iron ore. The objective is not to help to dispose of the basic commodities, which can be sold on the world market (albeit for a low price) but rather to build up exports of manufactures.

In addition, it is common for restrictions to be placed on the markets in which the manufactured goods can be sold so as to achieve **additionality** of exports, rather than having the manufactures disposed of in markets where cash buyers could be found independently of any countertrade deal.

b)   Forms of Countertrade

i)   **Counter-purchase** (also known as **link purchase**). This is the most common form of countertrade, especially with Eastern European countries and with developing countries such as Indonesia.

The exporter agrees, as a condition of obtaining the order, to arrange for purchase of goods or services from the importer's country.

The sequence of events is as follows:

1)   The exporter obtains an order subject to arranging for the disposal of goods or services from the importing country.

2)   Two parallel, but separate contracts are set up, one for the sale of goods to the importing country, and one for the counter-purchase of goods from the importing country.

The organization directly responsible for the counter-purchase will not necessarily be the exporter himself, but could be some other trading house or trader. There is normally recourse to the original exporter if the counter-purchase obligations are not fulfilled.

ii)   **Barter**. Barter involves a single contract for the simultaneous exchange of goods for goods between two parties. An example would be British exports of machinery to Zambia, paid for by a simultaneous shipment of wood or bitumen. Straightforward barter is popular with some African and Latin American countries, especially those with a shortage of hard currency, but pure barter deals are rare.

iii)   **Compensation or buyback deals**. Buyback is a form of barter which is favoured by some Eastern European countries. Suppliers of capital goods agree to be paid by the future output of the factory they are supplying. For example, ICI could sell a chemical processing plant and take part of the plant's future output of chemicals as payment.

iv)   **Barter by means of trust accounts**. A typical example would be the sale of trucks by a UK manufacturer to an African country, such as Kenya, with payment to come from the sale proceeds of local produce, say coffee.

The sequence of events is as follows:

1)   The coffee is shipped to the UK and the payment is retained in a UK bank in a trust account, also called an escrow account.

2)   The Kenyans arrange a documentary credit in favour of the UK truck manufacturer. The credit will be confirmed by the UK bank which maintains the escrow account, once there are sufficient funds from the sale of the coffee to cover the credit.

3)   The credit is then advised to the UK manufacturer who ships his goods and then presents the required documents to obtain payment.

v) **Offset**. Offset is widely used in high-technology products. Export orders are given for items such as aircraft on condition that the exporter incorporates components or sub-assemblies manufactured in the importing country.

vi) **Switch trading**. This is best described by way of example. Colombia could sell coffee to Hungary and instead of being paid builds up a credit balance. If Colombia then wishes to import coal from Poland, arrangements can be made to use the credit balance from the coffee sales to pay for the coal. Hungary would thus settle with Poland.

A market is becoming established for dealing with such credit balances, presumably along the lines of the secondary market which is now developing in Third World loans.

vii) **Evidence accounts**. Companies with a significant level of continuing business in certain markets may be required to arrange for counter-purchase of goods from that market. For example, a multinational company with a subsidiary in a Third World country may be required to counter-purchase goods from the Third World country to match the value of the subsidiary's import of raw materials. It may not be practical to balance this kind of trade item by item so the company may maintain an **evidence account** of all transactions. Usually this account must be kept in balance on a year-by-year basis.

Countertrade is becoming more innovative as it adapts to the changing international market-place. In addition to the above, new forms of financial countertrade are emerging, such as debt/equity swaps which have been pioneered by certain Latin American countries. Also, many countries are adopting official countertrade policies, e.g. Thailand. This all seems a far cry from the predictions of a steep decline in countertrade operations following the break-up of the Soviet Union – particularly, in reality, where this occurrence only served to increase countertrade deals and their international popularity.

c) Pitfalls of Countertrade for the Exporter

The main problems that can arise are:

i) Contractual commitments to purchase large quantities of unmarketable goods without any means of selling them.

ii) Penalty payments because the party to whom the counter-purchase has been committed has not honoured his obligations.

iii) Loss of profits on the sale of the principal goods because the costs of arranging the counter-purchase have not been considered.

iv) The discount between the face value of the goods taken in countertrade and the actual sale proceeds available.

When the counter-purchase goods are raw materials or commodities such as soya beans, a discount of 2% may be sufficient to cover the exporter. However, in the case of manufactured goods, a discount of 40%-50% can sometimes arise.

As a general rule, the nearer the counter-purchase goods are to commodities, the better.

v) The costs involved in marketing counter-purchased goods is continually rising. Exporters are therefore seeking alternative methods of meeting their countertrade obligations, e.g. training the importer's employees.

d)   Sources of Help for the Countertrade Exporter

i) **Bank**. Banks have many advantages that make them highly suitable for countertrade operations:

- A massive computer database which is already used to match potential buyers and sellers.

- A huge customer base.

- Expertise gained already from experience in arranging ECGD buyer credit facilities.

- Ability to innovate and arrange an imaginative deal in the circumstances that apply. In particular, banks can advise the exporter on the premium to be included in the export price to offset the discount on counter-purchase goods.

- Ability to provide guarantees or bonds to cover the exporter's liability under a counter-purchase agreement.

Some banks have representative offices in cities such as Moscow, Hong Kong or Singapore.

(ii) **ECGD**. The ECGD may provide insurance and financial guarantees for countertrade deals, but only in limited circumstances.

The most important proviso is that the payment obligation of the buyer (or borrower in the case of buyer credit guarantees) must be totally independent of the provisions of the counterpurchase agreement. In other words, for ECGD support to be available, the covered transaction must have all the characteristics and effect of a transaction to which no countertrade arrangements are related.

The ECGD is not prepared to involve itself in deals where payment for the export sale depends on fulfilment of the counterpurchase obligation, largely because the risks are unquantifiable. In addition, the ECGD does not wish to be seen to contravene EU or Berne Union agreements.

The ECGD will never become involved in insuring successful disposal of counterpurchase goods, although such insurance is available from specialist brokers or from countertrade specialists known as trading houses.

Exhibit 7 Tender Guarantee

OUR GUARANTEE (GUARANTEE NUMBER)

We do understand that (APPLICANT'S NAME) ('the Applicant') (APPLICANT'S ADDRESS) are tendering for the (DESCRIPTION OF GOODS) under your invitation to Tender (TENDER/CONTRACT NUMBER ETC.) and that a Bank Guarantee is required for (AGREED PERCENTAGE OF CONTRACT)% of the amount of their tender.

We, BANK PLC, overseas Branch, London HEREBY GUARANTEE the payment to you on demand of up to (AMOUNT IN FIGURES) (say, (AMOUNT IN WORDS)) in the event of your awarding the relative contract to the Applicant and of its failing to sign the Contract in the terms of its tender, or in the event of the Applicant withdrawing its tender before expiry of this guarantee without your consent.

This guarantee shall come into force on (COMMENCEMENT DATE) being the closing date for tenders, and will expire at close of banking hours at this office on (EXPIRY DATE) ('EXPIRY').

Our liability is limited to the sum of (AMOUNT IN FIGURES) and your claim hereunder must be received in writing at this office before Expiry accompanied by your signed statement that the Applicant has been awarded the relative contract and has failed to sign the contract awarded in the terms of its tender or has withdrawn its tender before Expiry without your consent, and such claim and statement shall be accepted as conclusive evidence that the amount claimed is due to you under this guarantee.

Claims and statements as aforesaid must bear the confirmation of your Bankers that the signatories thereon are authorized so to sign.

Upon Expiry this guarantee shall become null and void, whether returned to us for cancellation or not and any claim or statement received after Expiry shall be ineffective.

This guarantee is personal to yourselves and is not transferable or assignable.

This guarantee shall be governed by and construed in accordance with the Laws of England.

Exhibit 8 Performance Bond

OUR GUARANTEE(GUARANTEE NUMBER)

We understand that you have entered into a Contract (TENDER/CONTRACT NUMBER ETC.) (the Contract) with (APPLICANT'S NAME) (APPLICANT'S ADDRESS)(the Applicant) for the (DESCRIPTION OF GOODS) and that under such Contract the Applicant must provide a Bank Performance Guarantee for an amount of (AMOUNT IN FIGURES) being (AGREED PERCENTAGE OF CONTRACT)% of the value of the contract.

We, BANK PLC, overseas Branch, London, HEREBY GUARANTEE payment to you on demand of up to (AMOUNT IN FIGURES) (say, (AMOUNT IN WORDS)) in the event of the Applicant failing to fulfil the said Contract, provided that your claim hereunder is received in writing at this office accompanied by your signed statement that the Applicant has failed to fulfil the Contract. Such claim and statement shall be accepted as conclusive evidence that the amount claimed is due to you under this guarantee.

Claims and statements as aforesaid must bear the confirmation of your Bankers that the signatories thereon are authorized so to sign.

This guarantee shall expire at close of banking hours at this office on (EXPIRY DATE) ('EXPIRY') and any claim and statement hereunder must be received at this office before Expiry and after Expiry this guarantee shall become null and void whether returned to us for cancellation or not and any claim or statement received after Expiry shall be ineffective.

This guarantee is personal to yourselves and is not transferable or assignable.

This guarantee shall be governed by and construed in accordance with the Laws of England.

Exhibit 9 Advance Payment Guarantee

OUR GUARANTEE (GUARANTEE NUMBER)

We understand that you have entered into a Contrast (TENDER/CONTRACT NUMBER ETC.) with (APPLICANT'S NAME) (the Applicant (APPLICANT'S ADDRESS) for the (DESCRIPTION OF GOODS) and that under the Contract the sum of (AMOUNT IN FIGURES) being (AGREED PERCENTAGE OF CONTRACT)% of the total contract value is payable in advance against a Bank Guarantee.

In consideration of your making an Advance Payment of (AMOUNT IN FIGURES) (the Advance Payment) to the Applicant we, BANK PLC, overseas Branch, London, HEREBY GUARANTEE to refund to you on demand up to (AMOUNT IN FIGURES) (say, (AMOUNT IN WORDS)) in the event of the Applicant failing to fulfil the Contract.

Our maximum liability hereunder shall automatically reduce by (REDUCTION PERCENTAGE) of the value of (SERVICE/GOODS TO EFFECT REDUCTION) as evidenced by presentation to us by (PRESENTER FOR REDUCTION) of (DOCUMENTS FOR REDUCTION) showing the (EVIDENCE PRESENTED BY DOCUMENTS) which we shall be entitled to accept as conclusive evidence that the (CONCLUSIVE EVIDENCE OF) has been effected.

This guarantee shall remain valid until reduced to nil in accordance with the foregoing procedure or until close of banking hours at this office on (EXPIRY DATE) ('EXPIRY') whichever shall first occur. Any claim hereunder must be received in writing at this office before Expiry accompanied by your signed statement that the Applicant has failed to fulfil the Contract, and such claim and statement shall be accepted as conclusive evidence that the amount claimed is due to you under this guarantee.

Claims and statements as aforesaid must bear the confirmation of your Bankers that the signatories thereon are authorized so to sign.

This guarantee shall become operative upon issue of our amendment making it effective, which will be issued upon receipt by us of written confirmation from the Applicant that the latter has received the Advance Payment.

Upon Expiry, this guarantee shall become null and void, whether returned to us for cancellation or not and any claim or statement received after Expiry shall be ineffective.

This guarantee is personal to yourselves and is not transferable or assignable.

This guarantee shall be governed by and construed in accordance with the Laws of England.

* ALTERNATIVE

*This guarantee shall become operative automatically on receipt of the Advance of Payment of (AMOUNT IN FIGURES) on the account of (APPLICANT'S NAME) at our (BRANCH) Branch.

Exhibit 10 Progress Payment Guarantee

OUR GUARANTEE (GUARANTEE NUMBER)

We understand that you have entered into a Contract (the Contract) (TENDER/ CONTRACT NUMBER ETC.) with (APPLICANT'S NAME) (the Applicant) (APPLICANT'S ADDRESS) for the (DESCRIPTION OF GOODS) and that under the Contract a Progress Payment of (AMOUNT IN FIGURES) the Progress Payment being (AGREED PERCENTAGE OF CONTRACT)% of the total contract value is payable to the Applicant against a Bank Guarantee.

In consideration of your making a Progress Payment of (AMOUNT IN FIGURES) (the Progress Payment) to the Applicant we, BANK PLC, overseas Branch, London, HEREBY GUARANTEE to refund to you to demand up to (AMOUNT IN FIGURES) (say, (AMOUNT IN WORDS)) in the event of the Applicant failing to fulfil the Contract.

Our maximum liability hereunder shall automatically reduce by (REDUCTION PERCENTAGE)% of the value of (SERVICE/GOODS TO EFFECT REDUCTION) as evidenced by presentation to us by (PRESENTER FOR REDUCTION) of DOCUMENTS FOR REDUCTION) showing the (EVIDENCE PRESENTED BY DOCUMENTS) which we shall be entitled to accept as conclusive evidence that the (CONCLUSIVE EVIDENCE OF) has been effected.

This guarantee shall remain valid until reduced to nil in accordance with the foregoing procedure or until the close of banking hours at this office on (EXPIRY DATE) ('EXPIRY'), whichever shall first occur. Any claim hereunder must be received in writing at this office before Expiry accompanied by your signed statement that the Applicant has failed to fulfil the Contract, and such claim and statement shall be accepted as conclusive evidence that the amount claimed is due to you under this guarantee.

Claims and statements as aforesaid must bear the confirmation of your Bankers that the signatories thereon are authorized so to sign.

This guarantee shall become operative upon issue of our amendment making it effective, which will be issued upon receipt by us of written confirmation from the Applicant that the latter has received the Progress Payment.

Upon Expiry this guarantee shall become null and void, whether returned to us for cancellation or not and any claim or statement received after Expiry shall be ineffective.

This guarantee is personal to yourselves and is not transferable or assignable.

This guarantee shall be governed by and construed in accordance with the Laws of England.

* ALTERNATIVE

*This guarantee shall become operative automatically on receipt of the Progress Payment of (AMOUNT IN FIGURES) on the account of (APPLICANT'S NAME) at our (BRANCH) Branch.

Exhibit 11 Retention Monies Bond

OUR GUARANTEE (GUARANTEE NUMBER)

We understand that under the terms of your Contract (TENDER/CONTRACT NUMBER ETC.) with (APPLICANT'S NAME) (the Applicant) (APPLICANT'S ADDRESS) for the (DESCRIPTION OF GOODS) you are retaining the sum of (AMOUNT IN FIGURES) being (AGREED PERCENTAGE OF CONTRACT)% of the Contract value by way of retention monies (the Retention Monies) and that you are prepared to release the said retention monies against a Bank Guarantee.

In consideration of your releasing the sum of (AMOUNT IN FIGURES) to the Applicant we, BANK PLC, overseas Branch, London HEREBY GUARANTEE repayment to you on demand of up to (AMOUNT IN FIGURES) (say, (AMOUNT IN WORDS)) in the event of the Applicant failing to fulfil the Contract.

This guarantee shall remain valid until close of banking hours at this office on (EXPIRY DATE) ('EXPIRY'). Any claim hereunder must be received in writing at this office before Expiry accompanied by your signed statement that the Applicant has failed to fulfil the Contract, and such claim and statement shall be accepted as conclusive evidence that the amount claimed is due to you under this guarantee.

Claims and statements as aforesaid must bear the confirmation of your Bankers that the signatories thereon are authorized so as to sign.

*This guarantee shall become operative upon issue of our amendment making it effective, which will be issued upon receipt by us of written confirmation from the Applicant that the latter has received the Retention Monies.

Upon Expiry, this guarantee shall become null and void, whether returned to us for cancellation or not any claim or statement received after Expiry shall be ineffective.

This guarantee is personal to yourselves and is not transferable or assignable.

This guarantee shall be governed by and construed in accordance with the Laws of England.

* ALTERNATIVE

*This guarantee shall become operative automatically on receipt of the Retention Monies of (AMOUNT IN FIGURES) on the account of (APPLICANT'S NAME) at our (BRANCH) Branch.

Exhibit 12 Overdraft Guarantee

OUR GUARANTEE (GUARANTEE NUMBER)

In consideration of your granting advances by way of (TYPE OF BORROWING) on the account of (BORROWER) we hereby guarantee on demand being made to us in writing the due repayment of such advances in the event of (BORROWER) failing to repay such advances when required to do so by yourselves provided that the amount for which we shall be liable under his guarantee shall not exceed the sum of (AMOUNT IN FIGURES) (say, (AMOUNT IN WORDS)) *inclusive of interest and Bank charges.

Unless previously renewed by us, this guarantee is to be determined on (EXPIRY DATE) ('EXPIRY') subject to your right to cancel the facility prior to that date if you should think fit so to do, and to our right to determine our liability hereunder by giving notice in writing and upon receipt of such notice by you no further advances are to be made with recourse to us.

Claims under this guarantee must incorporate your declaration that the amount claimed represents outstanding advances by way of (TYPE OF BORROWING) on the account of (BORROWER) as aforesaid, *inclusive of interest and Bank charges, which have not been repaid by (BORROWER) as requested by you, and must be received by us at this office in writing or by authenticated telex/cable not later than 30 days after the above-mentioned expiry date, or not more than 40 days after the date of our prior notice of determination of liability, after which time this guarantee shall become null and void, whether returned to us for cancellation or not, and our liability hereunder shall terminate.

This guarantee is personal to yourselves and is not transferable or assignable.

This guarantee shall be governed by and construed in accordance with the Laws of England.

* ALTERNATIVE

* and in addition interest and Bank charges for a period not exceeding six months.

Exhibit 13 Warranty Bond

OUR GUARANTEE (GUARANTEE NUMBER)

We understand that you have entered into a Contract (the Contract) (TENDER/ CONTRACT NUMBER ETC.) with (APPLICANT'S NAME) (the Applicant) (APPLICANT'S ADDRESS) for the (DESCRIPTION OF GOODS) and that under the Contract the Applicant must provide a Bank Warranty Bond for an amount of (AMOUNT IN FIGURES) being (AGREED PERCENTAGE OF CONTRACT)% of the value of the Contract.

We, BANK PLC, overseas Branch, London, HEREBY GUARANTEE payment to you on demand of up to (AMOUNT IN FIGURES) (say, (AMOUNT IN WORDS)) in the event of the Applicant failing to fulfil the terms of the Warranty obligations under the Contract. Any claim hereunder must be received in writing at this office before Expiry accompanied by your signed statement that the Applicant has failed to fulfil the Warranty obligations under the Contract and such statement and claim shall be conclusive evidence that the amount claimed is due to you under the warranty.

Claims and statements as aforesaid must bear the confirmation of your Bankers that the signatories thereon are authorized so to sign.

This guarantee shall remain valid until close of banking hours at this office on (EXPIRY DATE) ('EXPIRY'). After Expiry this guarantee shall become null and void whether returned to us for cancellation or not and any claim or statement received after Expiry shall be ineffective.

This guarantee is personal to yourselves and is not transferable or assignable.

This guarantee shall be governed by and construed in accordance with the Laws of England.

PART FIVE

Introduction

This fifth and final part of the book is concerned with two major aspects of the syllabus:

a) Bank services for importers, including all relevant aspects of documentary collections and documentary credits;

b) Transferable and back-to-back credits.

Note
The Uniform Rules for Collections, Uniform Customs and Practice for Documentary Credits and Uniform Rules for Bank-to-Bank Reimbursements under Documentary Credits are set out in full in Appendices 3, 4 and 5 to this book. In addition. there are appendices covering correspondent banking and electronic commerce.

21

INWARD DOCUMENTARY COLLECTIONS

Objectives

On completion of this chapter the student should be able to:

- explain the difference between a clean and a documentary collection;
- understand and explain the responsibilities of all parties to a collection as stated in the Uniform Rules for Collection (URC);
- explain the process of presenting a bill of exchange for payment or acceptance;
- explain what action must be taken when a bill of exchange is dishonoured;
- explain the procedure for dealing with goods consigned to the collecting bank;
- explain how offers of partial payment are handled under URC and UK banking practice;
- appreciate the significance of 'avalization' of inward bills for collection;
- explain how banks can help importers when bills of lading have gone missing;
- explain how the produce loan procedure can be used to provide finance to importers who buy on documents against payment terms.

1   Introduction to Importing

Every vessel or aircraft arriving in the UK from a foreign departure point must report its arrival to the UK Customs authorities, and all goods must be **entered** into Customs on the prescribed form. There may be various levies such as VAT and excise duties to pay. Finally, it may be necessary to obtain an import licence for certain categories of goods, such as arms, drugs and livestock. However, most goods imported into the UK fall under the category of **open general licence**, which means that no licensing formalities are required.

Importers must conform to the Customs procedures, otherwise they cannot obtain possession of the goods. However, a detailed knowledge of Customs regulations is not required by the International Trade Finance syllabus, and questions on these matters do not appear on the exam papers.

Once Customs formalities have been completed, the importer will present an original bill of lading (made out to order and blank endorsed) to the carrier who will authorize the Docks Superintendent to release the goods. If waybills apply, the importer will present the waybill to the carrier, who will authorize the Docks Superintendent to release the goods, provided the importer is named as consignee.

Similar procedures apply when the goods come by air, but in this case the transport document will be an air waybill.

2 General Rules for the Handling of Inward Collections

The handling of inward collections received by UK banks from their overseas correspondents (banks) is considered to be a very important service which, if not taken seriously, can result in monetary loss and also damage a banking relationship.

A collection can be:

Clean – a bill of exchange or cheque unsupported by documents; or

Documentary – documents supported (or unsupported) by a bill of exchange.

All documents sent for collection must be accompanied by a collection instruction giving complete and precise instructions. Banks are permitted to act only upon the instructions given in such collection instructions and in accordance with these rules.

Any deviation from these instructions at the request of the drawee will be at the responsibility of the collecting bank.

The instructions of the remitting bank override the banking relationship, if any, between drawee and collecting bank.

Banks will act in good faith and exercise reasonable care and must verify that the documents received appear to be as listed in the collection instruction and must immediately advise the party from whom the collection instruction was received of any documents missing. Banks have no further obligation to examine the documents.

All UK banks will act in accordance with URC unless UK law or the collection instruction prevents this.

In the case of documents payable at sight, the presenting bank must make presentation for payment without delay and, in the case of documents payable at a tenor other than sight, the presenting bank must, where acceptance is called for, make presentation for acceptance without delay and where payment is called for, make presentation for payment not later than the appropriate maturity date.

In respect of a documentary collection including a bill of exchange payable at a future date, the collection instruction should state whether the commercial documents are to be released to the drawee against acceptance (D/A) or against payment (D/P). In the absence of such statement, the commercial documents will be released only against payment.

3 Procedure for Obtaining Acceptance of a Bill of Exchange

Acceptance of a bill of exchange is an unconditional undertaking to pay the bill on maturity. The drawee should not, therefore, when accepting the bill, impose any conditions on payment. Acceptances citing for instance:

a)   lesser amount

b)   payable at a different date

are referred to as 'qualified acceptances' and would not be acceptable to the remitting bank.

The bill may be accepted payable at a place other than the acceptor's address, normally at his bank, viz. 'Accepted payable at Barclays Bank plc...' This practice should be encouraged because the procedure for obtaining payment at maturity is greatly simplified; the bill needs only to be presented at the bank counters for payment.

The presenting bank is responsible for seeing that the form of the acceptance of a bill of exchange appears to be complete and correct, but is not responsible for the genuineness of any signature or for the authority of any signatory to sign the acceptance.

However, when the drawee is a customer, good banking practice dictates that the signature must be checked against the mandate.

Strict control must be maintained over an accepted bill which must not be presented for payment at maturity through the post.

4 Action to be Taken in the Event of Dishonour

A bill of exchange is dishonoured when a sight draft is unpaid on presentation or when a tenor draft is unaccepted on presentation or unpaid at maturity.

When an inward collection is dishonoured, the presenting bank must examine the collection order to see whether the bill is to be protested. Protesting a bill provides legal evidence of dishonour acceptable to a court of law.

If protest is to be carried out, a Notary Public will personally call upon the drawee/acceptor and demand payment or acceptance. If the payment/acceptance is not forthcoming, the Notary Public will draw up a **deed of Protest** which will give the reasons stated for dishonour. A bill should be protested within one working day of dishonour, otherwise, under the Bills of Exchange Act 1882 (S51), all signatories are freed from liability on that bill.

a)   Noting

Protesting is expensive and must be done within one working day of dishonour. To save money, it is possible to ask the Notary Public to note the dishonour. At maturity of an accepted bill, the Notary will present the bill either at the drawee's address or at the bank if payable there. If a bill is noted, the right to protest at a later date remains without any time limit.

b)   Householder's Protest

When a Notary Public is not available, a member of the bank staff can make a formal protest. Two ratepayers resident in the area of the drawee must witness the formal document. This is a valid form of Protest.

SPECIMEN FORM OF HOUSEHOLDER'S PROTEST

Date:...................................

Know all persons that

I..

householder of...   in the County

of............................

in the United Kingdom, at the request of Midland Bank plc, there being no Notary Public available, did on the ....   day of..........20

at..

demand............................*Payment/Acceptance of the Bill of Exchange hereunder written

from..

to which demand answer was

made...

Wherefore I now in the presence

of..

and...do protest the said Bill of Exchange.

*Delete as appropriate

        Signature:..

....)

Name..)

....)

Address

....)

....)

....)Two Witnesses

Name...)

....)

Address

....)

....)

....)

Copy of the Bill of Exchange

c) UK Practice

UK practice with inward documentary collections that are dishonoured is to note them if the collection order does not give any instructions regarding protest. This will retain the liability of all parties. This practice overrules Article 24 of URC which states that in the absence of specific instructions there is no need to note or protest a dishonoured bill of exchange. It is important that the remitting bank is kept fully informed of the situation in accordance with their instructions. If applicable, the **case of need** should also be advised, depending on his powers (Article 25).

5   Protection of Goods

Banks have no obligation to take any action in respect of the goods to which a documentary collection relates. Nevertheless, in the case that banks take action for the protection of the goods, whether instructed or not, they assume no liability or responsibility with regard to the fate and/or condition of the goods and/or for any acts and/or omissions on the part of any third parties entrusted with the custody and/or protection of the goods. However, collecting bank(s) must immediately advise the bank from which the collection order was received of any such action taken.

Any charges and/or expenses incurred by banks in connection with any action for the protection of the goods will be for the account of the principal.

In practice, however, the collecting bank will take reasonable care when entrusting the goods to a warehouse agent.

6   Goods Consigned to the Collecting Bank

Goods should not be despatched direct to the address of a bank or consigned to a bank without prior agreement on the part of that bank.

In the event of goods being despatched direct to the address of a bank or consigned to a bank for delivery to a drawee against payment or acceptance or upon other terms without prior agreement on the part of that bank, the bank has no obligation to take delivery of the goods, which remain at the risk and responsibility of the party despatching the goods (Article 10).

In practice, great care is required when goods are consigned to the bank because large losses have resulted from incorrect procedures being followed.

Quite often, goods consigned to the bank will arrive by air before the supporting documents have been received. At this stage we will have little indication of the value of the collection other than the declared value of the goods for Customs purposes. It is, therefore, important that a letter of release is handed only to the drawee who is undoubted and is prepared to sign an irrevocable undertaking to honour the documents upon presentation **regardless of the terms of those documents.**

Decisions of this nature will need to be made by a member of management.

7   Procedure for Dealing with Offers of Partial Payment

In respect of clean collections, partial payments may be accepted if and to the extent to which and on the conditions on which partial payments are authorized by the law in force in the place of payment. The documents will be released to the drawee only when full payment thereof has been received.

In respect of documentary collections, partial payments will be accepted only if specifically authorized in the collection order. However, unless otherwise instructed, the presenting bank will release the documents to the drawee only after full payment has been received.

Where a customer offers a part payment after accepting a bill of exchange and taking control of the goods, it is **UK banking practice** to accept the payment (even though the collection order may state that part payments are not allowed), note/protest **the bill** for dishonour, and hold the part payment on a suspense account, pending further instructions from the remitting bank.

Note
The bill is protested, not the **balance of the bill**, because it is the bill which is dishonoured and not a part of the bill.

8   Charges

Banks may deliver documents against payment or acceptance without collecting charges unless the collection instruction specifically states that the documents must not be released unless charges are paid. Where no specific instructions are given, the bank is in order to release the documents without collecting charges which are for account of the remitting bank.

9   Settlement

Settlement of an inward collection must be carried out strictly in accordance with the instructions contained in the collection instruction. Students must be familiar with the requirements laid down in URC.

Some overseas countries have specific exchange control laws that insist on all payments first of all being paid in local currency and then being subject to an application to that country's Central Bank for conversion and remittance abroad. Where such laws exist, they will prevail over URC, but there are no such rules in the UK.

10   Avalization of Inward Collections

Let us briefly recall the parties to an inward collection in connection with imports to the UK.

They are:

Principal – the overseas exporter;

Remitting bank – the exporter's bank;

Collecting/presenting bank – the importer's bank;

Drawee – the importer.

From the point of view of inward collections, avalization can be defined as 'the addition of the presenting bank's name to a bill of exchange with the intention of guaranteeing payment at maturity'. It will usually take the form of the following words being placed on the reverse of the bill of exchange:

Endorsed by way of aval (for the acceptor) for and on behalf of

.... Bank plc (i.e. UK presenting bank)

.... Authorized Signature

The practice of avalization is not recognized within the UK Bills of Exchange Act, nevertheless when a UK bank avalizes a bill of exchange, that bank in practice guarantees payment.

Avalization involves a contingent liability, and a bank will consider the granting of such a facility in the same way as it considers any lending facility. In other words, the bank will consider the creditworthiness of its importer customer. If the bank avalizes a bill of exchange, it will require the customer to complete an authority whereby the bank is irrevocably authorized to debit the customer's account upon presentation of the bill at maturity.

A brief comparison of avalization and documentary credit facilities appears in Chapter 22.

Note
Large losses have resulted from the failure to recognize the words **aval, pour aval** and **avalization** appearing on inward collection schedules received from banks abroad – the documents being released to the drawee merely against his acceptance and without the bank's agreement to **avalize** the accepted bill of exchange.

11 How Banks Can Help Importers When Bills of Lading Have Gone Missing

Any failure by the importer to remove his goods from the dockside within a specified time will result in demurrage charges. Demurrage is a storage charge made by dock authorities on importers who fail to remove their goods.

One of the most common causes of a demurrage charge is the arrival of goods before the relevant bills of lading have reached the importer. A typical situation is set out at 21.12, which shows how a bank indemnity can solve the problem.

12   Use of a Bank Indemnity when Bills of Lading are Missing

A typical question could be set on the following lines:

Your customer telephones to say that a machine which he is importing has arrived in this country. However, he is unable to take delivery because the bills of lading have not arrived.

The machine is incurring demurrage charges. How can the bank help the customer to obtain the machine and what precautions are involved?

An answer along the following lines is required:

a)   The bank could join in an indemnity to the freight company (carrier) requesting the release of the machine without the bills of lading, and promising to reimburse the carrier if he suffered any loss.

b)   The customer must sign a counter-indemnity authorizing the bank to pay any claims and debit the customer's account in reimbursement.

c)   The counter-indemnity will also promise that the importer will immediately send the missing bills of lading to the bank, should they come to hand.

d)   The bank will also ascertain whether the customer has paid for the machine, and, if not, what terms of payment have been agreed. If payment is by documentary collection, the customer must sign an irrevocable authority to honour the terms of the collection when presented. The bank could ask for the customer to place money on a suspense account earmarked to pay the collection, if the terms are D/P. Whether the bank insists on this will depend on the integrity and creditworthiness of the customer.

e)   The bank will issue the indemnity, provided the customer is creditworthy and trustworthy. The amount of the indemnity will be similar to the value of the goods. The indemnity must be in standard form so as not to impose any unreasonable obligations on the bank. The bank will consider the same principles as apply to consideration of the issue of bonds on behalf of a customer (see Chapter 20).

f)   The bank will make a charge for the indemnity, and can justify that charge by pointing out the saving on demurrage.

g)   If the missing bills of lading do subsequently come to hand, the bank will give them up to the carrier in exchange for cancellation of the indemnity.

h)   Indemnities such as these represent a contingent liability on the part of the importer, since at some future date there could be a claim from the carrier. However, most banks would regard the real risk as being very low or non-existent.

In practice, the bills of lading usually turn up and are surrendered in exchange for the cancelled indemnity.

13   Produce Loan Procedure

Sometimes importers buy goods on D/P collection terms for resale to a third party in the same country. It can happen that the importer requires finance to bridge the gap between payment of the sight draft, and receipt of funds from the ultimate buyer.

In such cases a produce loan facility can enable the importer's bank to advance funds against the security of goods and/or their sale proceeds. The procedure is as follows:

a)   Take a letter of pledge from the customer. This will state that the documents and/or goods are pledged as security to the bank.

b)   Pay the bill of exchange in accordance with the instructions on the collection order.

c)   Debit a produce loan and credit the customer's current account with the agreed amount of the advance.

d)   The documents will be retained by the bank. The bank will arrange with its agents to have the goods warehoused in the **bank's** name.

e)   The goods must be insured at the customer's expense.

f)   A status enquiry will be made on the supplier of goods to ensure that the goods should be of sound quality and on the ultimate buyer to ensure that he should be able to pay for the goods.

g)   The goods remain in the warehouse until the time comes for delivery to the ultimate buyer. When that time comes, the customer must sign a trust receipt. The bank will then issue a delivery order to enable the customer to obtain the goods and take them to the ultimate buyer. The trust receipt states that the customer holds the goods as trustee for the bank.

The bank has now lost physical control of the goods and relies on the customer to deliver them to the ultimate buyer.

h)   The ultimate buyer pays directly to the bank and the proceeds are used to clear the produce loan, including interest and charges.

14   Special Forms of Finance for Imports

Apart from produce loans, which have just been described, the main specialist forms of finance are:

a)   Factoring or Invoice Discounting

This applies when the goods are to be on-sold to other business organizations usually, but not necessarily always, located in the same country as the importer.

Note
UK factors will also provide finance to overseas exporters who have a good spread of UK

debtors. The overseas exporter sends the invoices to the UK factor.

The principles are the same as those described in Part Two of this book.

b)   Acceptance Credit Facilities

Again, these facilities apply when the goods are to be on-sold.
Normally the bank would lend unsecured, but it could conceivably require the security of the goods under a produce loan type facility.

The procedure is similar to that already described for exporters in Part Two of the book. The importer draws a bill of exchange (minimum £100,000) on the bank, the bank accepts the bill, and the importer discounts it. Provided the tenor of the bill is below 180 days, it will be classed as a bank bill and thus can be discounted at fine rates.

c)   Documentary Credits Payable after Sight but which Contain a Negotiation Clause

When the seller is in a strong enough bargaining position to insist on documentary credits, there can be a problem if the seller requires payment immediately on presentation of documents and the buyer requires credit terms.

One possible solution is a documentary credit that calls for term drafts, but which contains an authority for the advising bank to negotiate against correct presentation of documents. Provided that the applicant has agreed to be responsible for all discount costs, this credit will meet the requirements of the beneficiary.

From the importer's point of view, this facility is more generous than open account terms or documentary collection terms with overdraft/loan or factoring or acceptance credit facilities to allow for payment to the supplier on shipment.

d)   VAT deferment

In the absence of any arrangement to the contrary, importers will have to pay VAT on goods as they are cleared through Customs. However, it is possible for importers to arrange to open an account with the VAT authorities so that VAT is settled on a monthly basis. Usually all VAT incurred in January would be settled on 15 February, and all VAT incurred in February would be settled on 15 March and so on.

The importer would require a bank indemnity in favour of HM Customs to cover any non-payment of VAT incurred on the monthly settlement. The bank would apply normal credit criteria when deciding whether to grant the indemnity, would require a counter-indemnity from the importer and would charge a fee. These considerations will follow the principles described in Chapter 20, concerning the issue of bonds on behalf of customers.

The importer must decide whether the cash-flow gains, interest savings and convenience outweigh the bank's fee for the indemnity. The earlier in the month the goods clear Customs, the greater the cash flow and interest benefits.

An additional means of legally avoiding VAT is available in connection with goods that are being brought into the UK from abroad, and temporarily warehoused in the UK pending re-export. Such goods should be kept in a customs or bonded warehouse while in the UK. This will legally avoid the need to pay VAT, so long as the goods remain there until subsequent re-export. A variation of this method is the 'E' type warehouse, which can be located at the importer's own premises. Provided computerized stock control methods, backed up by periodic spot checks, show that the goods are accounted for separately, then there will be no VAT to pay so long as the goods are exported when they leave the control of the importer.

DELIVERY ORDER

No. 107   4th July

To The Superintendent of London Warehouses Ltd.

PLEASE DELIVER TO Alexander Productions   or Order

the undermentioned Goods,

ex Ship Mustansir   Rotation No.   6640L

Charges to be paid by consignee

Marks and Numbers M M M M M M	Quantity	Description
	One case	Photographic spools

S P E C I M E N

Per pro
NATIONAL WESTMINSTER BANK LIMITED

Chesil Beach

....Office or Branch

....Manager

430-1-9 69

Exhibit 14: Delivery Order

SIVEWRIGHT TRANSPORT & STORAGE LIMITED

SPECIMEN ONLY OF **ADVICE OF GOODS RECEIVED**

R 8067
R 8067

Into......Morpeth Tongue......WAREHOUSE, BIRKENHEAD.

On (date)......25th June, 1977......   I. No......12554

Sender or Ex......ex. 'TOKIO EXPRESS'......   M/C No......

A/c......Messrs. Black & Sons Ltd.,......

Senders Ref.	Marks and or Numbers	Quantity of Packages	WEIGHTS				Descriptions or other particulars (provided by senders)	Remarks
			Tons	Cwts.	Qts.	Lbs.		
1231	BLACK/BLUE	4	400 Kilos				Pallets Empty Glass Ink Bottles.	
							A number of bottles broken.	
							UNEXAMINED	
	TOTALS	(-4-) FOUR						

OBSERVATIONS.   E. & O. E., and subject to our Conditions of Storage.

For SIVEWRIGHT TRANSPORT & STORAGE LTD.

Exhibit 15: Warehouse Receipt

NWB1044 Trust Certificate

To Rimmer Glendz & Co
   9, Trottingham Park
   London E. 1.   3rd May .... —

The Customer ....

....

....

Dear Sir,

We hand you herewith the undermentioned documents of title to the undermentioned goods (now in pledge to us as security for advances) on the following terms and conditions:—

You undertake to hold the documents of Title and the said goods when received (and the proceeds thereof when sold) as trustees for NATIONAL WESTMINSTER BANK LIMITED (the Bank).

(a) (b) (c)
one or more of
these to be deleted.

(a) As you require the said documents in order to obtain delivery of the said goods you undertake to warehouse them in the name of the Bank and to hand us the Warrants forthwith; also to insure the goods against all risks to their full insurable value and to hold the policies on our behalf and in case of loss to pay the Insurance moneys to us in the same manner as proceeds of sales.

(b) As you require the said goods in order to despatch the same to your agents for the purpose of sale or for processing printing or for the further preparation of the said goods in any manner whatsoever for immediate or eventual sale you undertake to hand us the receipts of your agents for the said goods and at all times to keep the goods fully insured against all risks however caused and to hold the policies on our behalf and in case of loss to pay the Insurance money to us in the same manner as proceeds of sales.

Insert number
of days

(c) As you require the said goods in order to deliver the goods to the Buyers you undertake to pay us the proceeds of sales without deduction of any expenses and immediately upon the receipt thereof or of each portion thereof, as the case may be within 15 days days from the date hereof and to give us on request full authority to receive from any person or persons the purchase moneys of such goods or any of them and in the meantime to hold the goods in trust for us.

You undertake also to keep this transaction separate from all other transactions.

We authorise you to take delivery of the goods on our behalf and to act as our trustees in the custody and realisation of the same and we request you to pay the proceeds of all sales to us immediately and specifically as received by you and to act on the above terms.

Yours faithfully,

NATIONAL WESTMINSTER BANK LIMITED

PRINCES STREET OFFICE .... Branch

.... Manager

Exhibit 16: Trust Receipt (front)

The Schedule of Documents and Goods

Description of Documents	Description of Goods	Vessel	Name of Buyer	Invoice Price
3/3 B/Ls Insurance Pol. Invoice in trip	Tinned peaches	Flemmington	Andrew Sprite & Son	£2,400

To The Manager,

7th May _____ 19__

National Westminster Bank Limited

PRINCES STREET OFFICE

1, PRINCES STREET, E.C.2. _____ Branch

Dear Sir,

I/We acknowledge receipt of the above-mentioned documents relating to the above-mentioned goods of the Bank which I/we receive and/or will deal with upon the above terms and conditions giving as I/we do hereby all the undertakings mentioned above.

(*)to be deleted if (c) above is deleted

(*) I/We hereby declare that I am/ we are not indebted to the Buyers of the goods.

Yours faithfully,

For & on behalf of
Rimmer Glendz & Co.

Secretary

Exhibit 17: Trust Receipt (back)

22

DOCUMENTARY CREDITS FOR IMPORTS

Objectives

On completion of this chapter the student should be able to:

- appreciate the risks that a bank undertakes when issuing a documentary credit on behalf of an importer;

- explain how some of these risks can be reduced;

- understand and explain the technicalities that must be resolved to ensure that the documentary credit is logical and workable;

- understand and explain the effects of Uniform Customs and Practice for Documentary Credits on the issuing of the credit and the responsibilities of the applicant and issuing bank.

1 The Risks that a Bank Runs when it Issues a Documentary Credit

When a bank issues a documentary credit, it guarantees payment if the correct documents are presented in conformity with all the terms and conditions of the credit. Normally, the issuing bank would obtain reimbursement by debiting the customer's account in accordance with the authority (please see item (a) in the terms and conditions of the specimen authority at Figure 2).

However, the issuing bank must honour the credit, provided its terms have been fulfilled, irrespective of whether the applicant has funds in his account. As a result, the issuing bank treats the documentary credit in much the same way as any other lending facility, and a limit will be marked on the account.

2 How the Issuing Bank Can Reduce its Risks under Documentary Credits

As with any lending facility, the bank's prime considerations are the creditworthiness and integrity of its customer. However, an additional consideration is that the underlying goods can be used as security, provided the correct formalities are observed.

Thus, the considerations apart from general creditworthiness and integrity are:

a) The nature of the goods. Are they easily saleable if the bank has to sell them to cover its liability in the event of the applicant's default?

b) Should the credit call for a third-party inspection certificate? If such a document is called for and is produced, the goods should be of the required standard. If the document is not produced, the issuing bank is free of liability and will refuse payment because of a discrepancy in the presentation of documents.

c) The beneficiary should be well known, or a good status report should be held regarding his commercial reliability and integrity.

d) The bank could insist on a measure of cash cover from the applicant. Please see clause (f) on the terms and conditions of the specimen application form (Figure 2).

e) The goods must be insured. If the credit calls for an insurance document, which would be the case if the underlying sale contract were CIF, then all is well. If the credit does not call for an insurance document, as would be the case with an FOB sale contract, the bank must satisfy itself that the applicant is to effect the necessary insurance.

f) If air waybills are called for, the issuing bank must decide whether it wants to be named as consignee. If the bank feels it is necessary to retain control of the goods, the credit must stipulate that the air waybill shows the bank as consignee.

g) If the goods come by sea, it is in the interests of both bank and customer for the credit to call for a complete set of clean, shipped on board, bills of lading, made out to order and blank endorsed.

3 The Authority that the Applicant Completes

Once an importer and exporter have agreed to deal on documentary credit terms, the importer must request his bank to arrange the credit. You will recall from Part Three of the course that the importer is the applicant and his bank is the issuing bank.

From the specimen application form reproduced at Figure 1, you will see that the main details required are:

1 Full name and address of beneficiary.

FOR BANK USE ONLY

		Branch Ref.	ISB Ref.
DOCUMENTARY CREDIT APPLICATION ✠ **BARCLAYS**			

To
BARCLAYS BANK PLC _____ Branch

Date

Customer/Applicant:	Name and address of beneficiary
Address:	
Customer's Reference:	

Please open an *IRREVOCABLE* Letter of Credit by *(see note 1)*

☐ Mail Only   ☐ Mail with brief details Teletransmitted   ☐ Full details Teletransmitted with no mail confirmation

Advising Bank:
(Bank use only)

Amount (see note 1)
(in words and figures)
(specify currency)   ☐ Up to   ☐ About

Available by drafts on Barclays Bank PLC or its correspondents at *(see note 1)*

☐ sight   ☐ ____days sight   ☐ ____ days after ____

for ____ per cent of the _____ invoice value, accompanied by the following documents:
(see note 2)

Invoice *(see note 3)*
Full set of clean on board blank endorsed BILLS OF LADING *(see note 4)* marked notify:

INSURANCE policy or certificate *(in duplicate)* endorsed in blank for the invoice value of the goods plus _____ per cent, covering:
(see note 5)

Any Other Documents:

Brief description of goods:
(see note 6)

Shipment from:	Partshipments	Transhipments
to	☐ Allowed	☐ Allowed
At latest by:	☐ Prohibited	☐ Prohibited
	See note 1	

Documents to be presented within _____ days of shipment but in any event within the validity of the credit.

Credit to expire on _____ in the beneficiary's country.

Additional Information *(see note 7)*

37514/R5L/CBF 201

Figure 1: Specimen Authority

Finance of International Trade

▼ IF APPLICABLE PLEASE INDICATE

☐ Forward Contract No. _____ Maturity _____ Rate _____

☐ CFC Account No.

TERMS AND CONDITIONS

In consideration of your issuing this Letter of Credit:

a) We authorise you to debit our account with all your commissions/charges and expenses together with those of your correspondents where applicable as and when they become due and with drawings either: (i) on presentation if drafts are drawn at sight or where no drafts are involved, or, (ii) at maturity in respect of accepted drafts in which case we hereby undertake to provide you with funds not later than 3 days before maturity, unless you have been previously provided with funds for this purpose.

b) Where drafts are drawn in a currency other than Sterling, your demand for reimbursement from us will be calculated, unless previously agreed to the contrary, at your selling rate of exchange for the currency concerned, for the day you effect payment, or receive advice from your branch or correspondent that payment has been made. Interest where applicable is payable by us from the date of payment by your branch/correspondent until the reimbursement currency is available to you, and any exchange risks are for our account.

c) Where the beneficiary is not required to provide an insurance document, we undertake to arrange such insurance and deliver the relative policies/certificates to you on request. If the insurance is not arranged to your satisfaction you are authorised to arrange such insurance at our expense.

d) The relative shipping documents, as and when received by you, are to be delivered to us provided all costs, expenses and interest have been paid. If we fail to pay, you are authorised to sell the goods, and we undertake to pay on demand the amount of any deficiency on such sale.

e) It is agreed that this credit is subject to Uniform Customs and Practice for Documentary Credits (1983 Revision) I.C.C. Publication No. 400.

Clause (f) below should only be completed when full or part cash cover is being provided

f) To provide you with security you are authorised immediately to

(i) debit our account with _____ (say _____

_____)

(ii) buy the sum of _____ (say _____

_____)

on our behalf and debit our account with the Sterling equivalent.

Such sums to be held by you until all claims regarding this Letter of Credit have been satisfied.

For and on behalf of _____

(Insert Company Name)

Capacity of Signatory(ies) _____

NOTES

ALL DELETIONS AND ALTERATIONS TO BE INITIALLED

1) Indicate instruction to be followed by placing a tick or cross in appropriate box. One item only is to be completed in each section.
2) Insert Term of Contract, C.I.F., F.O.B., etc.
3) Indicate if required in duplicate, triplicate etc.
4) If Bill of Lading not required delete and insert other transport document (e.g. Air Waybill, Forwarding Agents Receipts etc.) indicating name and address of consignee.
5) If the insurance is being arranged by the beneficiary, complete this clause and state risks to be covered, Marine/Air/War etc. If insurance is being arranged by applicant, see note (c) above.
6) Goods description may include reference to proforma invoices or contracts but such documents should not be attached.
7) Include any additional information such as whether beneficiary has agreed to pay bank charges outside the U.K. and beneficiary's bankers (if known).

FOR BANK USE ONLY

BRANCH AUTHORISATION

AUTHORISING BRANCH TO INDICATE BELOW BY PLACING TICK IN BOX IF FULLY CASH COVERED ☐

ISB USE ONLY

SIGNATURES VERIFIED

TO INTERNATIONAL SERVICES BRANCH

Figure 2: Specimen Authority (continued)

FOLD ALONG THIS LINE

2   Whether the credit is revocable or irrevocable (Article 6). (On the Barclays authority, only irrevocable credits can be issued.)

3   Whether the details are to be passed to the advising bank by mail or teletransmission. If mail is to be used, check that there is adequate time before the expiry date (Article 11).

4   The amount of the credit. If the word 'about' is used, then a 10% deviation either way will be allowed (Article 39).

5   The documents called for. These must be logical. For instance, if the goods are coming by air, it would be illogical to call for bills of lading.

6   The description of the goods is important, because on presentation of documents the invoice must describe the goods in exactly the same way, whereas the transport document can describe the goods in general terms not inconsistent with this wording on the credit (Article 37).

7   The latest date of shipment and the expiry date. It is not necessary to show a latest date of shipment, but if one is shown it must be not later than the expiry date of the credit. If a latest date of shipment is shown and it is more than 21 days before the expiry date, then there is a danger that all documents would be stale (Article 43).

8   If the credit amount is expressed in foreign currency, both the bank and the customer must decide whether it is necessary to cover the exchange risk.

Note
The International Chamber of Commerce has produced a series of standardized documentary credit forms which will enable all types of form (e.g. application, advice to bank) to be produced from a single input of data.

4   Re-instatement Documentary Credits

Re-instatement documentary credits are best explained through an example. The 'Flotsam and Jetsam Ltd' question provides a good illustration of the use of such techniques.

Question
Flotsam and Jetsam Ltd imports a range of consumer items from many overseas countries. The directors have recently asked you to arrange an irrevocable letter of credit in favour of an overseas supplier to cover the company's imports for the next 12 months. Bank facilities are fully utilized and you are reluctant to issue an irrevocable letter of credit covering shipments valued in excess of £50,000 in any one month for the next 12 months. You are, however, prepared to issue an irrevocable letter of credit covering up to three months' shipments for a maximum of £150,000 (or the foreign currency equivalent), but you are not prepared to go beyond that limit. Nevertheless, the supplier has insisted that a bank undertaking should be issued in its favour, otherwise the company's source of supply will dry up.

Required

a) Specify the banking instruments that would satisfy the customer's needs utilizing irrevocable letters of credit, but which would not extend the bank facilities beyond the limit you are prepared to sanction.

b) Briefly describe how these banking instruments would operate.

c) Make brief notes showing the explanation you would give to the directors describing the advantages and disadvantages to the company, and the beneficiary (its supplier), of each of the methods described in (a) and (b) above.

Introduction to Flotsam and Jetsam Question

A documentary credit is a real liability to the issuing bank, because the bank must pay if the correct documents are tendered at the correct time.

The overseas supplier requires a documentary credit for a total sum of £600,000 which will allow part shipment against pro rata drawings. The supplier then knows that payment of his full year's sales to Flotsam is guaranteed, provided he conforms to the terms of the credit.

However, our bank is prepared to sanction only a maximum liability of £150,000 on behalf of Flotsam.

The supplier is in a strong bargaining position, so if Flotsam is to obtain the supplies, a documentary credit will be required.

Basically, the question asks what compromise is available whereby the supplier obtains a documentary credit, but our bank's liability is restricted to £150,000 maximum.

Answer

a) i) A re-instatement letter of credit;
   or
   ii) A stand-by letter of credit.

b) i) Operation of a re-instatement documentary credit.
   The terms of the credit would be as follows:

   1 Expiry date in 12 months' time.

   2 Maximum amount £150,000 (i.e. three months' shipments).

   3 The credit will call for a specific sum, say £50,000 in value, to be shipped each month.

   4 The credit will state that the value of any documents, drawn in accordance with the terms of the credit, will be **re-instated** provided that Flotsam agrees.

   5 The credit will state that if documents are presented which do not conform

to the credit, then either the bank or Flotsam could refuse to re-instate and would allow no further drawings.

6   The credit will state that Flotsam has the right to refuse re-instatement.

ii)   Operation of stand-by letter of credit.

1   Our bank is the issuing bank and Flotsam is the applicant.

2   The credit would be for a maximum of £150,000.

3   The credit could guarantee payment against presentation of an invoice and copy bill of lading, together with a signed certificate from the supplier certifying that payment had not been made. Alternatively, payment could be guaranteed against a dishonoured, protested, bill of exchange drawn on Flotsam.

4   The supplier would then trade on an open account basis, but he would be able to claim under the stand-by letter of credit if Flotsam did not pay. Alternatively, the supplier would trade on a documentary collection basis, and in the event of dishonour would then use the stand-by credit to obtain payment.

Note
The standby letter of credit could state 'issued subject to the Uniform Customs and Practice for Documentary Credits (1993 revision)' or it could be stated to be 'issued subject to ISP 1998'. The differences between the rules have been fully covered in Chapter 19 and the reader is invited to refer back to that chapter for any further examination of this aspect. For the purcposes of the points illustrated above, it is not necessary to consider which rules might apply.

c)   *The Advantages of Re-instatement Documentary Credit for Flotsam (Importer/Applicant)*

1)   The bank regards this facility as a liability of £150,000, rather than £600,000.

Hence borrowing facilities are a much lower amount and bank charges are reduced.

2)   Flotsam has the right to refuse to authorize re-instatement of any amount drawn under the credit. Thus, Flotsam are committed only to three months' purchases and could cancel the facility if alternative supplies were available.

3)   The credit is subject to UCP, and so payment can only be made against stipulated documents.

b)   *Disadvantage of Re-instatement Documentary Credit for Flotsam*
As with all documentary credits, payment is made against documents, not against goods. Hence, payment will be made against the correct documents even if the goods prove to be faulty.

iii) *Advantages of Re-instatement Documentary Credit to the Supplier/Beneficiary*
As with all documentary credits, payment of the amount (£150,000) is guaranteed against presentation of documents.

iv) *Disadvantages of Re-instatement Credit for Supplier/Beneficiary*
Only three months' sales are guaranteed, not twelve, because Flotsam could refuse to re-instate drawings.

Note
Importers prefer to issue 'ordinary' credits, which can be extended by amendment.

Advantages of Stand-by Letter of Credit to Buyer/Applicant

i) If Flotsam refuses, for whatever reason, to honour invoices on open account or bills under documentary collection, payment will be delayed until the supplier can assemble the documents to claim under the stand-by credit.

Disadvantages of Stand-by Letter of Credit to Applicant

i) If bills of exchange are used, dishonour will result in protest. This will damage Flotsam's credit.

Advantages of Stand-by Credit to Beneficiary

i) Good security up to £150,000.

ii) If the buyer does not honour the 'open account' or 'documentary collection' claim, this will act as a warning not to ship any further goods in excess of the £150,000 available under the limit.

Disadvantages of Stand-by Credit to Beneficiary

i) In effect, only three months' sales are guaranteed. Thus, the seller cannot rely upon a guarantee of payment for a full 12 months' sales

5 Comparison of Avalization and Documentary Credit Facilities from the Point of View of the Importer's Bank

a) Similarities

Each facility involves the bank in guaranteeing the indebtedness of the customer. Therefore, the facilities are available only to good customers.

b) Differences

i)   Avalization is usually unsecured, in that the collection is clean, or documents are released on acceptance.

ii)   The issuing bank can gain a measure of protection by calling for suitable documents under a documentary credit (e.g. third-party inspection certificate). Such protection is not available for avalization.

iii) Documentary credits can be issued on any mutually agreed terms between the bank and the applicant. Avalization is normally confined to bills of exchange of minimum amounts of £10,000.

iv)   Avalization facilities can be agreed quickly; documentary credits take more time to set up.

v)   In the UK, there is no statutory recognition of avalization. Thus, the UK bank will require a special indemnity from its customer to authorize reimbursement of any money paid by the bank to the presenter of the bill.

23

Transferable Letters of Credit and Back-to-back Letters of Credit

Objectives

On completion of this chapter the student should be able to:

● understand and explain the nature of transferable credits;

● differentiate between transferable and back-to-back credits;

● appreciate the differences between transferable credits, back-to-back credits, red clause credits and produce loans.

1   Description of a Transferable Credit and Situations when Transferable Credit Can be Used

A transferable credit is defined in Article 48 of the Uniform Customs and Practice for Documentary Credits (UCP). Under UCP a credit is transferable only if it is expressly designated transferable by the issuing bank. Terms such as 'divisible', 'assignable', 'transmissible' and 'fractionable' do not render a credit transferable.

The transferable credit will be used when the supplier of goods sells them through a middleman and does not deal directly with the ultimate buyer. If the supplier is in a strong bargaining position, he may insist that a documentary credit be set up in his favour.

The middleman may not wish to arrange a documentary credit himself, and his bankers in any case may not be willing to issue a credit on his behalf. Thus the middleman will approach the ultimate buyer and ask him to arrange a transferable documentary credit in his (the middleman's) favour. The middleman is known as the first beneficiary of the credit.

The credit will be designated transferable, and will allow the first beneficiary to request the bank authorized to pay, incur a deferred payment undertaking, accept or negotiate, or in the case of a freely negotiable credit the bank specifically authorized as the transferring bank to make the credit available to one or more third parties who are known as 'second beneficiaries'. Thus the original supplier of the goods is known as the second beneficiary.

2 The Terms on which the First Beneficiary Can Authorize Transfer of the Rights under the Credit to the Second Beneficiary

The transferring bank shall be under no obligation to transfer the credit, unless it agrees to do so. A transferable credit can be transferred only once, thus the second beneficiary or beneficiaries cannot transfer their rights to a third beneficiary.

The transfer will be in accordance with the terms of the original credit except for:

a) The name and address of the first beneficiary will be shown instead of that of the applicant.

b) The amount of the credit and unit price may be reduced to allow for the middleman's profit.

c) The expiry date (and last permissible date for shipment if one is stipulated) will be earlier than on the original credit.

d) The percentage for which insurance cover must be effected may be increased to provide the amount of cover stipulated in the original credit.

It is the transferring bank, acting on the instructions of the first beneficiary, who will advise the credit to the second beneficiary.

The first beneficiary must irrevocably instruct the transferring bank whether or not it may advise any subsequent amendments to the second beneficiary.

3 Operation of a Transferable Credit when the Second Beneficiary has Shipped the Goods and Presented the Documents

The second beneficiary will present his documents, usually via his own bankers, to the transferring bank. The invoice and bill of exchange will be for less than the amount advised to the first beneficiary. On receipt of the documents, the transferring bank will substitute the invoice of the first beneficiary and replace his bill of exchange with one for the full amount of the credit.

The transferring bank will then present the documents to the issuing bank and obtain payment. On receipt of the funds, the amount claimed by the second beneficiary will be paid to him, and the difference will be paid over to the middleman as his profit. If for any reason the first beneficiary fails to present his own invoices, the transferring bank may send to the issuing bank the documents it has received, including the second beneficiary's invoices without further responsibility to the first beneficiary.

4   Uniform Customs and Practice

Students should note the following points:

a)   UCP cover all aspects except those expressly covered by the terms of the credit.

b)   All authorities stipulate **subject to UCP 1993.**

c)   Transferable credits are covered in Article 48.

d)   A credit can be transferred only if it is expressly stated to be transferable.

e)   The first beneficiary can only request the bank to transfer. The bank is not obliged to do so.

f)   The first beneficiary must pay all charges and the bank need not effect the transfer until charges are paid.

g)   The credit can be transferred only on the terms and conditions specified in the original credit, except for lower amount, lower price per unit, earlier expiry date/date of shipment. The first beneficiary can call for the second beneficiary to provide the full amount of insurance, based on the price paid by the applicant.

h)   Under Article 49, the fact that a credit is not stated to be transferable shall not affect the beneficiary's right to assign any proceeds to which he may become entitled under the credit (see Chapter 17).

5   Transferable Credits: Flow Charts

a)   The Arrangements for Setting up the Credit

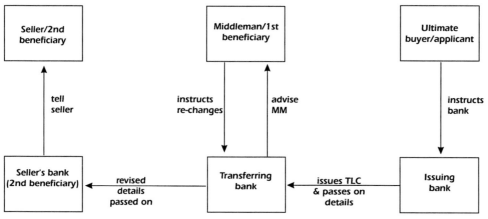

Changes in details when transferring bank pass on details:

a) 1st beneficiary's name substituted for applicant's;

b) Lower amount;

c) Earlier expiry date;

Note
Only credits that expressly say they are transferable can be transferred (Article 48 UCP).

b) Presentation of Documents under TLC

Changes in documents when transferring bank send them to issuing bank:

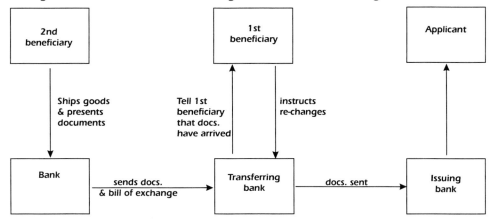

a) Substitutes 1st beneficiary's invoices which will be for a higher amount;

b) Substitutes a new bill of exchange for the full amount;

c) Payment under TLC (Ignore complexities of nostro/vostro accounts).

Note
Goods shipped direct from seller's country to ultimate buyer's country.

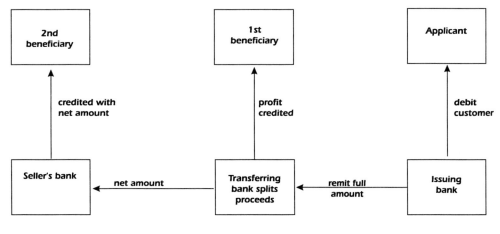

6 Back-to-back Credits

a) Description or Back-to-back Credits and Situations When they Can Be Used

Back-to-back credits consist of two entirely separate documentary credits, but one credit may act as security for the other. They apply in transactions when original suppliers and ultimate buyers deal through a middleman. In fact, back-to-back credits are used in the same situations as transferable credits, but the rights and obligations of the parties differ with the two types of credit.

If the supplier insists on a documentary credit, the middleman may apply to his bankers for them to issue one on his behalf. If the middleman's bankers are satisfied as to his creditworthiness, they will issue the credit in the normal way and no other formalities will apply. However, the 'back-to-back' aspect comes into play if the middleman's bankers insist that the middleman obtains a documentary credit in his favour from the ultimate buyer as security for one which the middleman has applied for in favour of the seller.

Only the middleman and his banker need know of the back-to-back aspect, and only they are concerned with the back-to-back aspect. The other parties, that is the ultimate buyer, the original supplier and their bankers, are not affected in any way whatsoever by the back-to-back aspect.

b) Procedure for Arranging Back-to-Back Credits When the Middleman's Bankers Require a Documentary Credit as Security for a Credit They Are Asked to Issue

i) The middleman asks the ultimate buyer to arrange a documentary credit in his favour. This is known as the 'first credit'.

ii) The middleman then requests his bankers to issue a credit in favour of the supplier of the goods. This is known as the 'second credit' and the middleman is the applicant for the second credit. The second credit will not be issued until the first one has been advised.

iii) The second credit must call for the same documents as the first credit, apart from the invoices, and must have an earlier expiry date and be for a lower amount than the first credit.

c) Procedure When the Original Supplier Ships his Goods and Presents the Documents in Accordance with the Second Credit

i) The documents are presented via the supplier's advising bank to the issuing bank which is the bank of the middleman. This issuing bank pays the supplier, debiting the middleman by way of a separate loan.

ii)   The middleman's bankers, who will be the advising bank of the first credit, substitute the middleman's invoices for those of the supplier. The bill of exchange will be for a higher amount and will agree with the amount on the new invoices.

iii)   The middleman's bankers, then, as advising bank of the first credit, present the documents to the issuing bank.

iv)   The issuing bank of the first credit pays in accordance with the terms, debiting the cost to the ultimate buyer.

v)   On receipt of the proceeds of the first credit, the middleman's bankers clear the loan account in the name of the middleman and any surplus represents the middleman's profit.

d)   Liabilities of the Parties with Back-to-back Credits

The credits are entirely separate instruments, and thus the middleman and his bank are responsible for paying the second credit irrespective of whether payment is subsequently received under the first credit.

The second credit must have an earlier expiry date than the first, otherwise the documents required to procure payment under the first credit would not be available in time. It is a good precaution to make the second credit expire in the place of issue otherwise the issuing bank is in the hands of the postal authorities, and delayed receipt of documents could mean non-payment under the first credit.

7   Comparison of Difference between Transferable and Back-to-back Credits

a)   With transferable credits the ultimate buyer is aware that he is dealing with a middleman; with back-to-back credits he is not.

(b)   With transferable credits the middleman and his bankers have no liability, but with back-to-back credits they are fully liable on the second credit.

8   Position when the First Credit Calls for an Insurance Document

a)   When the Second Credit Does Not Call for an Insurance Document

In this case the middleman's bankers must make sure that their customer has insured and can produce the appropriate document in time for presentation under the first credit.

b) Where the Second Credit Calls for an Insurance Document

Care must be taken to stipulate that the amount of insurance evidenced by the document required by the second credit is sufficient to meet the amount of insurance required by the first credit.

This may seem self-evident, but it must be remembered that the amount of cover is generally based on the amount of the invoice. Since the invoice value of the second credit is less than that of the first credit, the second credit must specify a sufficiently high amount of cover.

Note
There are no special rules in UCP to deal with back-to-back credits. Each credit stands on its own merits.

9   'Cash Flow' from the Point of View of the Middleman

a) Transferable Credits

There are no debits to the account at all. When the funds are paid over the middleman's bank credit him with the 'profit' and pay the balance to the second beneficiary. The only entry on the middleman's bank account will be a credit for the profit.

b) Back-to-back Credits

The middleman is the applicant for the second credit and the beneficiary of the first credit. The second credit has the earlier expiry date, and so the middleman will be debited with the full amount of the second credit, and shortly afterwards will be credited with payment of the full amount of the first credit. There will be two separate entries on the account:

a)   debit for the amount of the second credit;

b)   a credit for the amount of the first credit.

Appendix 1

ELECTRONIC COMMERCE (e-COMMERCE)

1   Background

With the advancement of modern technology international business is being conducted increasingly in a global market place. Business computerization continues at a phenomenal pace with estimates in excess of 250 million e-commerce users by 2003 being mooted. Also by 2003 it is expected that e-commerce will account for in excess of US $2,500 billion of the global economy. As a result, the use of paper-based systems is becoming outmoded and inefficient. The days of electronic commerce or 'paperless trading' are therefore upon us and will soon become the accepted norm.

2   Electronic Data Interchange (EDI)

EDI has existed in various forms for about thirty years. Because of the increase in trade, the amount of paperwork generated has slowed up the relevant processes and has added substantially to costs both in terms of financial and human resources. Consequently, interest in EDI has grown considerably.

EDI in the business world is the exchange of electronically-generated trade-related data, whether commercial or financial, between the computers of various parties. Such parties not only include buyers and sellers but also such organizations as freight forwarders, shipping companies, banks and credit insurers.

EDI is facilitated by using agreed message standards. These include EDIFACT (EDI for Administration, Commerce and Transport) and TRADACOMS (Trading Data Communication Standard).

3   Benefits of EDI

- Improvements in the time efficiency of trading processes. EDI negates the need to print details of a contract from one computer's file, which are then sent by post to a recipient who then inputs this information onto another computer file.

Errors from repeated manual input of data are reduced.

Cost reduction. It has been estimated that costs of processing paperwork in connection with orders can be reduced by up to 90%.

Automation provides more accurate information on which to base key decisions, e.g. cash flow needs, stock requirements.

By improving business efficiency and cost effectiveness, organizations can increase competitive advantage and profitability.

4   Problems Related to Full EDI Implementation

Initial cost of installing the relevant hardware and software for EDI to operate.

Additional training costs in ensuring that staff can operate the new systems.

Having alternative systems on hand in case of a technical breakdown.

Possibility of fraud due to bogus trade orders or unauthorized payment instructions.

All trading partners may not be operating EDI systems.

EDI is a business-to-business system and is therefore limited in its application by removing the ultimate retail buyer from the equation. Consequently, development of e-commerce via the internet, which is more flexible in its usage, is moving to replace the older EDI system.

5   The Internet

The Internet is a global communications system which links together a wide variety of computer networks throughout the world.

For exporters and importers, the Internet has two particular beneficial services – electronic mail (known as e-mail) and the World Wide Web (WWW).

E-mail allows parties to send electronic equivalents of letters or memoranda to one another via computer. Linked to this, complete computer files can be sent via e-mail.

WWW provides traders with an electronic shop window for their goods which can be regularly updated. Such traders can have their own WWW.page which can display both graphics and text and can include all relevant information about their goods and services including prices, delivery costs and payment terms. These are now proving to be the forum for global commercial trading and are creating commercial opportunities for business entities of all sizes.

6   Problems with Trading on the Internet

In order for any trade deal to be completed there must be absolute trust between the parties

to such a deal. When you are negotiating the purchase of goods face to
gain some impression of the person you are dealing with. To achieve a ⟨
is somewhat more difficult!

How do you know that the owner of a WWW page is authentic? H⟨
goods know that payment will be made? Coupled to these questions, wou⟨⟨ ⟩
sending details of your credit card via the Internet? What would happen if such details were
intercepted en route and became known by criminal elements?

In respect of the standing of suppliers or buyers, parties will still have to carry out status
enquiries via their banks or credit reference agencies. However, a greater potential problem
lies with the security of information supplied via the Internet.

A number of organizations have investigated this problem and produced various secure
systems. For example, Visa International and MasterCard developed a single technical
standard known as Secure Electronic Transaction (SET) which protects the use of payment
cards over the Internet.

SET involves the use of digital certificates which authenticate the identity of cardholders
making purchases. It therefore provides some security for all parties to such transactions.

However, 'hackers' are still breaching so-called safe security systems and therefore further
research into secure electronic commerce procedures is ongoing and readers should try to
keep abreast of developments in the financial press.

7   Current Electronic Commerce Developments

International Chamber of Commerce (ICC)

The ICC has under its Project E-100 looked into the development and promotion of electronic
alternatives to paper-based systems during the last few years. Under this project various
working parties examined such areas as electronic credits; open account trading; electronic
transport documents; legal and regulatory matters; and how electronic commerce could
interface with paper-based/auxiliary systems.

From this work has evolved the Electronic Commerce Project (ECP). ECP's main projects
involve the creation/development of international guidelines and policies on electronic
commerce and business services. By doing this, and working in partnership with other
electronic commerce initiatives, its intention is to aid a more secure transaction environment
and thereby develop worldwide trust in e-commerce transactions. ECP's initial activity was
to create General Usage for International Digitally Ensured Commerce (GUIDEC) which
was designed to clarify relevant rules and definitions in relation to electronic authentication
systems.

ECP has a number of working groups, one of which is the Electronic Trade Practices
working group. As most international rules are still based upon the use of paper

...entation, one of its objectives is to adapt current rules to comply with the new electronic ... In addition, it also seeks to improve efficiency in relation to trade deals.

Other constituent parts of the ICC are also involved in considering e-commerce and its implications. The ICC Banking Commission, for example, is currently deliberating over whether research needs to be undertaken in order to establish how ICC publication number 500, Uniform Customs and Practice for Documentary Credits, should be utilized in respect of electronic trade.

The E-Terms working group is looking at the setting up of an on-line repository for electronic terms. The repository is designed so that it can be accessed globally and that all contracting parties will be able to use clearly defined and understood terms in order to reduce possible legal risks to a minimum.

Finally, the ICC is currently working on new guidelines for electronic trade and settlements and, no doubt, is likely to continue to be a major player in the development of electronic commerce.

Bolero.Net

In September 1999, bolero.net was launched as a joint venture by S.W.I.F.T. (Society for Worldwide Interbank Financial Transactions) and the TT Club (Through Transport Mutual Insurance Association Limited). It is operated by Bolero International Limited.

Bolero.net provides a global e-commerce system for all parties to international trade including banks, freight forwarders, shipping companies, carriers, exporters and importers. Through its Core Messaging Platform (CMP) it provides a secure authentication and safe messaging service. It also has set up a central database known as the Title Registry which tracks and records changes of ownership/rights to the ownership of goods where goods are sold while in transit. Bolero Bills of Lading (BBL) are used for this purpose. BBLs are not bills of lading as such but are electronic documents that mirror the functions of their paper counterparts.

All subscribers to bolero.net agree to accept its 'Rulebook' which means that any likely legal problems can be minimized. The 'Rulebook' is expected to alter in conjunction with new legal legislation and technological developments as they occur.

Statutory and Legal Developments

With the growing prowess of e-commerce and its high profile in the global economy, governments are taking steps to aid its growth and security.

The UK government now has a Minister of E-commerce, and the Electronic Communications Bill is currently going through Parliament. The latter has among its provisions the statutory recognition of electronic signatures and procedures for eliminating legal problems linked to electronically agreed contracts.

The European Union has several pieces of legislation linked to e-commerce which are due to be introduced during 2000. Probably the most important of these is the European Commission Directive on e-commerce which will provide a regulatory framework for e-commerce business and therefore help to promote trust in on-line transactions.

This is a very volatile area and readers need to keep abreast of developments via the media, DTI or their local chamber of commerce.

Appendix 2

CORRESPONDENT BANKING AND COMPETITION BETWEEN BANKS

i)   What is Correspondent Banking?

Now that the whole of the services and facilities have been covered, the student needs to place correspondent banking in context.

In the 1980s, when capital was relatively cheap, many banks tried to expand their own operations abroad, by setting up new offices overseas, or by acquiring a ready-made banking network by means of a takeover. In many instances, these methods have proved to be too great a drain on capital and their operations in any event have not been too successful.

In today's more sober economic climate, some banks now provide an international service for their customers by means of correspondent banks. Correspondent banking simply means that the home country bank will aim to provide overseas services for its own customers by using an overseas, correspondent, bank as agent. Examples of the use of correspondent banks are:

● nostro/vostro accounts used in international settlement to facilitate international funds transfer;

● documentary credits advised via a correspondent bank, with a correspondent bank nominated to pay;

● special technology links (for example, NatWest Bank and Société Générale), to enable the banks to provide low-cost cross-border funds transfer for their respective customers;

● the willingness to recommend the services of the correspondent bank to facilitate a deal. For example, a UK bank may not wish to agree with a request to provide export factoring services, but it may well investigate whether the importer's bank could offer import factoring to its own customer so that the UK exporter can be paid upfront in cash by the importer.

In international trade, with the onset of the single European market and technology links between banks and customers, the correspondent banks have become an important part of the customer base of any bank with customers who have cross-border business. Fees received by banks for the provision of correspondent banking services can prove to be a significant contribution to total bank profits.

One problem relating to the use of correspondent banks has been the need to ensure that the standard of service of these banks was satisfactory. One major UK bank is currently negotiating a series of 'performance benchmarks' with its overseas correspondent banks. This will provide specific remedies against the correspondent bank should its service be substandard in any way.

The maintenance of a first-class network of correspondent banks will help a bank to gain a competitive edge and will generate a useful source of income from the services that the bank provides for its correspondents. Students should always be ready to suggest the use of a correspondent bank to deliver a customer service that our own bank cannot provide.

Management of the correspondent banking relationships is a very complex business. On the one hand, the correspondent is our bank's agent abroad helping our bank to deliver a complete service to our customers. On the other hand, that bank is a customer of ours (e.g. when our bank is collecting bank for an inward collection), and yet at the same time the correspondent is a potential competitor (e.g. our exporter customers may submit documentary collections directly to the overseas correspondent bank).

ii) Competition between Banks within the EU

Under the EU's Second Banking Co-ordination Directive, there is a 'single banking licence', under which any bank that is authorized to act as such in a member state will also be allowed to set up branches or to supply cross-border services in other member states.

Some European banks have set up pan-European banking groups, offering a wide range of services, both retail and corporate. Now that the single European market is upon us, competition from banks of other member states for UK customer business is bound to increase. Examples already occur whereby banks in Germany encourage UK exporters to route their documentary collections directly to the German bank where the importer maintains his account.

UK banks will no doubt use different strategies to counter the competition, and they will establish a credibility in overseas markets by a mixture of correspondent banking relationships, branch networks acquired via takeovers, or by means of representative offices. It is vital to the UK that the banking system as a whole continues to operate in such a way as to maintain the pre-eminence of London as a major international financial centre.

Appendix 3

UNIFORM RULES FOR
COLLECTIONS, ICC 522

A.   General Provisions and Definitions

Article 1
Application of URC 522

a)   The Uniform Rules for Collections, 1995 Revision, ICC Publication No 522, shall apply to all collections as defined in Article 2 where such rules are incorporated into the text of the 'collection instruction' referred to in Article 4 and are binding on all parties thereto unless otherwise expressly agreed or contrary to the provisions of a national, state or local law and/or regulation that cannot be departed from.

b)   Banks shall have no obligation to handle either a collection or any collection instruction or subsequent related instructions.

c)   If a bank elects, for any reason, not to handle a collection or any related instructions received by it, it must advise the party from whom it received the collection or the instructions by telecommunication or, if that is not possible, by other expeditious means, without delay.

Article 2
Definition of Collection

For the purposes of these Articles:

a)   'Collection' means the handling by banks of documents as defined in sub-Article 2(b), in accordance with instructions received, in order to

   i)   obtain payment and/or acceptance,

   or

   ii)   deliver documents against payment and/or against acceptance,

   or

   iii) deliver documents on other terms and conditions.

b) 'Documents' means financial documents and/or commercial documents:

   i) 'Financial documents' means bills of exchange, promissory notes, cheques, or other similar instruments used for obtaining the payment of money;

   ii) 'Commercial documents' means invoices, transport documents, documents of title or other similar documents, or any other documents whatsoever, not being financial documents.

c) 'Clean collection' means collection of financial documents not accompanied by commercial documents.

d) 'Documentary collection' means collection of:

   i) Financial documents accompanied by commercial documents;

   ii) Commercial documents not accompanied by financial documents.

Article 3
Parties to a Collection

a) For the purposes of these Articles the 'parties thereto' are:

   i. the 'principal' who is the party entrusting the handling of a collection to a bank;

   ii. the 'remitting bank' which is the bank to which the principal has entrusted the handling of a collection;

   iii) the 'collecting bank' which is any bank other than the remitting bank, involved in processing the collection;

   iv) the 'presenting bank' which is the collecting bank making presentation to the drawee.

b) The 'drawee' is the one to whom presentation is to be made in accordance with the collection instruction.

B. Form and Structure of Collections

Article 4
Collection Instruction

a) i) All documents sent tor collection must be accompanied by a collection instruction indicating that the collection is subject to URC 522 and giving complete and precise instructions. Banks are permitted to act only upon the instructions given in such collection instruction, and in accordance with these Rules.

   ii) Banks will not examine documents in order to obtain instructions.

   iii) Unless otherwise authorized in the collection instruction, banks will disregard any instructions from any party/bank other than the partyl/bank from whom they received the collection.

b)   A collection instruction should contain the following items of information, as appropriate:

    i)   Details of the bank from which the collection was received including full name, postal and SWIFT addresses, telex, telephone, facsimile numbers and reference.

    ii)   Details of the principal including full name, postal address, and if applicable telex, telephone and facsimile numbers.

    iii)   Details of the drawee including full name, postal address, or the domicile at which presentation is to be made and if applicable telex, telephone and facsimile numbers.

    iv)   Details of the presenting bank, if any, including full name, postal address, and if applicable telex, telephone and facsimile numbers.

    v)   Amount(s) and currency(ies) to be collected.

    vi)   List of documents enclosed and the numerical count of each document.

    vii)   a)   Terms and conditions upon which payment and/or acceptance is to be obtained.

            b)   Terms of delivery of documents against:

                1) payment and/or acceptance

                2) other terms and conditions

        It is the responsibility of the party preparing the collection instruction to ensure that the terms for the delivery of documents are clearly and unambiguously stated, otherwise banks will not be responsible for any consequences arising therefrom.

    viii)   Charges to be collected, indicating whether they may be waived or not.

    ix)   Interest to be collected, if applicable, indicating whether it may be waived or not, including:

        a.   rate of interest

        b.   interest period

        c.   basis of calculation (for example 360 or 365 days in a year as applicable).

    x)   Method of payment and form of payment advice.

    xi)   Instructions in case of non-payment, non-acceptance and/or non-compliance with other insfructions.

c)   i)   Collection instructions should bear the complete address of the drawee or of the domicile at which the presentation is to be made. If the address is incomplete or incorrect, the collecting bank may, without any liability and responsibility on its part, endeavour to ascertain the proper address.

ii)   The collecting bank will not be liable or responsible for any ensuing delay as a result of an incomplete/incorrect address being provided.

C.   Form of Presentation

Article 5
Presentation

a)   For the purposes of these Articles, presentation is the procedure whereby the presenting bank makes the documents available to the drawee as instructed.

b)   The collection instruction should state the exact period of time within which any acttion is to be taken by the drawee.

Expressions such as 'first', 'prompt', 'immediate' and the like should not be used in connection with presentation or with reference to any period of time within which documents have to be taken up or for any other action that is to be taken by the drawee. If such terms are used banks will disregard them.

c)   Documents are to be presented to the drawee in the form in which they are received except that banks are authorized to affix any necessary stamps at the expense of the party from whom they received the collection unless otherwise instructed, and to make any necessary endorsements or place any rubber stamps or other identifying marks or symbols customary to or required for the collection operation.

d)   For the purpose of giving effect to the instructions of the principal, the remitting bank will utilize the bank nominated by the principal as the collecting bank. In the absence of such nomination, the remitting bank will utilize any bank of its own, or another bank's choice in the country of payment or acceptance or in the country where other terms and conditions have to be complied with.

e)   The documents and collection instruction may be sent directly by the remitting bank to the collecting bank or through another bank as intermediary.

f)   If the remitting bank does not nominate a specific presenting bank the collecting bank may utilize a presenting bank of its choice.

Article 6
Sight/Acceptance

In the case of documents payable at sight the presenting bank must make presentation for payment without delay.

In the case of documents payable at a tenor other than sight the presenting bank must, where acceptance is called tor, make presentation for acceptance without delay and where payment is called for, make presentation for payment not later than the appropriate maturity date.

Article 7
Release of Commercial Documents
Documents Against Acceptance (D/A) *v.* Documents Against Payment (D/P)

a) Collections should not contain bills of exchange payable at a future date with instructions that commercial documents are to be delivered against payment.

b) If a collection contains a bill of exchange payable at a future date, the collection instruction should state whether the commercial documents are to be released to the drawee against acceptance (D/A) or against payment (D/P).

   In the absence of such statement commercial documents will be released only against payment and the collecting bank will not be responsible for any consequences arising out of any delay in the delivery of documents.

c) If a collection contains a bill of exchange payable at a future date and the collection instruction indicates that commercial documents are to be released against payment, documents will be released only against such payment and the collecting bank will not be responsible for any consequences arising out of any delay in the delivery of documents.

Article 8
Creation of Documents

Where the remitting bank instructs that either the collecting bank or the drawee is to create documents (bills of exchange, promissory notes, trust receipts, letters of undertaking or other documents) that were not included in the collection, the form and wording of such documents shall be provided by the remitting bank, otherwise the collecting bank shall not he liable or responsible for the form and wording of any such document provided by the collecting bank and/or the drawee.

D.   Liabilities and Responsibilities

Article 9
Good Faith and Reasonable Care

Banks will act in good faith and exercise reasonable care.

Article 10
Documents vs. Goods/Services/Performances

a) Goods should not be despatched directly to the address of a bank or consigned to or to the order of a bank without prior agreement on the part of that bank.

   Nevertheless, in the event that goods are despatched directly to the address of a bank or consigned to or to the order of a bank for release to a drawee against payment or acceptance or upon other terms and conditions without prior agreement on the part of that bank, such bank shall have no obligation to take delivery of the goods, which remain at the risk and responsibility of the party despatching the goods.

b)   Banks have no obligation to take any action in respect of the goods to which a documentary collection relates, including storage and insurance of the goods even when specific instructions are given to do so. Banks will take such action only if, when, and to the extent that they agree to do so in each case. Notwithstanding the provisions of sub-Article 1(c), this rule applies even in the absence of any specific advice to this effect by the collecting bank.

c)   Nevertleless, in the case that banks take action for the protection of the goods, whether instructed or not, they assume no liability or responsibility with regard to the fate and/ or condition of the goods and/or for any acts and/or omissions on the part of any third parties entrusted with the custody and/or protection of the goods. However, the collecting bank must advise without delay the bank from which the collection instruction was received of any such action taken.

d)   Any charges and/or expenses incurred by banks in connection with any action taken to protect the goods will be for the account of the party from whom they received the collection.

e)   i)   Notwithstanding the provisions of sub-Article 10(a), where the goods are consigned to or to the order of the collecting barlk and the drawee has honoured the collection by payment, acceptance or other terms and conditions, and the collecting bank arranges for the release of the goods, the remitting bank shall be deemed to have authorized the collecting bank to do so.

   ii)   Where a collecting bank on the instructions of the remitting bank or in terms of sub-Article 10(e)i arranges for the release of the goods, the remitting bank shall indemnify such collecting bank for all damages and expenses incurred.

Article 11
Disclaimer For Acts of an Instructed Party

a)   Banks utilizing the services of another bank or other banks for the purpose of giving effect to the instructions of the principal, do so for the account and at the risk of such principal.

b)   Banks assume no liability or responsibility should the instructions they transmit not be carried out even if they have themselves taken the initiative in the choice of such other bank(s).

c)   A party instructing another party to perform services shall be bound by and liable to indemnify the instructed party against all obligations and responsibilities imposed by foreign laws and usages.

Article 12
Disclaimer on Documents Received

a) Banks must determine that the documents received appear to be as listed in the collection instruction and must advise by telecommunication or, if that is not possible, by other expeditious means, without delay, the party from whom the collection instruction was received of any documents missing, or found to be other than listed.

   Banks have no further obligation in this respect.

b) If the documents do not appear to be listed the remitting bank shall be precluded from disputing the type and number of documents received by the collecting bank.

c) Subject to sub-Article 5(c) and sub-Articles 12(a) and 12(b) above, banks will present documents as received without further examination.

Article 13
Disclaimer on Effectiveness of Documents

Banks assume no liability or responsibility for the form, sufficiency, accuracy, genuineness, falsification or legal effect of any document(s), or for the general and/or particular conditions stipulated in the document(s) or superimposed thereon; nor do they assume any liability or responsibility for the description, quantity, weight, quality, condition, packing, delivery, value or existence of the goods represented by any document(s), or for the good faith or acts and/or omissions, solvency, performance or standing of the consignors, the carriers, the forwarders, the consignees or the insurers of the goods, or any other person whomsoever.

Article 14
Disclaimer on Delays, Loss in Transit and Translation

a) Banks assume no liability or responsibility for the consequences arising out of delay and/or loss in transit of any message(s), letter(s) or document(s), or for delay, mutilation or other error(s) arising in transmission of any telecommunication or for error(s) in translation and/or interpretation of technical terms.

b) Banks will not be liable or responsible for any delays resulting from the need to obtain clarification of any instructions received.

Article 15
Force Majeure

Banks assume no liability or responsibility for consequences arising out of the interruption of their business by Acts of God, riots, civil commotions, insurrections, wars, or any other causes beyond their control or by strikes or lockouts.

E.   Payment

Article 16
Payment Without Delay

a)   Amounts collected (less charges and/or disbursements and/or expenses where applicable) must be made available without delay to the party from whom the collection instruction was received in accordance with the terms and conditions of the collection instruction.

b)   Notwithstanding the provisions of sub-Article 1(c) and unless otherwise agreed, the collecting bank will effect payment of the amount collected in favour of the remitting bank only.

Article 17
Payment in Local Currency

In the case of documents payable in the currency of the country of payment (local currency), the presenting bank must, unless otherwise instructed in the collection instruction, release the documents to the drawee against payment in local currency only if such currency is immediately available for disposal in the manner specified in the collection instruction.

Article 18
Payment in Foreign Currency

In the case of documents payable in a currency other than that of the country of payment (foreign currency), the presenting bank must, unless otherwise instructed in the collection instruction, release the documents to the drawee against payment in the designated foreign currency only if such foreign currency can immediately be remitted in accordance with the instructions given in the collection instruction.

Article 19
Partial Payments

a)   In respect of clean collections, partial payments may be accepted if and to the extent to which and on the conditions on which partial payments are authorized by the law in force in the place of payment. The financial document(s) will be released to the drawee only when full payment thereof has been received.

b)   In respect of documentary collections, partial payments will be accepted only if specifically authorized in the collection instruction. However, unless otherwise instructed, the presenting bank will release the documents to the drawee only after full payment has been received, and the presenting bank will not be responsible for any consequences arising out of any delay in the delivery of documents.

c)   In all cases partial payments will be accepted only subject to compliance with the provisions of either Article 17 or Article 18 as appropriate.

Partial payment, if accepted, will be dealt with in accordance with the provisions of Article 16.

F. Interest, Charges and Expenses

Article 20
Interest

a) If the collection instruction specifies that interest is to be collected and the drawee refuses to pay such interest, the presenting bank may deliver the document(s) against payment or acceptance or on other terms and conditions as the case may be, without collecting such interest, unless sub-Article 20(c) applies.

b) Where such interest is to be collected, the collection instruction must specify the rate of interest, interest period and basis of calculation.

c) Where the collection instruction expressly states that interest may not be waived and the drawee refuses to pay such interest the presenting bank will not deliver documents and will not be responsible for any consequences arising out of any delay in the delivery of document(s). When payment of interest has been refused, the presenting bank must inform by telecommunication or, if that is not possible, by other expeditious means without delay the bank from which the collection instruction was received.

Article 21
Charges and Expenses

a) If the collection instruction specifies that collection charges and/or expenses are to be for account of the drawee and the drawee refuses to pay them, the presenting bank may deliver the document(s) against payment or acceptance or on other terms and conditions as the case may be, without collecting charges and/or expenses, unless sub-Article 21(b) applies.

Whenever collection charges and/or expenses are so waived they will be for the account of the party from whom the collection was received and may be deducted from the proceeds.

b) Where the collection instruction expressly states that charges and/or expenses may not be waived and the drawee refuses to pay such charges and/or expenses, the presenting bank will not deliver documents and will not be responsible for any consequences arising out of any delay in the delivery of the document(s). When payment of collection charges and/or expenses has been refused the presenting bank must inform by telecommunication or, if that is not possible, by other expeditious means without delay the bank from which the collection instruction was received.

c) In all cases where in the express terms of a collection instruction or under these Rules, disbursements and/or expenses and/or collection charges are to be borne by the principal, the collecting bank(s) shall be entitled to recover promptly outlays in respect of disbursements, expenses and charges from the bank from which the collection instruction was received, and the remitting bank shall be entitled to recover promptly from the principal any amount so paid out by it, together with its own disbursements, expenses and charges, regardless of the fate of the collection.

d)   Banks reserve the right to demand payment of charges/and expenses in advance from the party from whom the collection instruction was received, to cover costs in attempting to carry out any instructions, and pending receipt of such payment also reserve the right not to carry out such instructions.

G.   Other Provisions

Article 22
Acceptance

The presenting bank is responsible for seeing that the form of the acceptance of a bill of exchange appears to be complete and correct, but is not responsible for the genuineness of any signature or for the authority of any signatory to sign the acceptance.

Article 23
Promissory Notes and Other Instruments

The presenting bank is not responsible for the genuineness of any signature or for the authority of any signatory to sign a promissory note, receipt, or other instruments.

Article 24
Protest

The collection instruction should give specific instructions regarding protest (or other legal process in lieu thereof), in the event of non-payment or non-acceptance.

In the absence of such specific instructions, the banks concerned with the collection have no obligation to have the document(s) protested (or subjected to other legal process in lieu thereof) for non-payment or non-acceptance.

Any charges and/or expenses incurred by banks in connection with such protest, or other legal process, will be for the account of the party from whom the collection instruction was received.

Article 25
Case-of-Need

If the principal nominates a representative to act as case-of-need in the event of non-payment and/or non-acceptance the collection instruction should clearly and fully indicate the powers of such case-of-need. In the absence of such indication banks will not accept any instructions from the case-of-need.

Article 26
Advices

Collecting banks are to advise fate in accordance with the following rules:

a) **Form of Advice**

All advices or information from the collecting bank to the bank from which the collection instruction was received, must bear appropriate details including, in all cases, the latter bank's reference as stated in the collection instruction.

b) **Method of Advice**

It shall be the responsibility of the remitting bank to instruct the collecting bank regarding the method by which the advices detailed in (c)i, (c)ii and (c)iii are to be given. In the absence of such instructions, the collecting bank will send the relative advices by the method of its choice at the expense of the bank from which the collection instruction was received.

c)   i)   ADVICE OF PAYMENT

The collecting bank must send without delay advice of payment to the bank from which the collection instruction was received, detailing the amount or amounts collected, charges and/or disbursements and/or expenses deducted, where appropriate, and method of disposal of the funds.

     ii)   ADVICE OF ACCEPTANCE

The collecting bank must send without delay advice of acceptance to the bank from which the collection instruction was received.

     iii)   ADVICE OF NON-PAYMENT AND/OR NON-ACCEPTANCE

The presenting bank should endeavour to ascertain the reasons for non-payment and/or non-acceptance and advise accordingly, without delay, the bank from which it received the collection instruction.

The presenting bank must send without delay advice of non-payment and/or advice of non-acceptance to the bank from which it received the collection instruction.

On receipt of such advice the remitting bank must give appropriate instructions as to the further handling of the documents. If such instructions are not received by the presenting bank within 60 days after its advice of nonpayment and/or non-acceptance, the documents may be returned to the bank from which the collection instruction was received without any further responsibility on the part of the presenting bank.

Appendix 4

UNIFORM CUSTOMS AND PRACTICE FOR DOCUMENTARY CREDITS

A. General Provisions and Definitions

Article 1
Application of UCP

The Uniform Customs and Practice for Documentary Credits, 1993 Revision, ICC Publication no. 500, shall apply to all Documentary Credits (including to the extent to which they may be applicable, Standby Letter(s) of Credit) where they are incorporated into the text of the Credit. They are binding on all parties thereto, unless otherwise expressly stipulated in the Credit.

Article 2
Meaning of Credit

For the purposes of these Articles, the expressions 'Documentary Credit(s)' and 'Standby Letter(s) of Credit' (hereinafter referred to as 'Credit(s)'), mean any arrangement, however named or described, whereby a bank (the 'Issuing Bank') acting at the request and on the instructions of a customer (the 'Applicant') or on its own behalf,

i) is to make a payment to or to the order of a third party (the 'Beneficiary') or is to accept and pay bills of exchange (Draft(s)) drawn by the Beneficiary

or

ii) authorizes another bank to effect such payment, or to accept and pay such bills of exchange (Draft(s)),

or

iii) authorizes another bank to negotiate,

against stipulated document(s), provided that the terms and conditions of the Credit are complied with.

For the purposes of these Articles, branches of a bank in different countries are considered another bank.

Article 3
Credits v. Contracts

a) Credits, by their nature, are separate transactions from the sales or other contract(s) on which they may be based and banks are in no way concerned with or bound by such contract(s), even if any reference whatsoever to such contract(s) is included in the Credit. Consequently, the undertaking of a bank to pay, accept and pay Draft(s) or negotiate and/or to fulfil any other obligation under the Credit, is not subject to claims or defences by the Applicant resulting from his relationships with the Issuing Bank or the Beneficiary.

b) A Beneficiary can in no case avail himself of the contractual relationships existing between the banks or between the Applicant and the Issuing Bank.

Article 4
Documents v. Goods/Services/Performances

In Credit operations all parties concerned deal with documents, and not with goods, services and/or other performances to which the documents may relate.

Article 5
Instructions to Issue/Amend Credits

a) Instructions for the issuance of a Credit, the Credit itself, instructions for an amendment thereto, and the amendment itself, must be complete and precise.

   In order to guard against confusion and misunderstanding, banks should discourage any attempt:

   i)   to include excessive detail in the Credit or in any amendment thereto;

   ii)   to give instructions to issue, advise or confirm a Credit by reference to a Credit previously issued (similar Credit) where such previous Credit has been subject to accepted amendment(s), and/or unaccepted amendment(s).

b) All instructions for the issuance of a Credit and the Credit itself and, where applicable, all instructions for an amendment thereto and the amendment itself, must state precisely the document(s) against which payment, acceptance or negotiation is to be made

B.   Form and Notification of Credits

Article 6
Revocable v. Irrevocable Credits

a) A Credit may be either

i)   revocable,

or

ii)   irrevocable

b)   The Credit, therefore, should clearly indicate whether it is revocable or irrevocable.

c)   In the absence of such indication the Credit shall be deemed to be irrevocable.

Article 7
Advising Bank's Liability

a)   A Credit may be advised to a Beneficiary through another bank (the 'Advising Bank') without engagement on the part of the Advising Bank, but that bank, if it elects to advise the Credit, shall take reasonable care to check the apparent authenticity of the Credit which it advises. If the bank elects not to advise the Credit, it must so inform the Issuing Bank without delay.

b)   If the Advising Bank cannot establish such apparent authenticity it must inform, without delay, the bank from which the instructions appear to have been received that it has been unable to establish the authenticity of the Credit and if it elects nonetheless to advise the Credit it must inform the Beneficiary that it has not been able to establish the authenticity of the Credit.

Article 8
Revocation of a Credit

a)   A revocable Credit may be amended or cancelled by the Issuing Bank at any moment and without prior notice to the Beneficiary.

b)   However, the Issuing Bank must:

i)   reimburse another bank with which a revocable Credit has been made available for sight payment, acceptance or negotiation – for any payment, acceptance or negotiation made by such bank – prior to receipt by it of notice of amendment or cancellation against documents that appear on their face to be in compliance with the terms and conditions of the Credit;

ii)   reimburse another bank with which a revocable Credit has been made available for deferred payment, if such a bank has, prior to receipt by it of notice of amendment or cancellation, taken up documents that appear on their face to be in compliance with the terms and conditions of the Credit.

Article 9
Liability of Issuing and Confirming Banks

a)   An irrevocable Credit constitutes a definite undertaking of the Issuing Bank, provided that the stipulated documents are presented to the Nominated Bank or to the Issuing

Bank and that the terms and conditions of the Credit are complied with:

i)   if the Credit provides for sight payment: to pay at sight;

ii) if the Credit provides for deferred payment: to pay on the maturity date(s) determinable in accordance with the stipulations of the Credit;

iii) if the Credit provides for acceptance:

   a)   by the Issuing Bank: to accept Draft(s) drawn by the Beneficiary on the Issuing Bank and pay them at maturity,

   or

   b)   by another drawee bank: to accept and pay at maturity Draft(s) drawn by the Beneficiary on the Issuing Bank in the event the drawee bank stipulated in the Credit does not accept Draft(s) drawn on it, or to pay Draft(s) accepted but not paid by such drawee bank at maturity;

iv) if the Credit provides for negotiation: to pay without recourse to drawers and/or bona fide holders, Draft(s) drawn by the Beneficiary and/or document(s) presented under the Credit. A Credit should not be issued available by Draft(s) on the Applicant. If the Credit nevertheless calls for Draft(s) on the Applicant, banks will consider such Draft(s) as an additional document(s).

b)   A confirmation of an irrevocable Credit by another bank (the 'Confirming Bank') upon the authorization or request of the Issuing Bank, constitutes a definite undertaking of the Confirming Bank, in addition to that of the Issuing Bank, provided that the stipulated documents are presented to the Confirming Bank or to any other Nominated Bank and that the terms and conditions of the Credit are complied with.

i)   if the Credit provides for sight payment: to pay at sight;

ii) if the Credit provides for deferred payment: to pay on the maturity date(s) determinable in accordance with the stipulations of the Credit;

iii) if the Credit provides for acceptance:

   a.   by the Confirming Bank: to accept Draft(s) drawn by the Beneficiary on the Confirming Bank and pay them at maturity,

   or

   b.   by another drawee bank: to accept and pay at maturity Draft(s) drawn by the Beneficiary on the Confirming Bank, in the event the drawee bank stipulated in the Credit does not accept Draft(s) drawn on it, or to pay Draft(s) accepted but not paid by such drawee bank at maturity;

iv) if the Credit provides for negotiation: to negotiate without recourse to drawers and/or bona fide holders, Draft(s) drawn by the Beneficiary and/or document(s) presented under the Credit. A Credit should not be issued available by Draft(s) on the Applicant. If the Credit nevertheless calls for Draft(s) on the

Applicant, banks will consider such Draft(s) as an additional document(s).

c) i) If another bank is authorized or requested by the Issuing Bank to add its confirmation to a Credit but is not prepared to do so, it must so inform the Issuing Bank without delay.

ii) Unless the Issuing Bank specifies otherwise in its authorization or request to add confirmation, the Advising Bank may advise the Credit to the Beneficiary without adding its confirmation.

d) i) Except as otherwise provided by Article 48, an irrevocable Credit can neither be amended nor cancelled without the agreement of the Issuing Bank, the Confirming Bank, if any, and the Beneficiary.

ii) The Issuing Bank shall be irrevocably bound by an amendment(s) issued by it from the time of the issuance of such amendment(s). A Confirming Bank may extend its confirmation to an amendment and shall be irrevocably bound as of the time of its advice of the amendment. A Confirming Bank may, however, choose to advise an amendment to the Beneficiary without extending its confirmation and if so, must inform the Issuing Bank and the Beneficiary without delay.

iii) The terms of the original Credit (or a Credit incorporating previously accepted amendment(s)) will remain in force for the Beneficiary until the Beneficiary communicates his acceptance of the amendment to the bank that advised such amendment. The Beneficiary should give notification of acceptance or rejection of amendment(s). If the Beneficiary fails to give such notification, the tender of documents to the Nominated Bank or Issuing Bank, that conform to the Credit and to not yet accepted amendment(s), will be deemed to be notification of acceptance by the Beneficiary of such amendment(s) and as of that moment the Credit will be amended.

iv) Partial acceptance of amendments contained in one and the same advice of amendment is not allowed and consequently will not be given any effect.

Article 10
Types of Credit

a) All Credits must clearly indicate whether they are available by sight payment, by deferred payment, by acceptance or by negotiation.

b) i) Unless the Credit stipulates that it is available only with the Issuing Bank, all Credits must nominate the bank (the 'Nominated Bank') that is authorized to pay, to incur a deferred payment undertaking, to accept Draft(s) or to negotiate. In a freely negotiable Credit, any bank is a Nominated Bank.

Presentation of documents must be made to the Issuing Bank or the Confirming Bank, if any, or any other Nominated Bank.

ii) Negotiation means the giving of value for Draft(s) and/or document(s) by the bank authorized to negotiate. Mere examination of the documents without giving of value does not constitute a negotiation.

c) Unless the Nominated Bank is the Confirming Bank, nomination by the Issuing Bank does not constitute any undertaking by the Nominated Bank to pay, to incur a deferred payment undertaking, to accept Draft(s), or to negotiate. Except where expressly agreed to by the Nominated Bank and so communicated to the Beneficiary, the Nominated Bank's receipt of and/or examination and/or forwarding of the documents does not make that bank liable to pay, to incur a deferred payment undertaking, to accept Draft(s), or to negotiate.

d) By nominating another bank, or by allowing for negotiation by any bank, or by authorizing or requesting another bank to add its confirmation, the Issuing Bank authorizes such bank to pay, accept Draft(s) or negotiate as the case may be, against documents that appear on their face to be in compliance with the terms and conditions of the Credit and undertakes to reimburse such bank in accordance with the provisions of these Articles.

Article 11
Teletransmitted and Pre-Advised Credits

a) i) When an Issuing Bank instructs an Advising Bank by an authenticated teletransmission to advise a Credit or an amendment to a Credit, the teletransmission will be deemed to be the operative Credit instrument or the operative amendment, and no mail confirmation should be sent. Should a mail confirmation nevertheless be sent, it will have no effect and the Advising Bank will have no obligation to check such mail confirmation against the operative Credit instrument or the operative amendment received by teletransmission.

ii) If the teletransmission states 'full details to follow' (or words of similar effect) or states that the mail confirmation is to be the operative Credit instrument or the operative amendment, then the teletransmission will not be deemed to be the operative Credit instrument or the operative amendment. The Issuing Bank must forward the operative Credit instrument or the operative amendment to such Advising Bank without delay.

b) If a bank uses the services of an Advising Bank to have the Credit advised to the Beneficiary, it must also use the services of the same bank for advising an amendment(s).

c) A preliminary advice of the issuance or amendment of an irrevocable Credit (pre-advice), shall be given by an Issuing Bank only if such bank is prepared to issue the operative Credit instrument or the operative amendment thereto. Unless otherwise stated in such preliminary advice by the Issuing Bank, an Issuing Bank having given such pre-advice shall be irrevocably committed to issue or amend the Credit, in terms not inconsistent with the pre-advice, without delay.

Article 12
Incomplete or Unclear Instructions

If incomplete or unclear instructions are received to advise, confirm or amend a Credit, the bank requested to act on such instructions may give preliminary notification to the Beneficiary for information only and without responsibility. This preliminary notification should state clearly that the notification is provided for information only and without the responsibility of the Advising Bank. In any event, the Advising Bank must inform the Issuing Bank of the action taken and request it to provide the necessary information.

The Issuing Bank must provide the necessary information without delay. The Credit will be advised, confirmed or amended, only when complete and clear instructions have been received and if the Advising Bank is then prepared to act on the instructions.

C.   Liabilities and Responsibilities

Article 13
Standard for Examination of Documents

a)   Banks must examine all documents stipulated in the Credit with reasonable care, to ascertain whether or not they appear, on their face, to be in compliance with the terms and conditions of the Credit. Compliance of the stipulated documents on their face with the terms and conditions of the Credit shall be determined by international standard banking practice as reflected in these Articles. Documents that appear on their face to be inconsistent with one another will be considered as not appearing on their face to be in compliance with the terms and conditions of the Credit.

Documents not stipulated in the Credit will not be examined by banks. If they receive such documents, they shall return them to the presenter or pass them on without responsibility.

b)   The Issuing Bank, the Confirming Bank, if any, or a Nominated Bank acting on their behalf, shall each have a reasonable time, not to exceed seven banking days following the day of receipt of the documents, to examine the documents and determine whether to take up or refuse the documents and to inform the party from which it received the documents accordingly.

c)   If a Credit contains conditions without stating the document(s) to be presented in compliance therewith, banks will deem such conditions as not stated and will disregard them.

Article 14
Discrepant Documents and Notice

a)   When the Issuing Bank authorizes another bank to pay, incur a deferred payment Draft(s), or negotiate against documents that appear on their face to be the terms and conditions of the Credit, the Issuing Bank and the Confirming Bank, if any, are bound:

   i)   to reimburse the Nominated Bank that has paid, incurred a deferred payment undertaking, accepted Draft(s), or negotiated,

   ii) to take up the documents.

b)   Upon receipt of the documents the Issuing Bank and/or Confirming Bank, if any, or a Nominated Bank acting on its behalf, must determine on the basis of the documents alone whether or not they appear on their face to be in compliance with the terms and conditions of the Credit. If the documents appear on their face not to be in compliance with the terms and conditions of the Credit, such banks may refuse to take up the documents.

c)   If the Issuing Bank determines that the documents appear on their face not to be in compliance with the terms and conditions of the Credit, it may in its sole judgment approach the Applicant for a waiver of the discrepancy(ies). This does not, however, extend the period mentioned in sub-Article 13 (b).

d)   i)   If the Issuing Bank and/or Confirming Bank, if any, or a Nominated Bank acting on its behalf, decides to refuse the documents, it must give notice to that effect by telecommunication or, if that is not possible, by other expeditious means, without delay but no later than the close of the seventh banking day following the day of receipt of the documents. Such notice shall be given to the bank from which it received the documents, or to the Beneficiary, if it received the documents directly from him.

   ii) Such notice must state all discrepancies in respect of which the bank refuses the documents and must also state whether it is holding the documents at the disposal of, or is returning them to, the presenter.

   iii) The Issuing Bank and/or Confirming Bank, if any, shall then be entitled to claim from the remitting bank refund, with interest, of any reimbursement that has been made to that bank.

e)   If the Issuing Bank and/or Confirming Bank, if any, fails to act in accordance with the provisions of this Article and/or fails to hold the documents at the disposal of, or return them to the presenter, the Issuing Bank and/or Confirming Bank, if any, shall be precluded from claiming that the documents are not in compliance with the terms and conditions of the Credit

f)   If the remitting bank draws the attention of the Issuing Bank and/or Confirming Bank, if any, to any discrepancy(ies) in the document(s) or advises such banks that it has paid, incurred a deferred payment undertaking, accepted Draft(s) or negotiated under reserve or against an indemnity in respect of such discrepancy(ies), the Issuing Bank and/or Confirming Bank, if any, shall not be thereby relieved from any of their obligations under any provision of this Article. Such reserve or indemnity concerns only the relations between the remitting bank and the party towards whom the reserve was made, or from whom, or on whose behalf, the indemnity was obtained.

Article 15
Disclaimer on Effectiveness of Documents

Banks assume no liability or responsibility for the form, sufficiency, accuracy, genuineness, falsification or legal effect of any document(s), or for the general and/or particular conditions stipulated in the document(s) or superimposed thereon; nor do they assume any liability or responsibility for the description, quantity, weight, quality, condition, packing, delivery, value or existence of the goods represented by any document(s), or for the good faith or acts and/or omissions, solvency, performance or standing of the consignors, the carriers, the forwarders, the consignees or the insurers of the goods, or any other person whomsoever.

Article 16
Disclaimer on the Transmission of Messages

Banks assume no liability or responsibility for the consequences arising out of delay and/or loss in transit of any message(s), letter(s) or document(s), or for delay, mutilation or other error(s) arising in the transmission of any telecommunication. Banks assume no liability or responsibility for errors in translation and/or interpretation of technical terms, and reserve the right to transmit Credit terms without translating them.

Article 17
Force Majeure

Banks assume no liability or responsibility for the consequences arising out of the interruption of their business by acts of God, riots, civil commotions, insurrections, wars or any other causes beyond their control, or by any strikes or lockouts. Unless specifically authorized, banks will not, upon resumption of their business, pay, incur a deferred payment undertaking, accept Draft(s) or negotiate under Credits which expired during such interruption of their business.

Article 18
Disclaimer for Acts of an Instructed Party

a) Banks utilizing the services of another bank or other banks for the purpose of giving effect to the instructions of the Applicant do so for the account and at the risk of such Applicant.

b) Banks assume no liability or responsibility should the instructions they transmit not be carried out, even if they have themselves taken the initiative in the choice of such other bank(s).

c) i) A party instructing another party to perform services is liable for any charges, including commissions, fees, costs, or expenses incurred by the instructed party in connection with its instructions.

ii) Where a Credit stipulates that such charges are for the account of a party other than the instructing party, and charges cannot be collected, the instructing party remains ultimately liable for the payment thereof.

d) The Applicant shall be bound by and liable to indemnify the banks against all obligations and responsibilities imposed by foreign laws and usages.

Article 19
Bank-to-bank Reimbursement Arrangements

a) If an Issuing Bank intends that the reimbursement to which a paying, accepting or negotiating bank is entitled, shall be obtained by such bank (the 'Claiming Bank'), claiming on another party (the 'Reimbursing Bank'), it shall provide such Reimbursing Bank in good time with the proper instructions or authorization to honour such reimbursement claims.

b) Issuing Banks shall not require a Claiming Bank to supply a certificate of compliance with the terms and conditions of the Credit to the Reimbursing Bank

c) An Issuing Bank shall not be relieved from any of its obligations to provide reimbursement if and when reimbursement is not received by the Claiming Bank from the Reimbursing Bank

d) The Issuing Bank shall be responsible to the Claiming Bank for any loss of interest if reimbursement is not provided by the Reimbursing Bank on first demand, or as otherwise specified in the Credit, or mutually agreed, as the case may be.

e) The Reimbursing Bank's charges should be for the account of the Issuing Bank. However, in cases where the charges are for the account of another party, it is the responsibility of the Issuing Bank to so indicate in the original Credit and in the reimbursement authorization. In cases where the Reimbursing Bank's charges are for the account of another party they shall be collected from the Claiming Bank when the Credit is drawn under. In cases where the Credit is not drawn under, the Reimbursing Bank's charges remain the obligation of the Issuing Bank.

D.   Documents

Article 20
Ambiguity as to the Issuers of Documents

a) Terms such as 'first class', 'well known', 'qualified'. 'independent', 'official', 'competent', 'local' and the like, shall not be used to describe the issuers of any document(s) to be presented under a Credit. If such terms are incorporated in the Credit, banks will accept the relative document(s) as presented, provided that it appears on its face to be in compliance with the other terms and conditions of the Credit and not to have been issued by the Beneficiary

b)   Unless otherwise stipulated in the Credit, banks will also accept as an original document(s), a document(s) produced or appearing to have been produced

　　i)   by reprographic, automated or computerized systems, or

　　ii)   as carbon copies,

provided that it is marked as original and, where necessary, appears to be signed.

A document may be signed by handwriting, by facsimile signature, by perforated signature, by stamp, by symbol, or by any other mechanical or electronic method of authentication.

c)   i)   Unless otherwise stipulated in the Credit, banks will accept as a copy(ies), a document(s) either labelled copy or not marked as an original – a copy(ies) need not be signed Credits that require multiple document(s) such as 'duplicate', 'two fold', 'two copies' and the like, will be satisfied by the presentation of one original and the remaining number in copies except where the document itself indicates otherwise.

　　ii)   Credits that require multiple document(s) such as 'duplicate', 'two fold', 'two copies' and the like, will be satisfied by the presentation of one original and the remaining number in copies except where the document itself indicates otherwise.

d)   Unless otherwise stipulated in the Credit, a condition under a Credit calling for a document to be authenticated, validated, legalized, visaed, certified or indicating a similar requirement, will be satisfied by any signature, mark, stamp or label on such document that on its face appears to satisfy the above condition.

Article 21
Unspecified Issuers or Contents of Documents

When documents other than transport documents, insurance documents and commercial invoices are called for, the Credit should stipulate by whom such documents are to be issued and their wording or data content. If the Credit does not so stipulate, banks will accept such documents as presented, provided that their data content is not inconsistent with any other stipulated document presented.

Article 22
Issuance Date of Documents v. Credit Date

Unless otherwise stipulated in the Credit, banks will accept a document bearing a date of issuance prior to that of the Credit, subject to such document being presented within the time limits set out in the Credit and in these Articles.

Article 23
Marine/Ocean Bill of Lading

a)   If a Credit calls for a bill of lading covering a port-to-port shipment, banks will, unless otherwise stipulated in the Credit, accept a document, however named, which:

i)   appears on its face to indicate the name of the carrier and to have been signed or otherwise authenticated by:

-   the carrier or a named agent for or on behalf of the carrier, or

-   the master or a named agent for or on behalf of the master.

Any signature or authentication of the carrier or master must be identified as carrier or master, as the case may be. An agent signing or authenticating for the carrier or master must also indicate the name and the capacity of the party, i.e. carrier or master, on whose behalf that agent is acting,

and

ii) indicates that the goods have been loaded on board, or shipped on a named vessel. Loading on board or shipment on a named vessel may be indicated by pre-printed wording on the bill of lading that the goods have been loaded on board a named vessel or shipped on a named vessel, in which case the date of issuance of the bill of lading will be deemed to be the date of loading on board and the date of shipment.

In all other cases loading on board a named vessel must be evidenced by a notation on the bill of lading which gives the date on which the goods have been loaded on board, in which case the date of the on board notation will be deemed to be the date of shipment.

If the bill of lading contains the indication 'intended vessel', or similar qualification in relation to the vessel, loading on board a named vessel must be evidenced by an on-board notation on the bill of lading which, in addition to the date on which the goods have been loaded on board, also includes the name of the vessel on which the goods have been loaded, even if they have been loaded on the vessel named as the 'intended vessel'.

If the bill of lading indicates a place of receipt or taking in charge different from the port of loading, the on-board notation must also include the port of loading stipulated in the Credit and the name of the vessel on which the goods have been loaded, even if they have been loaded on the vessel named in the bill of lading. This provision also applies whenever loading on board the vessel is indicated by pre-printed wording on the bill of lading,

and

iii) indicates the port of loading and the port of discharge stipulated in the Credit, notwithstanding that it:

a)   indicates a place of taking in charge different from the port of loading, and/ or a place of final destination different from the port of discharge,

and/or

b) contains the indication 'intended' or similar qualification in relation to the port of loading and/or port of discharge, as long as the document also states the ports of loading and/or discharge stipulated in the Credit,

and

iv) consists of a sole original bill of lading or, if issued in more than one original, the full set as so issued,

and

v) appears to contain all of the terms and conditions of carriage, or some of such terms and conditions by reference to a source or document other than the bill of lading (short form/blank back bill of lading); banks will not examine the contents of such terms and conditions,

and

vi) contains no indication that it is subject to a charter party and/or no indication that the carrying vessel is propelled by sail only,

and

vii) in all other respects meets the stipulations of the Credit.

b) For the purpose of this Article, transhipment means unloading and reloading from one vessel to another vessel during the course of ocean carriage from the port of loading to the port of discharge stipulated in the Credit.

c) Unless transhipment is prohibited by the terms of the Credit, banks will accept a bill of lading which indicates that the goods will be transhipped, provided that the entire ocean carriage is covered by one and the same bill of lading.

d) Even if the Credit prohibits transhipment, banks will accept a bill of lading that:

i) indicates that transhipment will take place as long as the relevant cargo is shipped in Container(s), Trailer(s) and/or 'LASH' barge(s) as evidenced by the bill of Lading, provided that the entire ocean carriage is covered by one and the same bill of lading,

and/or

ii) incorporates clauses stating that the carrier reserves the right to tranship.

Article 24
Non-Negotiable Sea Waybill

a) If a Credit calls for a non-negotiable sea waybill covering a port-to-port shipment, banks will, unless otherwise stipulated in the Credit, accept a document, however named, which:

i) appears on its face to indicate the name of the carrier and to have been signed or otherwise authenticated by:

● the carrier or a named agent for or on behalf of the carrier, or

● the master or a named agent for or on behalf of the master,

Any signature or authentication of the carrier or master must be identified as carrier or master, as the case may be. An agent signing or authenticating for the carrier or master must also indicate the name and the capacity of the party. i.e. carrier or master, on whose behalf that agent is acting,

and

ii) indicates that the goods have been loaded on board, or shipped on a named vessel.

Loading on board or shipment on a named vessel may be indicated by pre-printed wording on the non-negotiable sea waybill that the goods have been loaded on board a named vessel or shipped on a named vessel, in which case the date of issuance of the non-negotiable sea waybill will be deemed to be the date of loading on board and the date of shipment.

In all other cases loading on board a named vessel must be evidenced by a notation on the non-negotiable sea waybill which gives the date on which the goods have been loaded on board, in which case the date of the on-board notation will be deemed to be the date of shipment.

If the non-negotiable sea waybill contains the indication 'intended vessel', or similar qualification in relation to the vessel, loading on board a named vessel must be evidenced by an on-board notation on the non-negotiable sea waybill which, in addition to the date on which the goods have been loaded on board, includes the name of the vessel on which the goods have been loaded, even if they have been loaded on the vessel named as the 'intended vessel'.

If the non-negotiable sea waybill indicates a place of receipt or taking in charge different from the port of loading, the on-board notation must also include the port of loading stipulated in the Credit and the name of the vessel on which the goods have been loaded, even if they have been loaded on a vessel named in the non-negotiable sea waybill. This provision also applies whenever loading on board the vessel is indicated by pre-printed wording on the non-negotiable sea waybill,

and

iii) indicates the port of loading and the port of discharge stipulated in the Credit, notwithstanding that it:

a) indicates a place of taking in charge different from the port of loading, and/or a place of final destination different from the port of discharge,

and/or

b) contains the indication 'intended' or similar qualification in relation to the port of loading and/or port of discharge, as long as the document also states the ports of loading and/or discharge stipulated in the Credit, and

iv) consists of a sole original non-negotiable sea waybill, or if issued in more than one original, the full set as so issued,

and

v) appears to contain all of the terms and conditions of carriage, or some of such terms and conditions by reference to a source or document other than the non-negotiable sea waybill (short form/blank back non-negotiable sea waybill); banks will not examine the contents of such terms and conditions,

and

vi) contains no indication that it is subject to a charter party and/or no indication that the carrying vessel is propelled by sail only,

and

vii) in all other respects meets the stipulations of the Credit.

b) For the purpose of this Article, transhipment means unloading and reloading from one vessel to another vessel during the course of ocean carriage from the port of loading to the port of discharge stipulated in the Credit.

c) Unless transhipment is prohibited by the terms of the Credit, banks will accept a non-negotiable sea waybill which indicates that the goods will be transhipped, provided that the entire ocean carriage is covered by one and the same non-negotiable sea waybill.

d) Even if the Credit prohibits transhipment, banks will accept a non-negotiable sea waybill that:

i) indicates that transhipment will take place as long as the relevant cargo is shipped in Container(s), Trailer(s) and/or 'LASH' barge(s) as evidenced by the non-negotiable sea waybill, provided that the entire ocean carriage is covered by one and the same non-negotiable sea waybill,

and/or

ii) incorporates clauses stating that the carrier reserves the right to tranship.

Article 25
Charter Party Bill of Lading

a) If a Credit calls for or permits a charter party bill of lading, banks will, unless otherwise stipulated in the Credit, accept a document, however named, which:

i) contains any indication that it is subject to a charter party,

and

ii) appears on its face to have been signed or otherwise authenticated by:

● the master or a named agent for or on behalf of the master, or

● the owner or a named agent for or on behalf of the owner.

Any signature or authentication of the master or owner must be identified as master or owner as the case may be. An agent signing or authenticating for the master or owner must also indicate the name and the capacity of the party, i.e. master or owner, on whose behalf that agent is acting,

and

iii) does or does not indicate the name of the carrier,

and

iv) indicates that the goods have been loaded on board or shipped on a named vessel.

Loading on board or shipment on a named vessel may be indicated by pre-printed wording on the bill of lading that the goods have been loaded on board a named vessel or shipped on a named vessel, in which case the date of issuance of the bill of lading will be deemed to be the date of loading on board and the date of shipment.

In all other cases loading on board a named vessel must be evidenced by a notation on the bill of lading which gives the date on which the goods have been loaded on board, in which case the date of the on-board notation will be deemed to be the date of shipment,

and

v) indicates the port of loading and the port of discharge stipulated in the Credit,

and

vi) consists of a sole original bill of lading or, if issued in more than one original, the full set as so issued,

and

vii) contains no indication that the carrying vessel is propelled by sail only,

and

viii) in all other respects meets the stipulations of the Credit.

b) Even if the Credit requires the presentation of a charter party contract in connection with a charter party bill of lading, banks will not examine such charter party contract, but will pass it on without responsibility on their part.

Article 26
Multimodal Transport Document

a) If a Credit calls for a transport document covering at least two different modes of transport (multimodal transport), banks will, unless otherwise stipulated in the Credit, accept a document, however named, that:

i) appears on its face to indicate the name of the carrier or multimodal transport operator and to have been signed or otherwise authenticated by:

- the carrier or multimodal transport operator or a named agent for or on behalf of the carrier or multimodal transport operator, or

- the master or a named agent for or on behalf of the master.

Any signature or authentication of the carrier, multimodal transport operator or master must be identified as carrier, multimodal transport operator or master, as the case may be. An agent signing or authenticating for the carrier, multimodal transport operator or master must also indicate the name and the capacity of the party, i.e. carrier, multimodal transport operator or master, on whose behalf that agent is acting,

and

ii)   indicates that the goods have been dispatched, taken in charge or loaded on board.

Dispatch, taking in charge or loading on board may be indicated by wording to that effect on the multimodal transport document and the date of issuance will be deemed to be the date of dispatch, taking in charge or loading on board and the date of shipment However, if the document indicates, by stamp or otherwise, a date of dispatch, taking in charge or loading on board, such date will be deemed to be the date of shipment,

and

iii)   a)   indicates the place of taking in charge stipulated in the Credit which may be different from the port, airport or place of loading, and the place of final destination stipulated in the Credit which may be different from the port, airport or place of discharge,

and/or

b)   contains the indication 'intended' or similar qualification in relation to the vessel and/or port of loading and/or port of discharge,

and

iv)   consists of a sole original multimodal transport document or, if issued in more than one original, the full set as so issued,

and

v)   appears to contain all of the terms and conditions of carriage, or some of such terms and conditions by reference to a source or document other than the multimodal transport document (short form/blank back multimodal transport document); banks will not examine the contents of such terms and conditions,

and

vi)   contains no indication that it is subject to a charter party and/or no indication that the carrying vessel is propelled by sail only,

and

vii) in all other respects meets the stipulations of the Credit.

b) Even if the Credit prohibits transhipment, banks will accept a multimodal transport document which indicates that transhipment will or may take place, provided that the entire carriage is covered by one and the same multimodal transport document.

Article 27
Air Transport Document

a) If a Credit calls for an air transport document, banks will, unless otherwise stipulated in the Credit, accept a document, however named, that:

   i) appears on its face to indicate the name of the carrier and to have been signed or otherwise authenticated by:

   - the carrier, or
   - a named agent for or on behalf of the carrier.

   Any signature or authentication of the carrier must be identified as carrier. An agent signing or authenticating for the carrier must also indicate the name and the capacity of the party, i.e. carrier, on whose behalf that agent is acting,

   and

   ii) indicates that the goods have been accepted for carriage,

   and

   iii) where the Credit calls for an actual date of dispatch, indicates a specific notation of such date, the date of dispatch so indicated on the air transport document will be deemed to be the date of shipment.

   For the purpose of this Article, the information appearing in the box on the air transport document (marked 'For Carrier Use Only' or similar expression) relative to the flight number and date will not be considered as a specific notation of such date of dispatch.

   In all other cases, the date of issuance of the air transport document will be deemed to be the date of shipment,

   and

   iv) indicates the airport of departure and the airport of destination stipulated in the Credit,

   and

   v) appears to be the original for consignor/shipper even if the Credit stipulates a full set of originals, or similar expressions,

   and

   vi) appears to contain all of the terms and conditions of carriage, or some of such terms and conditions, by reference to a source or document other than the air transport document; banks will not examine the contents of such terms and conditions,

and

vii) in all other respects meets the stipulations of the Credit.

b) For the purpose of this Article, transhipment means unloading and reloading from one aircraft to another aircraft during the course of carriage from the airport of departure to the airport of destination stipulated in the Credit.

c) Even if the Credit prohibits transhipment, banks will accept an air transport document which indicates that transhipment will or may take place, provided that the entire carriage is covered by one and the same air transport document.

Article 28
Road, Rail or Inland Waterway Transport Documents

a) If a Credit calls for a road, rail, or inland waterway transport document, banks will, unless otherwise stipulated in the Credit, accept a document of the type called for, however named, that:

i) appears on its face to indicate the name of the carrier and to have been signed or otherwise authenticated by the carrier or a named agent for or on behalf of the carrier and/or to bear a reception stamp or other indication of receipt by the carrier or a named agent for or on behalf of the carrier.

Any signature, authentication, reception stamp or other indication of receipt of the carrier, must be identified on its face as that of the carrier. An agent signing or authenticating for the carrier, must also indicate the name and the capacity of the party, i.e. carrier, on whose behalf that agent is acting,

and

ii) indicates that the goods have been received for shipment, dispatch or carriage or wording to this effect. The date of issuance will be deemed to be the date of shipment unless the transport document contains a reception stamp, in which case the date of the reception stamp will be deemed to be the date of shipment,

and

iii) indicates the place of shipment and the place of destination stipulated in the Credit,

and

iv) in all other respects meets the stipulations of the Credit.

b) In the absence of any indication on the transport document as to the numbers issued, banks will accept the transport document(s) presented as constituting a full set. Banks will accept as original(s) the transport document(s) whether marked as original(s) or not.

c)   For the purpose of this Article, transhipment means unloading and reloading from one means of conveyance to another means of conveyance, in different modes of transport, during the course of carriage from the place of shipment to the place of destination stipulated in the Credit.

d)   Even if the Credit prohibits transhipment, banks will accept a road, rail, or inland waterway transport document which indicates that transhipment will or may take place, provided that the entire carriage is covered by one and the same transport document and within the same mode of transport.

Article 29
Courier and Post Receipts

a)   If a Credit calls for a post receipt or certificate of posting, banks will, unless otherwise stipulated in the Credit, accept a post receipt or certificate of posting that:

   i)   appears on its face to have been stamped or otherwise authenticated and dated in the place from which the Credit stipulates the goods are to be shipped or dispatched and such date will be deemed to be the date of shipment or dispatch, and

   ii) in all other respects meets the stipulations of the Credit.

b)   If a Credit calls for a document issued by a courier or expedited delivery service evidencing receipt of the goods for delivery, banks will, unless otherwise stipulated in the Credit, accept a document, however named, that:

   i)   appears on its face to indicate the name of the courier/service, and to have been stamped, signed or otherwise authenticated by such named courier/service (unless the Credit specifically calls for a document issued by a named Courier/Service, banks will accept a document issued by any Courier/Service), and

   ii) indicates a date of pick-up or of receipt or wording to this effect, such date being deemed to be the date of shipment or dispatch, and

   iii) in all other respects meets the stipulations of the Credit.

Article 30
Transport Documents issued by Freight Forwarders

Unless otherwise authorized in the Credit, banks will only accept a transport document issued by a freight forwarder if it appears on its face to indicate:

i)   the name of the freight forwarder as a carrier or multimodal transport operator and to have been signed or otherwise authenticated by the freight forwarder as carrier or multimodal transport operator, or

ii)   the name of the carrier or multimodal transport operator and to have been signed or otherwise authenticated by the freight forwarder as a named agent for or on behalf of the carrier or multimodal transport operator.

Article 31
'On Deck', 'Shipper's Load and Count', Name of Consignor

Unless otherwise stipulated in the Credit, banks will accept a transport document that:

i)   does not indicate, in the case of carriage by sea or by more than one means of conveyance including carriage by sea, that the goods are or will be loaded on deck. Nevertheless, banks will accept a transport document which contains a provision that the goods may be carried on deck, provided that it does not specifically state that they are or will be loaded on deck,

and/or

ii)   bears a clause on the face thereof such as 'shipper's load and count' or 'said by shipper to contain' or words of similar effect,

and/or

iii)   indicates as the consignor of the goods a party other than the Beneficiary of the Credit.

Article 32
Clean Transport Documents

a)   A clean transport document is one that bears no clause or notation which expressly declares a defective condition of the goods and/or the packaging.

b)   Banks will not accept transport documents bearing such clauses or notations unless the Credit expressly stipulates the clauses or notations that may be accepted.

c)   Banks will regard a requirement in a Credit for a transport document to bear the clause 'clean on board' as complied with if such transport document meets the requirements of this Article and of Articles 23, 24, 25, 26, 27, 28 or 30.

Article 33
Freight Payable/Prepaid Transport Documents

a)   Unless otherwise stipulated in the Credit, or inconsistent with any of the documents presented under the Credit, banks will accept transport documents stating that freight or transportation charges (hereafter referred to as 'freight') have still to be paid.

b)   If a Credit stipulates that the transport document has to indicate that freight has been paid or prepaid, banks will accept a transport document on which words clearly indicating payment or prepayment of freight appear by stamp or otherwise, or on which payment or prepayment of freight is indicated by other means. If the Credit requires courier charges to be paid or prepaid banks will also accept a transport document issued by a courier or expedited delivery service evidencing that courier charges are for the account of a party other than the consignee.

c) The words 'freight prepayable' or 'freight to be prepaid' or words of similar effect, if appearing on transport documents, will not be accepted as constituting evidence of the payment of freight.

d) Banks will accept transport documents bearing reference by stamp or otherwise to costs additional to the freight, such as costs of, or disbursements incurred in connection with, loading, unloading or similar operations, unless the conditions of the Credit specifically prohibit such reference.

Article 34
Insurance Documents

a) Insurance documents must appear on their face to be issued and signed by insurance companies or underwriters or their agents.

b) If the insurance document indicates that it has been issued in more than one original, all the originals must be presented unless otherwise authorized in the Credit.

c) Cover notes issued by brokers will not be accepted, unless specifically authorized in the Credit.

d) Unless otherwise stipulated in the Credit, banks will accept an insurance certificate or a declaration under an open cover pre-signed by insurance companies or underwriters or their agents. If a Credit specifically calls for an insurance certificate or a declaration under an open cover, banks will accept, in lieu thereof, an insurance policy.

e) Unless otherwise stipulated in the Credit, or unless it appears from the insurance document that the cover is effective at the latest from the date of loading on board or dispatch or taking in charge of the goods, banks will not accept an insurance document which bears a date of issuance later than the date of loading on board or dispatch or taking in charge as indicated in such transport document.

f) i)   Unless otherwise stipulated in the Credit, the insurance document must be expressed in the same currency as the Credit.

  ii) Unless otherwise stipulated in the Credit, the minimum amount for which the insurance document must indicate the insurance cover to have been effected is the CIF (cost, insurance and freight (... 'named port of destination')) or CIP (carriage and insurance paid to (... 'named place of destination')) value of the goods, as the case may be, plus 10%, but only when the CIF or CIP value can be determined from the documents on their face. Otherwise, banks will accept as such minimum amount 110% of the amount for which payment, acceptance or negotiation is requested under the Credit, or 110% of the gross amount of the invoice, whichever is the greater.

Article 35
Type of Insurance Cover

a) Credits should stipulate the type of insurance required and, if any, the additional risks that are to be covered. Imprecise terms such as 'usual risks' or 'customary risks' shall not be used; if they are used, banks will accept insurance documents as presented, without responsibility for any risks not being covered.

b) Failing specific stipulations in the Credit, banks will accept insurance documents as presented, without responsibility for any risks not being covered.

c) Unless otherwise stipulated in the Credit, banks will accept an insurance document which indicates that the cover is subject to a franchise or an excess (deductible).

Article 36
All Risks Insurance Cover

Where a Credit stipulates 'insurance against all risks', banks will accept an insurance document which contains any 'all risks' notation or clause, whether or not bearing the heading 'all risks', even if the insurance document indicates that certain risks are excluded, without responsibility for any risk(s) not being covered.

Article 37
Commercial Invoices

a) Unless otherwise stipulated in the Credit, commercial invoices:

   i)   must appear on their face to be issued by the Beneficiary named in the Credit (except as provided in Article 48),

        and

   ii) must be made out in the name of the Applicant (except as provided in sub-Article 48 h)),

        and

   iii) need not be signed.

b) Unless otherwise stipulated in the Credit, banks may refuse commercial invoices issued for amounts in excess of the amount permitted by the Credit. Nevertheless, if a bank authorized to pay, incur a deferred payment undertaking, accept Draft(s), or negotiate under a Credit accepts such invoices, its decision will be binding upon all parties, provided that such bank has not paid, incurred a deferred payment undertaking, accepted Draft(s) or negotiated for an amount in excess of that permitted by the Credit.

c) The description of the goods in the commercial invoice must correspond with the description in the Credit. In all other documents, the goods may be described in general terms not inconsistent with the description of the goods in the Credit.

Article 38
Other Documents

If a Credit calls for an attestation or certification of weight in the case of transport other than by sea, banks will accept a weight stamp or declaration of weight that appears to have been superimposed on the transport document by the carrier or his agent unless the Credit specifically stipulates that the attestation or certification of weight must be by means of a separate document.

E.   Miscellaneous Provisions

Article 39
Allowances in Credit Amount, Quantity and Unit Price

a)   The words 'about', 'approximately', 'circa' or similar expressions used in connection with the amount of the Credit or the quantity or the unit price stated in the Credit are to be construed as allowing a difference not to exceed 10% more or 10% less than the amount or the quantity or the unit price to which they refer.

b)   Unless a Credit stipulates that the quantity of the goods specified must not be exceeded or reduced, a tolerance of 5% more or 5% less will be permissible, always provided that the amount of the drawings does not exceed the amount of the Credit. This tolerance does not apply when the Credit stipulates the quantity in terms of a stated number of packing units or individual items.

c)   Unless a Credit that prohibits partial shipments stipulates otherwise, or unless sub-Article (b) above is applicable, a tolerance of 5% less in the amount of the drawing will be permissible, provided that if the Credit stipulates the quantity of the goods, such quantity of goods is shipped in full, and if the Credit stipulates a unit price, such price is not reduced. This provision does not apply when expressions referred to in sub-Article (a) above are used in the Credit.

Article 40
Partial Shipments/Drawings

a)   Partial drawings and/or shipments are allowed, unless the Credit stipulates otherwise.

b)   Transport documents which appear on their face to indicate that shipment has been made on the same means of conveyance and for the same journey, provided they indicate the same destination, will not be regarded as covering partial shipments, even if the transport documents indicate different dates of shipment and/or different ports of loading, places of taking in charge, or despatch.

c)   Shipments made by post or by courier will not be regarded as partial shipments if the post receipts or certificates of posting or courier's receipts or dispatch notes appear to have been stamped, signed or otherwise authenticated in the place from which the Credit stipulates the goods are to be dispatched, and on the same date.

Article 41
Instalment Shipments/Drawings

If drawings and/or shipments by instalments within given periods are stipulated in the Credit and any instalment is not drawn and/or shipped within the period allowed for that instalment, the Credit ceases to be available for that and any subsequent instalments, unless otherwise stipulated in the Credit.

Article 42
Expiry Date and Place for Presentation of Documents

a)   All Credits must stipulate an expiry date and a place for presentation of documents for payment, acceptance, or with the exception of freely negotiable Credits, a place for presentation of documents for negotiation. An expiry date stipulated for payment, acceptance or negotiation will be construed to express an expiry date for presentation of documents.

b)   Except as provided in sub-Article 44 (a), documents must be presented on or before such expiry date.

c)   If an Issuing Bank states that the Credit is to be available 'for one month', 'for six months', or the like, but does not specify the date from which the time is to run, the date of issuance of the Credit by the Issuing Bank will be deemed to be the first day from which such time is to run. Banks should discourage indication of the expiry date of the Credit in this manner.

Article 43
Limitation on the Expiry Date

a)   In addition to stipulating an expiry date for presentation of documents, every Credit that calls for a transport document(s) should also stipulate a specified period of time after the date of shipment during which presentation must be made in compliance with the terms and conditions of the Credit. If no such period of time is stipulated, banks will not accept documents presented to them later than 21 days after the date of shipment. In any event, documents must be presented not later than the expiry date of the Credit.

b)   In cases in which sub-Article 40 (b) applies, the date of shipment will be considered to be the latest shipment date on any of the transport documents presented.

Article 44
Extension of Expiry Date

a)   If the expiry date of the Credit and/or the last day of the period of time for presentation of documents stipulated by the Credit or applicable by virtue of Article 43 falls on a day on which the bank to which presentation has to be made is closed for reasons other than those referred to in Article 17, the stipulated expiry date and/or the last day of the period of time after the date of shipment for presentation of documents, as the case may be, shall be extended to the first following day on which such bank is open.

b) The latest date for shipment shall not be extended by reason of the extension of the expiry date and/or the period of time after the date of shipment for presentation of documents in accordance with sub-Article (a) above. If no such latest date for shipment is stipulated in the Credit or amendments thereto, banks will not accept transport documents indicating a date of shipment later than the expiry date stipulated in the Credit or amendments thereto.

c) The bank to which presentation is made on such first following business day must provide a statement that the documents were presented within the time limits extended in accordance with sub-Article 44 (a) of the Uniform Customs and Practice for Documentary Credits, 1993 Revision, ICC Publication No. 500.

Article 45
Hours of Presentation

Banks are under no obligation to accept presentation of documents outside their banking hours.

Article 46
General Expressions as to Dates for Shipment

a) Unless otherwise stipulated in the Credit, the expression 'shipment' used in stipulating an earliest and/or a latest date for shipment will be understood to include expressions such as, 'loading on board', 'dispatch', 'accepted for carriage', 'date of post receipt', 'date of pickup', and the like, and in the case of a Credit calling for a multimodal transport document the expression 'taking in charge'.

b) Expressions such as 'prompt', 'immediately', 'as soon as possible', and the like should not be used. If they are used banks will disregard them.

c) If the expression 'on or about' or similar expressions are used, banks will interpret them as a stipulation that shipment is to be made during the period from five days before to five days after the specified date, both end days included.

Article 47
Date Terminology for Periods of Shipment

a) The words 'to', 'until', 'till', 'from' and words of similar import applying to any date or period in the Credit referring to shipment will be understood to include the date mentioned.

b) The word 'after' will be understood to exclude the date mentioned.

c) The terms 'first half', 'second half' of a month shall be construed respectively as the

1st to the 15th, and the 16th to the last day of such month, all dates inclusive.

d)   The terms 'beginning', 'middle', or 'end' of a month shall be construed respectively as the 1st to the 10th, the 11th to the 20th, and the 21st to the last day of such month, all dates inclusive.

F.   Transferable Credit

Article 48
Transferable Credit

a)   A transferable Credit is a Credit under which the Beneficiary (First Beneficiary) may request the bank authorized to pay, incur a deferred payment undertaking, accept or negotiate (the 'Transferring Bank'), or in the case of a freely negotiable Credit, the bank specifically authorized in the Credit as a Transferring Bank, to make the Credit available in whole or in part to one or more other Beneficiary(ies) (Second Beneficiary(ies)).

b)   A Credit can be transferred only if it is expressly designated as 'transferable' by the Issuing Bank. Terms such as 'divisible', 'fractionable', 'assignable', and 'transmissible' do not render the Credit transferable. If such terms are used they shall be disregarded.

c)   The Transferring Bank shall be under no obligation to effect such transfer except to the extent and in the manner expressly consented to by such bank.

d)   At the time of making a request for transfer and prior to transfer of the Credit, the First Beneficiary must irrevocably instruct the Transferring Bank whether or not he retains the right to refuse to allow the Transferring Bank to advise amendments to the Second Beneficiary(ies). If the Transferring Bank consents to the transfer under these conditions, it must, at the time of transfer, advise the Second Beneficiary(ies) of the First Beneficiary's instructions regarding amendments.

e)   If a Credit is transferred to more than one Second Beneficiary(ies), refusal of an amendment by one or more Second Beneficiary(ies) does not invalidate the acceptance(s) by the other Second Beneficiary(ies) with respect to whom the Credit will be amended accordingly. With respect to the Second Beneficiary(ies) who rejected the amendment, the Credit will remain unamended

f)   Transferring Bank charges in respect of transfers including commissions, fees, costs or expenses are payable by the First Beneficiary, unless otherwise agreed. If the Transferring Bank agrees to transfer the Credit it shall be under no obligation to effect the transfer until such charges are paid.

g)   Unless otherwise stated in the Credit, a transferable Credit can be transferred once only. Consequently, the Credit cannot be transferred at the request of the Second Beneficiary to any subsequent Third Beneficiary. For the purpose of this Article, a retransfer to the First Beneficiary does not constitute a prohibited transfer.

Fractions of a transferable Credit (not exceeding in the aggregate the amount of the Credit) can be transferred separately, provided partial shipments/drawings are not prohibited, and the aggregate of such transfers will be considered as constituting only one transfer of the Credit.

h) The Credit can be transferred only on the terms and conditions specified in the original Credit, with the exception of:

- the amount of the Credit,
- any unit price stated therein,
- the expiry date,
- the last date for presentation of documents in accordance with Article 43,
- the period for shipment,

any or all of which may be reduced or curtailed.

The percentage for which insurance cover must be effected may be increased in such a way as to provide the amount of cover stipulated in the original Credit, or these Articles.

In addition, the name of the First Beneficiary can be substituted for that of the Applicant, but if the name of the Applicant is specifically required by the original Credit to appear in any document(s) other than the invoice, such requirement must be fulfilled.

i) The First Beneficiary has the right to substitute his own invoice(s) (and Draft(s)) for those of the Second Beneficiary(ies), for amounts not in excess of the original amount stipulated in the Credit and for the original unit prices if stipulated in the Credit, and upon such substitution of invoice(s) (and Draft(s)) the First Beneficiary can draw under the Credit for the difference, if any, between his invoice(s) and the Second Beneficiary's(ies') invoice(s).

When a Credit has been transferred and the First Beneficiary is to supply his own invoice(s) (and Draft(s)) in exchange for the Second Beneficiary's(ies') invoice(s) (and Draft(s)) but fails to do so on first demand, the Transferring Bank has the right to deliver to the Issuing Bank the documents received under the transferred Credit, including the Second Beneficiary's(ies') invoice(s) (and Draft(s)) without further responsibility to the First Beneficiary.

j) he First Beneficiary may request that payment or negotiation be effected to the Second Beneficiary(ies) at the place to which the Credit has been transferred up to and including the expiry date of the Credit, unless the original Credit expressly states that it may not be made available for payment or negotiation at a place other than that stipulated in the Credit. This is without prejudice to the First Beneficiary's right to substitute subsequently his own invoice(s) (and Draft(s)) for those of the Second Beneficiary(ies) and to claim any difference due to him.

G. Assignment of Proceeds

Article 49
Assignment of Proceeds

The fact that a Credit is not stated to be transferable shall not affect the Beneficiary's right to assign any proceeds to which he may be, or may become, entitled under such Credit, in accordance with the provisions of the applicable law. This Article relates only to the assignment of proceeds and not to the assignment of the right to perform under the Credit itself.

ICC Arbitration

Contracting parties that wish to have the possibility of resorting to ICC Arbitration in the event of a dispute with their contracting partner should specifically and clearly agree upon ICC Arbitration in their contract or, in the event no single contractual document exists, in the exchange of correspondence that constitutes the agreement between them. The fact of issuing a letter of credit subject to the UCP 500 does NOT by itself constitute an agreement to have resort to ICC Arbitration. The following standard arbitration clause is recommended by the ICC:

> *All disputes arising in connection with the present contract shall be finally settled under the Rules of Conciliation and Arbitration of the International Chamber of Commerce by one or more arbitrators appointed in accordance with the said Rules.*

ICC Uniform Customs and Practice for Documentary Credits – 1993 Revision ICC Publication 500 - ISBN 92.842.1155.7

Published in its official English version by the International Chamber of Commerce, Paris

© 1993 – International Chamber of Commerce (ICC)

Available from: ICC Publishing SA, 38 Cours Albert 1ᵉʳ, 75008 Paris, France, and from: ICC United Kingdom, 14/15 Belgrave Square, London SW1X 8PS.

Appendix 5

UNIFORM RULES FOR BANK-TO-BANK REIMBURSEMENTS UNDER DOCUMENTARY CREDITS

A. General Provisions and Definitions

Article 1
Application of URR

The Uniform Rules for Bank-to-Bank Reimbursements under Documentary Credits ('Rules'), ICC Publication No. 525, shall apply to all Bank-to-Bank Reimbursements where they are incorporated into the text of the Reimbursement Authorization. They are binding on all parties thereto, unless otherwise expressly stipulated in the Reimbursement Authorization. The Issuing Bank is responsible for indicating in the Documentary Credit ('Credit') that Reimbursement Claims are subject to these Rules.

In a Bank-to-Bank Reimbursement subject to these Rules, the Reimbursing Bank acts on the instructions and/or under the authority of the Issuing Bank.

These Rules are not intended to override or change the provisions of the ICC Uniform Customs and Practice for Documentary Credits.

Article 2
Definitions

As used in these Rules, the following terms shall have the meanings specified in this Article and may be used in the singular or plural as appropriate:

a) 'Issuing Bank' shall mean the bank that has issued a Credit and the Reimbursement Authorization under that Credit.

b) 'Reimbursing Bank' shall mean the bank instructed and/or authorized to provide reimbursement pursuant to a Reimbursement Authorization issued by the Issuing Bank.

c) 'Reimbursement Authorization' shall mean an instruction and/or authorization, independent of the Credit, issued by an Issuing Bank to a Reimbursing Bank to reimburse a Claiming Bank, or, if so requested by the Issuing Bank, to accept and pay a time draft(s) drawn on the Reimbursing Bank.

d) 'Reimbursement Amendment' shall mean an advice from the Issuing Bank to a Reimbursing Bank stating changes to a Reimbursement Authorization.

e) 'Claiming Bank' shall mean a bank that pays, incurs a deferred payment undertaking, accepts draft(s), or negotiates under a Credit and presents a Reimbursement Claim to the Reimbursing Bank. 'Claiming Bank' shall include a bank authorized to present a Reimbursement Claim to the Reimbursing Bank on behalf of the bank that pays, incurs a deferred payment undertaking, accepts draft(s), or negotiates.

f) 'Reimbursement Claim' shall mean a request for reimbursement from the Claiming Bank to the Reimbursing Bank.

g) 'Reimbursement Undertaking' shall mean a separate irrevocable undertaking of the Reimbursing Bank, issued upon the authorization or request of the Issuing Bank, to the Claiming Bank named in the Reimbursement Authorization, to honour that bank's Reimbursement Claim provided the terms and conditions of the Reimbursement Undertaking have been complied with.

h) 'Reimbursement Undertaking Amendment' shall mean an advice from the Reimbursing Bank to the Claiming Bank named in the Reimbursement Authorization, stating changes to a Reimbursement Undertaking.

i) For the purposes of these Rules branches of a bank in different countries are considered separate banks.

Article 3
Reimbursement Authorization Versus Credits

A Reimbursement Authorization is separate from the Credit to which it refers, and a Reimbursing Bank is not concerned with or bound by the terms and conditions of the Credit, even if any reference whatsoever to the terms and conditions of the Credit is included in the Reimbursement Authorization.

B.   Liabilities and Responsibilities

Article 4
Honour of a Reimbursement Claim

Except as provided by the terms of its Reimbursement Undertaking a Reimbursing Bank is not obligated to honour a Reimbursement Claim.

Article 5
Responsibilities of the Issuing Bank

The Issuing Bank is responsible for providing the information required in these Rules in both the Reimbursement Authorization and Credit and is responsible for any consequences resulting from non-compliance with this provision.

C.   Form and Notification of Authorizations, Amendments and Claims

Article 6
Issuance and Receipt of a Reimbursement Authorization or Reimbursement Amendment

a)   All Reimbursement Authorizations and Reimbursement Amendments must be issued in the form of an authenticated teletransmission or a signed letter.

When a Credit, or an amendment thereto that has an effect on the Reimbursement Authorization, is issued by teletransmission, the Issuing Bank should advise its Reimbursement Authorization or Reimbursement Amendment to the Reimbursing Bank by authenticated teletransmission. The teletransmission will be deemed the operative Reimbursement Authorization or the operative Reimbursement Amendment and no mail confirmation should be sent. Should a mail confirmation nevertheless be sent, it will have no effect and the Reimbursing Bank will have no obligation to check such mail confirmation against the operative Reimbursement Authorization or the operative Reimbursement Amendment received by teletransmission.

b)   Reimbursement Authorizations and Reimbursement Amendments must be complete and precise. To guard against confusion and misunderstanding, Issuing Banks must not send to Reimbursing Banks:

   i)   a copy of the Credit or any part thereof or a copy of an amendment to the Credit in place of, or in addition to, the Reimbursement Authorization or Reimbursement Amendment. If such copies are received by the Reimbursing Bank they shall be disregarded.

   ii)   multiple Reimbursement Authorizations under one teletransmission or letter, unless expressly agreed to by the Reimbursing Bank.

c)   Issuing Banks shall not require a certificate of compliance with the terms and conditions of the Credit in the Reimbursement Authorization.

d)   All Reimbursement Authorizations must (in addition to the requirement of Article 1 for incorporation of reference to these Rules) state the following:

   i)   Credit number;

   ii)   currency and amount;

   iii)   additional amounts payable and tolerance, if any;

   iv)   Claiming Bank or, in the case of freely negotiable credits, that claims can be made by any bank. In the absence of any such indication the Reimbursing Bank is authorized to pay any Claiming Bank;

v) parties responsible for charges (Claiming Bank's and Reimbursing Bank's charges) in accordance with Article 16 of these Rules.

Reimbursement Amendments must state only the relative changes to the above and the Credit number.

e) If the Reimbursing Bank is requested to accept and pay a time draft(s), the Reimbursement Authorization must indicate the following, in addition to the information specified in (d) above:

i) tenor of draft(s) to be drawn;

ii) drawer;

iii) party responsible for acceptance and discount charges, if any.

Reimbursement Amendments must state the relative changes to the above.

Issuing Banks should not require a sight draft(s) to be drawn on the Reimbursing Bank.

f) Any requirement for:

i) pre-notification of a Reimbursement Claim to the Issuing Bank must be included in the Credit and not in the Reimbursement Authorization;

ii) pre-debit notification to the Issuing Bank must be indicated in the Credit.

g) If the Reimbursing Bank is not prepared to act for any reason whatsoever under the Reimbursement Authorization or Reimbursement Amendment, it must so inform the Issuing Bank without delay.

h) In addition to the provisions of Articles 3 and 4, Reimbursing Banks are not responsible for the consequences resulting from non-reimbursement or delay in reimbursement of Reimbursement Claims, where any provision contained in this Article is not followed by the Issuing and/or Claiming Bank.

Article 7
Expiry of a Reimbursement Authorization

Except to the extent expressly agreed to by the Reimbursing Bank, the Reimbursement Authorization must not have an expiry date or latest date for presentation of a claim except as indicated in Article 9.

Reimbursing Banks will assume no responsibility for the expiry date of Credits and if such date is provided in the Reimbursement Authorization it will be disregarded.

The Issuing Bank must cancel its Reimbursement Authorization for any unutilized portion of the Credit to which it refers, informing the Reimbursing Bank without delay.

Article 8
Amendment or Cancellation of Reimbursement Authorizations

Except where the Issuing Bank has authorized or requested the Reimbursing Bank to issue a Reimbursement Undertaking as provided in Article 9 and the Reimbursing Bank has issued a Reimbursement Undertaking:

a) The Issuing Bank may issue a Reimbursement Amendment or cancel a Reimbursement Authorization at any time upon sending notice to that effect to the Reimbursing Bank.

b) The Issuing Bank must send notice of any amendment to a Reimbursement Authorization that has an effect on the reimbursement instructions contained in the Credit to the nominated bank or, in the case of a freely negotiable Credit, the advising bank. In the case of cancellation of the Reimbursement Authorization prior to expiry of the Credit, the Issuing Bank must provide the nominated bank or the advising bank with new reimbursement instructions.

c) The Issuing Bank must reimburse the Reimbursing Bank for any Reimbursement Claims honoured or draft(s) accepted by the Reimbursing Bank prior to the receipt by it of notice of cancellation or Reimbursement Amendment.

Article 9
Reimbursement Undertakings

a) In addition to the requirements of sub-Article 6(a), (b) and (c) of these Rules, all Reimbursement Authorizations authorizing or requesting the issuance of a Reimbursement Undertaking must comply with the provisions of this Article.

b) An authorization or request by the Issuing Bank to the Reimbursing Bank to issue a Reimbursement Undertaking is irrevocable ('Irrevocable Reimbursement Authorization') and must (in addition to the requirement of Article 1 for incorporation of reference to these Rules) contain the following:

   i)   Credit number;

   ii)   currency and amount;

   iii) additional amounts payable and tolerance, if any;

   iv)   full name and address of the Claiming Bank to whom the Reimbursement Undertaking should be issued;

   v)   latest date for presentation of a claim including any usance period;

   vi)   parties responsible for charges (Claiming Bank's and Reimbursing Bank's charges and Reimbursement Undertaking fee) in accordance with Article 16 of these Rules.

c) If the Reimbursing Bank is requested to accept and pay a time draft(s), the Irrevocable Reimbursement Authorization must also indicate the following, in addition to the information contained in (b) above:

    i)   tenor of draft(s) to be drawn;

    ii)   drawer;

    iii)   party responsible for acceptance and discount charges, if any.

Issuing Banks should not require a sight draft(s) to be drawn on the Reimbursing Bank.

d)   If the Reimbursing Bank is authorized or requested by the Issuing Bank to issue its Reimbursement Undertaking to the Claiming Bank but is not prepared to do so, it must so inform the Issuing Bank without delay.

e)   A Reimbursement Undertaking must indicate the terms and conditions of the undertaking and:

    i)   Credit number and Issuing Bank;

    ii)   currency and amount of the Reimbursement Authorization;

    iii)   additional amounts payable and tolerance if any;

    iv)   currency and amount of the Reimbursement Undertaking;

    v)   latest date for presentation of a claim including any usance period;

    vi)   party to pay the Reimbursement Undertaking fee, if other than the Issuing Bank. The Reimbursing Bank must also include its charges, if any, that will be deducted from the amount claimed.

f)   If the latest date for presentation of a claim falls on a day on which the Reimbursing Bank is closed for reasons other than those mentioned in Article 15, the latest date for presentation of a claim shall be extended to the first following day on which the Reimbursing Bank is open.

g)   i)   An Irrevocable Reimbursement Authorization cannot be amended or cancelled without the agreement of the Reimbursing Bank.

    ii)   When an Issuing Bank has amended its Irrevocable Reimbursement Authorization, a Reimbursing Bank which has issued its Reimbursement Undertaking may amend its undertaking to reflect such amendment. If a Reimbursing Bank chooses not to issue its Reimbursement Undertaking Amendment it must so inform the Issuing Bank without delay.

    iii)   An Issuing Bank that has issued its Irrevocable Reimbursement Authorization Amendment shall be irrevocably bound as of the time of its advice of the Irrevocable Reimbursement Authorization Amendment.

    iv)   The terms of the original Irrevocable Reimbursement Authorization (or an Authorization incorporating previously accepted Irrevocable Reimbursement

Authorization Amendments) will remain in force for the Reimbursing Bank until it communicates its acceptance of the amendment to the Issuing Bank.

v) A Reimbursing Bank must communicate its acceptance or rejection of an Irrevocable Reimbursement Authorization Amendment to the Issuing Bank. A Reimbursing Bank is not required to accept or reject an Irrevocable Reimbursement Authorization Amendment until it has received acceptance or rejection from the Claiming Bank to its Reimbursement Undertaking Amendment.

h) i) A Reimbursement Undertaking cannot be amended or cancelled without the agreement of the Claiming Bank.

ii) A Reimbursing Bank that has issued its Reimbursement Undertaking Amendment shall be irrevocably bound as of the time of its advice of the Reimbursement Undertaking Amendment.

iii) The terms of the original Reimbursement Undertaking (or a Reimbursement Undertaking incorporating previously accepted Reimbursement Authorizations) will remain in force for the Claiming Bank until it communicates its acceptance of the Reimbursement Undertaking Amendment to the Reimbursing Bank.

iv) A Claiming Bank must communicate its acceptance or rejection of a Reimbursement Undertaking Amendment to the Reimbursing Bank.

Article 10
Standards for Reimbursing Claims

a) The Claiming Bank's claim for reimbursement:

i) must be in the form of a teletransmission, unless specifically prohibited by the Issuing Bank, or an original letter. A Reimbursing Bank has the right to request that a Reimbursement Claim be authenticated and in such case the Reimbursing Bank shall not be liable for any consequences resulting from any delay incurred. If a Reimbursement Claim is made by teletransmission, no mail confirmation is to be sent. In the event such a mail confirmation is sent, the Claiming Bank will be responsible for any consequences that may arise from a duplicate reimbursement;

ii) must clearly indicate the Credit number and Issuing Bank (and Reimbursing Bank's reference number, if known);

iii) must separately stipulate the principal amount claimed, any additional amount(s) and charges;

iv) must not be a copy of the Claiming Bank's advice of payment, deferred payment, acceptance or negotiation to the Issuing Bank;

v) must not include multiple Reimbursement Claims under one teletransmission or letter;

vi) must, in the case of a Reimbursement Undertaking, comply with the terms and conditions of the Reimbursement Undertaking.

b) In cases where a time draft is to be drawn on the Reimbursing Bank, the Claiming Bank must forward the draft with the Reimbursement Claim to the Reimbursing Bank for processing, and include the following in its claim if required by the Credit and/or Reimbursement Undertaking:

i) general description of the goods and/or services;

ii) country of origin;

iii) place of destination/performance;

and if the transaction covers the shipment of merchandise.

iv) date of shipment;

v) place of shipment.

c) Claiming Banks must not indicate in a Reimbursement Claim that a payment, acceptance or negotiation was made under reserve or against an indemnity.

d) Reimbursing Banks assume no liability or responsibility for any consequences that may arise out of any non-acceptance or delay of processing should the Claiming Bank fail to follow the provisions of this Article.

Article 11
Processing Reimbursement Claims

a) i) Reimbursing Banks shall have a reasonable time, not to exceed three banking days following the day of receipt of the Reimbursement Claim, to process claims. Reimbursement Claims received outside banking hours are deemed to be received on the next banking day.

If a pre-debit notification is required by the Issuing Bank, this pre-debit notification period shall be in addition to the processing period mentioned above.

ii) If the Reimbursing Bank determines not to reimburse, either because of a non-conforming claim under a Reimbursement Undertaking, or for any reason whatsoever under a Reimbursement Authorization, it shall give notice to that effect by telecommunication or, if that is not possible, by other expeditious means, without delay, but no later than the close of the third banking day following the day of receipt of the claim (plus any additional period mentioned in sub-Article (i) above). Such notice shall be sent to the Claiming Bank and the Issuing Bank and, in the case of a Reimbursement Undertaking, it must state the reasons for non-payment of the claim.

b) Reimbursing Banks will not process requests for back value (value dating prior to the date of a Reimbursement Claim) from the Claiming Bank.

c)   Where a Reimbursing Bank has not issued a Reimbursement Undertaking and a reimbursement is due on a future date:

   i)   The Reimbursement Claim must specify the predetermined reimbursement date.

   ii)   The Reimbursement Claim should not be presented to the Reimbursing Bank more than ten (10) of its banking days prior to such predetermined date. If a Reimbursement Claim is presented more than ten (10) banking days prior to the predetermined date, the Reimbursing Bank may disregard the Reimbursement Claim. If the Reimbursing Bank disregards the Reimbursement Claim it must so inform the Claiming Bank by teletransmission or other expeditious means without delay.

   iii) If the predetermined reimbursement date is more than three banking days following the day of receipt of the Reimbursement Claim, the Reimbursing Bank has no obligation to provide notice of non-reimbursement until such predetermined date, or no later than the close of the third banking day following the receipt of the Reimbursement Claim plus any additional period mentioned in (a)(i) above, whichever is later.

d)   Unless otherwise expressly agreed to by the Reimbursing Bank and the Claiming Bank, Reimbursing Banks will effect reimbursement under a Reimbursement Claim only to the Claiming Bank.

e)   Reimbursing Banks assume no liability or responsibility if they honour a Reimbursement Claim that indicates that a payment, acceptance or negotiation was made under reserve or against an indemnity and shall disregard such indication. Such reserve or indemnity concerns only the relations between the Claiming Bank and the party towards whom the reserve was made, or from whom, or on whose behalf, the indemnity was obtained.

Article 12
Duplications of Reimbursement Authorizations

An Issuing Bank must not, upon receipt of documents, give a new Reimbursement Authorization, or additional instructions, unless they constitute an amendment to, or a cancellation of an existing Reimbursement Authorization. If the Issuing Bank does not comply with the above and a duplicate reimbursement is made, it is the responsibility of the Issuing Bank to obtain the return of the amount of the duplicate reimbursement. The Reimbursing Bank assumes no liability or responsibility for any consequences that may arise from any such duplication.

D.   Miscellaneous Provisions

Article 13
Foreign Laws and Usages

The Issuing Bank shall be bound by and shall indemnify the Reimbursing Bank against all obligations and responsibilities imposed by foreign laws and usages.

Article 14
Disclaimer on the Transmission of Messages

Reimbursing Banks assume no liability or responsibility for the consequences arising out of delay and/or loss in transit of any message(s), letter(s) or document(s), or for delay, mutilation or other errors arising in the transmission of any telecommunication. Reimbursing Banks assume no liability or responsibility for errors in translation.

Article 15
Force Majeure

Reimbursing Banks assume no liability or responsibility for the consequences arising out of the interruption of their business by acts of God, riots, civil commotions, insurrections, wars or any other causes beyond their control, or by any strikes or lockouts.

Article 16
Charges

a)   The Reimbursing Bank's charges should be for the account of the Issuing Bank. However, in cases where the charges are for the account of another party, it is the responsibility of the Issuing Bank to so indicate in the original Credit and in the Reimbursement Authorization.

b)   When honouring a Reimbursement Claim, a Reimbursing Bank is obligated to follow the instructions regarding any charges contained in the Reimbursement Authorization.

c)   In cases where the Reimbursing Bank's charges are for the account of another party, they shall be deducted when the Reimbursement Claim is honoured. Where a Reimbursing Bank follows the instructions of the Issuing Bank regarding charges (including commission, fees, costs or expenses) and these charges are not paid or a Reimbursement Claim is never presented to the Reimbursing Bank under the Reimbursement Authorization, the Issuing Bank remains liable for such charges.

d)   Unless otherwise stated in the Reimbursement Authorization, all charges paid by the Reimbursing Bank will be in addition to the amount of the Authorization provided that the Claiming Bank indicates the amount of such charges.

e)   If the Issuing Bank fails to provide the Reimbursing Bank with instructions regarding charges, all charges shall be for the account of the Issuing Bank.

Article 17
Interest Claims/Loss of Value

All claims for loss of interest, loss of value due to any exchange rate fluctuations, revaluations or devaluations are between the Claiming Bank and the Issuing Bank, unless such losses result from the non-performance of the Reimbursing Bank's obligation under a Reimbursement Undertaking.

Index

new exporters, help from bank 217
non-bank sources of help for exporters 218
non-financial services for exporters 211–223
non-negotiable sea waybill 182
nostro 94
  and vostro accounts 94
Notary Public 246
notes, sterling and foreign currency 212
notification date 56
noting a bill of exchange 246

O

ocean bill of lading 113, 181
offset 233
on demand bonds 226
open account 141
  payment terms, definition 108
  terms 145
    major risks 145
    reducing risk 146
open credit for travellers 215
open general licence 244
opener 174
operational risk 69
option
  forward contracts, calculating 44
  premium 54
options 52
Ordinary SWIFT 96
over-the-counter options (OTC options) 57
overdraft guarantee, example 240
overdrafts for exporters 192
Overseas Investment Insurance Scheme,
    ECGD 152

P

packing list 123
palletized cargoes 113
parcel post receipt 116
partial payment, procedure for offers of 249
payment 178
  in advance 142
performance bonds 225
  example 236
placement 93
post-shipment finance 190
pour aval 196
pre-paid transport documents 183
pre-shipment finance 190, 210
Prevention of Terrorism Act (Temporary
    Provisions) 92

price elasticity of demand 14
priority SWIFT 100
pro forma invoice 119
produce loan facility 252
Progress Payment Guarantee, example 238
project lines of credit 206
Project Participants' Insolvency Cover, ECGD
    151
protection of goods and inward collections 248
protest instructions 196
purchaser 54
purchasing power parity 73
  theory 29, 72
pure options 52
put option 54

Q

qualified acceptances 246

R

rail consignment notes 116
rates of exchange
  quoting 40
  spot, and the exchange risk 41
re-instatement documentary credits 263
receipts, truck/carrier 116
recourse bonds 225
red clause documentary credits 198
relative inflation rates 26
remitting bank, duties 163
retention
  bonds 225
  money guarantee 229
  monies bond, example 239
revocable, definition 175
risks that apply to open account terms 145
road consignment notes 116

S

sea waybill 113
Second Banking Directive 94
settlement
  date 56
  international, through banks 92
  of
    inward collection 249
    inward payments to UK beneficiaries 101
    overseas debt with cheques 103
shipment terms 126
shipping documents, specimen set 166
ship's waybill 113